BARNEY, BRADLEY, AND MAX

BOOKS BY WHITNEY BALLIETT

BARNEY, BRADLEY, AND MAX

Sixteen Portraits in Jazz

WHITNEY BALLIETT

New York   Oxford
OXFORD UNIVERSITY PRESS
1989

OXFORD UNIVERSITY PRESS

Oxford   New York   Toronto
Delhi   Bombay   Calcutta   Madras   Karachi
Petaling Jaya   Singapore   Hong Kong   Tokyo
Nairobi   Dar es Salaam   Cape Town
Melbourne   Auckland

and associated companies in
Berlin   Ibadan

Published by Oxford University Press, Inc.,
200 Madison Avenue, New York, New York 10016

Library of Congress Cataloging-in-Publication Data
Balliett, Whitney.
Barney, Bradley, and Max : sixteen portraits in jazz / Whitney Balliett.
p.   cm.
"With the exception of the chapter on Buddy De Franco, the
contents of this book first appeared in the New Yorker,
in somewhat different form."—T.P. verso.
ISBN 0–19–506124–1
1. Jazz musicians—United States—Biography.   I. Title.
ML385.B25   1989
89–9387   781.65′092′273—dc20   CIP   MN

With the exception of the chapter on Buddy De Franco,
the contents of this book first appeared in *The New Yorker*,
in somewhat different form.

2 4 6 8 9 7 5 3 1

Printed in the United States of America
on acid-free paper

For Barney,
Bradley, and
Max—and Jean

NOTE

This book, written between 1971 and 1988, is intended as a supplement to my *American Musicians*, published by Oxford in 1986. It includes eight portraits that have never been in book form (the chapter on Buddy De Franco has not been printed anywhere) and seven that have been rescued and refurbished from earlier volumes of mine that are either out of print or out of mind. One more portrait, of George Shearing, is reprinted from *American Singers*. There, Shearing the singer was star; here, updated, it is Shearing the pianist. The book moves from the edges of jazz to its heart. There is a chapter on an elegant jazz fan (Jean Bach); a chapter on three men who have run wonderful and very different jazz night clubs (Max Gordon, Barney Josephson, Bradley Cunningham); a chapter on a jazz musician who has lived a serene life on the outskirts of the big time (Marie Marcus); three chapters on virtuosos who have successfully worked both sides of the jazz-classical fence (Benny Goodman, Harvey Phillips, Mel Powell); a chapter of a virtuoso who has stayed on the jazz side (Louis Bellson); chapters on two of the greatest jazz clarinettists (Goodman and De Franco); and a chapter on Charlie Parker, who, thirty-three years after his death, has at last been made famous—by, of all people, Clint Eastwood. Six of the portraits concern pianists, which is and isn't accidental, since jazz pianists, orchestras in themselves, have often been brilliant bellwethers. The title of the book, chosen some time ago, has suddenly become eerie. Within the past nine months, Barney, Bradley, and Max have all died—in that order.

May 1989   W. B.
New York City

CONTENTS

BARNEY, BRADLEY,
AND MAX

FAN

~~~

E. B. White suggests in his essay "Here Is New York" that there are three New Yorks—that of the native-born New Yorker, that of the commuter, and that of "the person who was born somewhere else and came to New York in quest of something." He continues, "Of these three trembling cities the greatest is the last—the city of final destination, the city that is a goal. It is this third city that accounts for New York's high-strung disposition, its poetical deportment, its dedication to the arts, and its incomparable achievements. Commuters give the city its tidal restlessness, natives give it solidity and continuity, but the settlers give it passion." One of the settlers who have given New York immeasurable passion during the past thirty-five years is a pretty, witty, quick, indefatigable woman named Jean Bach. She is a Boswell, for, not widely known herself, she spends much of her time cosseting and studying the great and near-great, the famous and almost famous. She does this in two ways, both of which Boswell would have admired, for each smooths egos and stays vanity. She produces the "Arlene Francis Show," a radio interview program that has been heard five days a week over WOR for the past twenty-three years, and she gives—often with her husband, Bob Bach—countless select, sought-after parties at her house in Greenwich Village. She picks out the guests for the

3

radio show, reads their books, sees their movies, attends their plays or ballets or art shows, writes the introduction to each interview, and frames questions that Arlene Francis might ask. When a guest fails to appear or Arlene Francis is away, Jean Bach goes on the air, and the show takes on a special sparkle. She talks in a fast, assured Mid-western way, and she has an open, rich voice—the kind that gives the impression of being constantly on the edge of laughter. She has her own patois, made up of a jazz lingo and of her own quick and funny imagery (a good party "flies," a bad one is "a pancake"; a press agent has to "keep all flags flying"; celebrities always "keep their pores open"; her first husband, the late trumpeter Shorty Sherock, was "the first Mr. Bach"). She is also an expert autobiographer. Listeners to the Arlene Francis program know about Jean Bach's feet, which bother her a lot; about her cats, Lena and Lana, who replaced Seymour Katz when he died; about Bob Bach, who is an independent television producer; about her small cinder-block weekend house in the hills of northern Westchester ("It's painted black and green. It looks French. It has angles and corners everywhere that cast pretty shadows"); and about her mother, a beautiful and energetic woman of ninety-one who lives in a Georgian mansion in the middle of Milwaukee. Sometimes people on the show turn up at Jean Bach's parties, and sometimes the people at her parties turn up on the show. She breathes parties, and has for most of her life. She also breathes jazz, which she began to listen to when she was a teenager. Her parents gave parties constantly, and she began giving her own when she was fourteen or fifteen. She gave parties for the various sections of the big band that Shorty Sherock had when they were married, and she immediately started giving parties after she and Bob Bach were married, in the late forties. They held charades at their house on Charles Street, and they invited the Herbert Bayard Swopes and the James Downeys and the William Harbachs and the Robert Sarnoffs. The pianist Barbara Carroll provided the first music they had, and she was followed by the likes of Cy Walter and Walter Gross. After Cy

Walter played, he would leave a five-dollar bill on the piano—an upright with a short keyboard—as a contribution toward a new piano. They gave a party for Judy Garland. The composer Willard Robison came not because he admired Judy Garland but because he loved the shape of Jean Bach's head, which reminded him of Wendell Willkie's. (Robison drove to the party from White Plains, where he lived, and parked near Jean Bach's house. When he left, he forgot he had driven down and took the train home. Next morning, finding his car missing, he called the police and reported it stolen.) Here are some of the people who have gone to Jean Bach's parties: Geoffrey Holder, Duke Ellington, Billy Strayhorn, Gene Austin, James Mason, Jack Lemmon, Walter Winchell, Vic Damone, Harold Arlen, Yip Harburg, Johnny Mercer, Geraldine Page, Tommy Dorsey, Daphne Hellman, Artie Shaw, James Baldwin, George Wein, Norman Mailer, Burt Bacharach, Rex Reed, Gloria Vanderbilt, Juliette Greco, Randolph Churchill, Sammy Davis, Jr., Mica and Ahmet Ertegun, Nesuhi Ertegun, Lena Horne, Lee and Bob Elliott, and Bobby Short. Short was co-host with Jean Bach of one of the greatest of all Bach parties—a celebration of their forty years of friendship. It was a black-tie dance, and it was given in the winter of 1981 at the Carlyle, and it was presided over by Count Basie's band. The guest list caromed from Tony Bennett to Kurt Vonnegut to Jack Lemmon to Ira Gitler. Jean Bach wore a brilliant full-skirted red dress with a half-moon neck and puffed sleeves, and she looked like an anemone. She has, she has said, been compared with every famous blonde of the twentieth century, among them Doris Day, Shirley Temple, and Ingrid Bergman. She has a handsome nose and blue eyes and a square face, and her smile slips to one side.

Bobby Short recently talked about his old friend: "Jean and I met in the winter of 1942 at the Sherman Hotel in Chicago. She was married to Shorty Sherock, who was in the Alvino Rey band, and I was singing in the Dome in the hotel. I was a baby just out of high school, and what drew me to Jean was not only her love for Duke Ellington but the fact that she could sing note

for note Ben Webster solos and Cootie Williams solos and Johnny
Hodges solos. And—she *knew* my idol, Ivie Anderson. Jean was
by far the most elegant and beautiful and sharply intelligent
person I had ever met. We resumed our friendship in Southern
California the following year; then I lost track of her and didn't
see her again until Paris in 1952, when our friendship got off on
a good adult level. In December of 1981, we celebrated its fortieth anniversary with the dance at the Carlyle. The Basie band's
sheer aural power, contained and condensed in those small
rooms, was mind-blowing. Jean and I talk at least once a week,
and we have never had a quarrel or a disagreement. She never
schemes, never makes demands. She's very human, so she's vul-
nerable; and she's very courageous. She's also loyal and un-
changing. She's not one way in Albany one week and another
way in New York the next week. And her energy is boundless.
She passes information on in the most unassuming manner—it
never comes across as a lesson or as an act of self-aggrandize-
ment. She still corrects me, but in the gentlest way. In earlier
days, I was sometimes out of work, and I'd always turn to Jean
and she'd tell me what to do, and what she told me was invariably right. Our friendship always makes me think how awfully
difficult it is to let your friends know in what high esteem you
hold them."

Jean Bach's urge to pass information on resulted four years
ago in her writing a unique sixty-four-page paperback book
called *200 Ways to Conquer "The Blues."* It was sold in super-
markets and fit in a woman's purse. It sets forth advice on how
to fight depression—a condition that 25 percent of the nation is
said to be sometimes sunk in. The book is full of folk (and ur-
ban) wisdom:

> USE THE STAIRS. Whenever possible, use your legs instead of
> the elevator. It's good for the circulation and, as you de-
> velop your vigor, your spirits will rise.
>
> CONCEAL EYESORES. A worn place in the rug doesn't mean
> much to the casual visitor, but it can become a horror for
> the person who lives with it and has to see it every time

she walks across the room. Think about placing a small scatter rug over it. A folding screen is very useful for hiding all kinds of eyesores. Be imaginative. What about a potted palm?

OPEN A WINDOW. Let some fresh air into the place. A nice breeze feels good and you never know what wonderful, new ideas will blow in on it.

FAKE FEELING GOOD. You may have the most legitimate reason in the world to be unhappy. You may have lost someone important to you, you may have lost your job, you may be a stranger in town, you may be recovering from a broken romance. But when you're with people, don't wear your depression like a badge. You're going to have to learn to fake cheerfulness. Believe it or not, eventually that effort will pay off: you'll actually start feeling happier.

DON'T leave your bed unmade.

Absorbing the information she dispenses is an act Jean Bach loves. She said recently, "I was sitting in bed one night doing my homework for the show—reading Peter Prescott's memoir about Choate, as a matter of fact—and suddenly I thought, This is the essence, the best thing in the world, the reason I do what I do: acquiring information."

One spring afternoon in 1983, after a quiet Arlene Francis show, Jean Bach walked from the WOR studios, at Broadway and Forty-first Street, to Lord & Taylor, where she had an appointment to have her nails done. First, she had lunch at the Café, on the fifth floor. She ordered the sandwich platter and talked about Shorty Sherock, who had died not long before. "He was darling," she said. "He was of Polish and Czech extraction, and he was very handsome. I met him at the Three Deuces in Chicago in 1941, and we were married a few weeks later. He was with Gene Krupa at the time, but he spent every extra moment at the feet of Roy Eldridge, whom he worshipped. When Krupa went out of town for one-nighters, Roy started coming along and sitting in, and the next thing we knew Shorty was out and Roy had been hired. It was simply: Who needs this im-

postor when we have the real thing right there? Shorty and I
had a little apartment we'd paid a month's rent for, and we
hocked the golf sticks and my pearls. Then Shorty got a call
from Tommy Dorsey, and we joined him in Bluefield, West
Virginia. Raymond Scott was next, and, after that, Bob Strong,
and Alvino Rey, and, finally, Horace Heidt. By this time, we
were living in Malibu in a roomy house, and I was giving
parties. Horace Heidt turned the band over to Shorty in 1945,
and we got the summer booking at the Glen Island Casino, in
New Rochelle. Travel was still very slow and difficult because
of the war, so we took only our key men. Shorty and I were
jammed into a drawing room with all the band parts, and I'd
have nightmares about losing the fourth-trombone book. A big
picnic basket Ivie Anderson gave us lasted the whole trip. We
rented a house in New Rochelle, and I became band manager.
We went on the road in the fall, stopping at places like Selma,
Alabama, where I remember hanging clothes to dry on a ceiling
fan. We had either kids or old cripples in the band, and when
we didn't have enough money to pay everybody I'd ask the kids
if they minded being paid next week, and they'd get real con-
cerned and ask me if I had money for breakfast. It was a strange
band. We had a soft, floating Basie-type rhythm section and an
Italianate trumpet section that played a little sharp and real
loud, and it was constant war. By 1948, I'd had enough. I'd had
measles on the road, and I was tired. Shorty and I were divorced, and I married Bob Bach. We lived on West Fourth Street
at first; then we moved to Charles Street. I got a job at WNEW
as a scriptwriter. Radio still had live music, and everything was
scripted—the badinage between the announcer and the bandleader, the introductions to recordings. I went on to Edward
Bernays, in his public-relations business, and from him to an
early television show called 'Okay, Mother.' Dennis James was
the host, and we had a guest mother every day. People from the
audience were asked questions, and if they got them right they
won a sewing machine or a Ronson lighter. The show finally
sank of its own dreadful weight. I worked for Dick Kollmar's art

gallery, and then went with another press agent. One of the clients was a record producer, and part of my job was to go around to radio stations and hand out payola to disk jockeys. I was supposed to figure out on the spot what a particular d.j. was worth—twenty-five, fifty, or a hundred dollars—and hand him the money. I think Dick Clark was the only one who ever refused me. I was with Harry Sobol after that; then I did a year with Rheingold. I started doing the 'Arlene Francis Show' in 1960. We broadcast from Sardi's at the beginning, but it got too difficult. One of our early guests was Carl Sandburg, and when Arlene asked him if God was dead he picked up a piece of celery and started eating it, and all you heard over the air while the great man pondered was *crunch, crunch, crunch.*"

After lunch, Jean Bach descended to the beauty salon, and had her nails done. Then she took a Fifth Avenue bus to Eighth Street, and walked a couple of blocks to her house. It was once the studio of Gertrude Vanderbilt Whitney, and it still looks like a studio. The living room is two stories high, and has a huge north window. The room has a fireplace, a grand piano, and assorted pictures (ink drawings by Salvador Dali, a pencil self-portrait by E. E. Cummings), and to one side there is a tiny bedroom and bath known as the Blossom Dearie Suite—so named because the singer had been wont, after practicing on Jean Bach's piano, to stay the night. A stairway leads down to a dining room and kitchen, and another stairway leads up to the master bedroom. Jean Bach was greeted by Lena and Lana. Curtains were drawn over the great window, and the room was cool and dim. Jean Bach made some tea, and then sat down on a sofa, pulled off her shoes, and put her feet on a coffee table.

"I was born in Chicago," she said, "but I grew up on the east side of Milwaukee. I was an only child, and my parents were a Scott Fitzgerald couple. They associated with the well-fixed. They were blue-eyed and good-looking. They rode well. They sang and played the piano. They loved to dance and had a passion for dance bands. When I was ten and eleven, they'd take me with them to hear Ben Bernie and Hal Kemp. They'd invite the bands to dinner or to late-Sunday-morning champagne breakfasts. My father was George Enzinger, Jr., and he'd grown up in St. Louis. His father was a piano teacher and church organist. Daddy remembered a policeman knocking on the screen door and asking 'the professor' if he would teach him to play the 'Maple Leaf Rag.' He did, note by note, and it took six months. Old Mr. Enzinger was plugged into Bach, though, and I remember him whistling Bach fugues up and down the halls. My father was plugged into anything that was avant-garde or anti-establishment. He'd gone to the University of Missouri School of Journalism, and he had his own advertising company. He made monthly trips to New York, where he hung out with the now people of then, like Marion Morehouse, who married E. E. Cummings. She was a fashion model, and Cecil Beaton, or someone like that, said she was one of the two great beauties of the twentieth century. My father would bring back sheet music from the newest shows—songs like Dietz and Schwartz's 'Smokin' Reefers.' And he'd pick up the newest records—Louis Armstrong Hot Fives and Ethel Waters's 'Shake That Thing.' Once, my mother went to California and took the Waters record with her, and when she got back it was broken. My father got very pale and took it into his office and closed the door and spent hours trying to put it together with glue and cardboard. But ordinarily he was a gay, light-hearted man. He'd sit down at the piano at cocktail time and play Chopin, and dinner would be announced and we'd all have to sit and wait, whether the soufflé fell or not. My mother was Gertrude Cole. She was born in Canada, where she lived until she was twelve. Her father was F. F. Cole, the buckwheat king. She was the fourth of six children and the one with all the pizzazz and good looks. When Cole died, the whole troupe moved to Chicago, where they owned land but never seemed to have enough money. Mother taught nursery school at the Hebrew Institute, and she went to the University of Chicago for a while. She had a sister, Viola Cole-Audet, who had trained to be a concert pianist with Harold Bauer. Aunt Viola had a salon in her studio in the Fine Arts Building, and

that's where Daddy first met my mother. She thought his name
was Anderson, and she told Aunt Viola later that 'that nice Mr.
Anderson looked so clean I bet I could have used his tooth-
brush.' The twenties were a goofy time. There seemed to be
nothing but house parties and evening clothes day and night. I
remember walking past the music room in our house in Milwaukee on the way to kindergarten and seeing a man in white
tie and tails passed out under the piano. There was so much
drinking! A German gentleman named Best would go down in
our cellar and make liebfraumilch and put it in nice long bottles.
So my parents' marriage turned out to be founded on sand. It
had no substance. As long as there were parties, they were all
right. They were divorced in 1936, and a year later my mother
married Eric William Passmore. He was a lawyer and a liberal
and a fashion plate, and he eventually became very powerful.
He had met Mother when I was one, and had always adored
her. In the fifties, he bought her the house she lives in now, and
it has Tiffany stair rails and thirteen fireplaces and I don't know
how many bathrooms. Eric died in 1979, so I go out on weekends a lot to see her. My father married Irene Castle in 1946.
They lived near Chicago, and her friends were famous movie
stars. She gave Sunday-evening soirées and posh charity balls,
and she'd be invited to the South Side to judge dance contests.
Then she and my father moved to Arkansas, where she built a
house. He died there in 1959, at the age of sixty-six.

"We moved back to Chicago when I was thirteen, and I went
to the University School for Girls. I was class president and
editor of the year-book. I went to Vassar, but I wasn't the
drudge I am now, and when my parents were divorced I dropped
out and moved into a two-story house with my father in midtown Chicago. I got a job on the Chicago *Times* as a kind of
society columnist for young people—for débutantes, who were
very big then. Then I moved over to the Chicago *American*. I
was already into jazz, and I'd report on the music they had at
the deb parties. Jonah Jones told me a little while ago that I
gave him the first mention he ever had in a newspaper. My by-

line was simply Jean, and I also had a record-review column. I guess I was the first jazz groupie. I'd heard Benny Goodman at the Congress Hotel in 1935 and 1936, and Jimmy Dorsey had taken me to hear Earl Hines at the Grand Terrace. When I was at Vassar, I heard Charlie Barnet at Yale and the old Count Basie band at the University of Virginia. Billie Holiday was singing with him, and I ran into her in the ladies' room. I was gushy, and she wasn't too enchanted. I went out with Roy Eldridge in my late teens. He had a La Salle convertible, and I remember one night he had the guitarist John Collins and the drummer Doc West in the back seat and they'd missed a couple of days of 'Terry and the Pirates' and he filled them in on what had happened—but in swing talk: 'This little cat, he had eyes for this chick. But, man, you know, she was called the Dragon Lady, and she was sly . . .' He went on like that, with passion, for half an hour. I also went out with John Bubbles, who had been Sportin' Life in *Porgy and Bess*. Daddy knew Abbie Mitchell, who was in *Porgy*, too, and she introduced us. I visited New York in 1938, and I was backstage at the theatre Bubbles was playing when Stepin Fetchit sent word by one of his footmen that if I wanted his autograph I should stop by where he was working and he'd give it to me and take me on a tour of Harlem. So I went, and what a scene! Stepin Fetchit was slithering around his dressing room in one of the brand-new cashmere suits he'd inherited from the tailor he shared with Rudolph Valentino—who had died before he could wear them. Stepin Fetchit had a piano, and Herman Chittison was sitting at it. Chittison had worked for him early in the thirties, and later Stepin Fetchit had rescued him from some disaster in Egypt. When I arrived, Stepin Fetchit said, 'What do you want to hear? "Tea for Two"? Fine. "Tea for Two," Chittison,' and Chittison played 'Tea for Two.' Then we toured Harlem in his car and wound up at Jimmy Daniels'.

"In my day, Chicago was very important musically. There was the Club DeLisa and the Grand Terrace and the Regal Theatre, where it was essential to know the stage doorman, Bob

Redcross. There was the Three Deuces, where Roy Eldridge and Art Tatum played, and the Congress Hotel and the Pump Room, where John Kirby was, all got up in white tie and tails, and the Panther Room in the Hotel Sherman. Ellington spent a month there in 1940, and I went every night, except the one night when Daddy *made* me stay home. I became the No. 1 Ellington fan. I was in the recording studio the day the band did 'Conga Brava,' and Ellington was already dispensing his jive. They'd do a take, and he'd say, as if it mattered, 'Now, Jean, how's the tempo? Should it be slower or faster?' I'd take him seriously and say, 'Well, maybe it should be slower . . .' I was in the studio when Duke and Jimmy Blanton recorded their famous duets. Ellington had told me, "Come around. I have a novelty— a bass player who plays in tune.' And there was this kid in a crazy navy-blue pin-striped suit that would knock your eye out. When I first knew Ellington and was a fat eighteen-year-old, I told him that he and Stravinsky were my favorite composers, and he said, 'I'm jealous of Stravinsky.' "

Jean Bach laughed and looked at her watch and said that she had to go to a Fortune Society meeting. She explained that she was on the executive board, that the society had been founded by a former theatrical press agent named David Rothenberg, and that its purpose was to help rehabilitate former convicts. She said that after the meeting it was early to bed, so that she could get rested for a party she was giving the next night. "It's more or less built around Henry Quarles. He's a lawyer and an Ellington scholar I met recently in Milwaukee when I went to visit my mother. Milwaukee can be very heavy going some- times. There are a lot of right-wing Republicans and people who like to run down Jews and blacks, and I was going crazy, so I called Henry and he asked me to an Ellington Study Group meeting. They played records and told stories and cheered me up. Later, he wrote and asked me if I was going to their annual meeting in Washington, D.C., and I wrote back and said that I couldn't but that the Blossom Dearie Suite would be vacant and wouldn't he come and stay and I'd give a little party for the group after the Washington meeting. About fifty are coming, including Pat Willard, who's doing an Ellington biography; members from Holland, Belgium, and West Germany; Joya Sherrill, the Ellington singer; Steve James, Duke's nephew; Brooks Kerr; Harold Taylor, who used to be head of Sarah Lawrence and played clarinet at Ellington's seventieth-birthday party at the White House; and such locals as Richard Sudhalter and Dan Morgenstern and Ira Gitler. We'll have ham and macaroni-and-cheese and thin-sliced cucumbers in vinegar. I'm aiming at quantity, because I'm panicked about running out of food. I don't know why, but Ellington fans are heavy eaters." Jean Bach picked up her pocketbook and said: "Someone from out of town I met last night asked me why I live in New York. I told him I live here because of the tempo and the fast track, because there are always so many more choices. I live here because it ruins you for any other place."

[1983]

JAZZ CLUBS

~~

The owners of the night clubs where jazz has been a staple have ranged from Capone mobsters to sleazeballs of various grades to decent men, even outright moralists. Here are three of the last. They share certain things—all are honest, all love the music, and all have more or less backed into their line of work. The first is the venerable and indomitable Max Gordon.

I

He is short and bent and gnomish. His hands and feet are child-like, and he is dominated by a large head, which in turn is dominated by a broad brow and heavy white receding hair. His eyes are sad, and prunelike wrinkles course down his face. (When the comedian Joe Frisco visited Gordon's first club, the Village Fair Coffee House, in the early thirties, he pointed to Gordon and asked a friend, "Who's that miserable guy by the door? He looks like the Wailing Wall in Jerusalem.") But Gordon, like many hesitant, inward-gazing people, glows. His Solomonlike visage is constantly ruffled by smiles and laughter, and if he gets excited his voice, which creaks when he breaks one of his occasional long silences, booms. He is a funny, dreaming man who shrugs off victory and laughs at defeat, and who invariably treats the weaknesses in others with respect. One of his many admirers has said of him, "If I had to spend the rest of my days on a desert island and could take just five people, Max would top the list."

Gordon lives in an airy, high-ceilinged apartment on East Seventy-ninth Street with his wife, Lorraine, and his daughters, Rebecca and Deborah. Gordon talked about his life one morning: "We've lived here twelve years. Two years ago the building was coöpted, but we didn't buy. A lady named McDonald bought the apartment. We've never seen her and I don't know if she's seen the apartment. It worries Lorraine that she might throw us out. But it doesn't bother me—the places I've lived in. When I came to New York in 1926 I lived in furnished rooms. I must have lived in twenty or more of them, and they were mostly in a complex, a rabbit warren owned by a man named Albert Strunsky. The N.Y.U. Law School is there now. The side facing Washington Square had big studios where fancy people paid seventy-five dollars a month, but we lived on the other side, in rooms with hall toilets, for six dollars a week. There was no central heating, just gas heaters, and you took your life in your hands if you went to sleep in the winter and left the gas on. Strunsky was a marvellous man. He'd known Jack London, and he loved creative people. You could always owe him money. He looked like an Irishman, with his beet face and polished scalp. A cousin, Simeon, was an editorial writer with the *Times,* and another relative, Anna, was a Yiddish writer. I think one of his daughters married Ira Gershwin. Strunsky was always around, and when someone asked him where his beautiful wife was, he'd say, 'Oh, Palm Beach.' I was walking down the street a while ago, and there was an old sofa, all broken down and gaping, sitting by the curb. It made me laugh. It was authentic Strunsky period.

"I'd come to New York from Portland, Oregon, ostensibly to go to Columbia Law School. I was raised in Portland, but I was born in 1903 in Svir in Lithuania. I was the third of four children. My mother brought us over to Providence, Rhode Island,

in 1908. My father had already established himself in the dairy
and delicatessen business. I remember him churning butter in
the window of his shop, and going for rides on Sunday in a
surrey with a fringe on top. We spoke Yiddish at home, but my
Yiddish fell away. I have no memory of the lack of English. I
can't read Yiddish now, although I speak it haltingly, and I
probably could enjoy a play in Yiddish. We stayed in Providence several years. Then my father moved to Portland, and we
followed him. He became a kind of peddler, and he'd go out to
the eastern part of the state and buy furs from trappers. He used
a horse and wagon first, and then he had a Ford pickup truck.
We were poor, and we hustled as children. I sold papers, and
we'd save all kinds of boxes during the year and sell them for
people to sit at the Rose Festival parade. Mark Rothko, the
great painter, was related to us, and we sold papers together.
We talked about it on the phone the day before he committed
suicide, just a little while ago. I couldn't understand him doing
that. He had a big studio, a home, money. When I went to the
funeral his elder brothers were there, and I asked them why
they had let Mark sell papers and run the streets when they
already owned a drugstore. They shrugged and said, 'What did
we know in those days?' My mother and father were separated
off and on when I was growing up. I never knew why. My
father worked hard, and he was a good, gentle man. But my
mother was hard-bitten. She was not a happy woman. She had
a goiter and a heart condition. But she had that Jewish drive to
educate her children, and I think I broke her heart when I
didn't become a lawyer. When I was in high school I hung
around with people who read novels and poetry, and I never
studied. But I went to Reed College in Oregon, and when I was
a junior I got fed up. I wanted to get away, to lash out, so I
matriculated at Stanford and then ran out of money. I got a job
in an all-night cigar store, saved some money, and went back
to Reed and graduated. I only lasted at Columbia six weeks. I
lived on the campus for a while after I'd dropped out, and I got
to know the intellectuals, like Gus Solomon, who's a federal

judge in Oregon, and Furner Nuhn, who contributed to the
American Mercury. Then I moved down to Strunsky's. I didn't
know what I wanted to do. All I knew was that work was un-
worthy of me. What *was* worthy I didn't know. So I wouldn't
work until I really had to, and then I'd get a job in a mail-order
place, running an addressograph machine or licking envelopes.
When I tired of one place I'd go to another, or if I had scraped
enough money together I'd lay off a couple of months. I spent
my days in the Public Library and my nights at Paul's on
Wooster Street or Sam Johnson's on Third Street. I stayed up
until three or four in the morning and slept until two or three
in the afternoon. Paul's and Sam Johnson's were coffeehouses
with poetry. Eli Siegel, who has a movement called Aesthetic
Realism now, ran Sam Johnson's. He'd won the *Nation* poetry
prize in 1925 for 'Hot Afternoons Have Been in Montana.'
There would be poetry readings and lots of discussion groups,
and I met people like Joe Gould and John Rose Gildea and
Harry Kemp and Max Bodenheim, whom I'd read in college.
There was a lot of drinking—wine, or alcohol mixed with the
essence of juniper. It was Prohibition that did that. The minute
repeal came, everybody went on the wagon. Gildea was a wonderful man. He married an East Side girl, and he'd come to the
Village in tails and stay three days. He improvised poetry for
drinks, and some of it was marvellous. I don't think he ever
published anything. I remember taking him home and walking
under the Sixth Avenue 'L' on a freezing winter night while he
spouted this great poetry at the top of his lungs. I took Joe
Gould home, too. Malcolm Cowley would give him piles of
books to review, but he read very fast, skipping a lot, and his
reviews were short and sketchy. Harry Kemp, whose poems you
can find in the old anthologies, was a huge, heavyweight strap-
ping guy. A big, real, impossible man. He'd had an affair with
Upton Sinclair's wife, and in 1922 he published *Tramping on
Life*, a very successful autobiography. He followed it with *More
Miles*, but that flopped. He ran Harry Kemp's One-Act Playhouse, where Clifford Odets started as an actor. Kemp lived on

the dunes at Provincetown, and he helped start the Province-town Playhouse. When he came back to town he'd look for me in the coffeehouses and he'd shout, 'Max! Where are you? I have a new poem to read to you!' and crush me with an embrace. I was enchanted with Provincetown when I went up there in the thirties. Kemp would roar down Commercial Street, talking, talking, talking, and it was like the Village, only with water."

Gordon went out to the kitchen and made a pot of tea. "I'm not much at this sort of thing," he said when he came back, "but it's real tea and it's hot." He lit a big cigar. It made him look top-heavy. He puffed for a while, his eyes narrowed against the smoke, and then put the cigar down and took a sip of tea.

"In 1929 I went home. It was frustration and fatigue, and I went home to recharge my batteries. I stayed four or five months and came back in November of that year and drifted into my old life of odd jobs with mail-order outfits and writing for little puff magazines. By this time I had vague visions of being a writer. For the puff magazines, which were a racket, we'd pick out people of the second and third echelon who had been in the news and write congratulatory biographies, about three hundred words or so, and then call them up and read them what we'd written and ask them how many copies they wanted at thirty-five cents a throw. I also wrote a humorous essay which had to do with a *schnorrer*, a Yiddish word for a phony promoter. It was printed in the *Menorah Journal*, which was edited by Eliott Cohen, who later edited *Commentary*. Albert Halper, the novelist, was in the same issue, and I noticed a while ago that he's just published an autobiography. I knew I wasn't a writer, but I also knew I had to be *some*thing. I had got to the point where I was sick worrying about my mother, about what she was thinking of me. People didn't have contempt for their parents then, and this guilt was engulfing me. Ann Andreas, who was a good friend of mine, saved me. She suggested I start a decent coffeehouse, since Sam Johnson's and Paul's had gone downhill. My sister had moved to New York, and between us we raised four or five hundred dollars. I found a half basement on Sullivan Street that seated about seventy-five. I think it's a fraternity house now. We opened in the latter part of 1932, and we called it the Village Fair Coffee House. We served tea and coffee and sandwiches and setups. The waitresses wore pajama-type pants, and it was the sort of place where they'd sit and talk with the customers if they were invited to. But it was all very innocent. The poets, who were always looking for new places, started coming in, and I hired Ivan Black, the press agent, as a master of ceremonies and a bouncer. I fed him and give him five bucks a week, and he organized everything. He was a newspaperman and a poet and he read his own stuff, including a risqué parody of Joyce and Gertrude Stein that had run in *Transition*. I came across a reprint of it the other day in an old file, and, you know, it's pretty funny. It's called 'Mister Weirdy at Home.' "

Gordon shuffled some papers, cleared his throat, and read aloud:

> At that time he was constipaching, ins aferment outs abloat, his faceskin a ptomaine green Oily. He was about to write his gratest poem. Pianowing was his livelihoodway and even more his lifeleewayhoot but when he got leadbelly he verscript. He put on a Beethovenfrown as browclasp. He dipt his pen and poised.

Gordon laughed. "It really went over big, and when he'd finish, Ivan would call on poets in the audience to read. They'd get food or liquor or fifty cents. Graham Norwell, a Canadian painter, did the murals in the place. He was a wonderful, handsome man, but he'd lost his teeth and he was a drunk. I paid him in gin. Once, when he had an exhibition of his stuff over in Brooklyn, he went to the opening, and he looked so awful—I think he'd dyed his hair orange—that they wouldn't let him in. We had other entertainment besides the poets. The late Michael Field's wife danced to records, and so did the painter Oronzo Gasparro. Maggie Egri sang Hungarian folk songs that she said she had learned at her mother's breast in Joplin, Missouri. She was a real, bona-fide witch. I used to stand on the side and wonder what it all meant, and yet in a way I was part of it, too. After a while, things got sort of drunken and evil-seeming. Uptown people started coming down so they could say they'd bought John Rose Gildea a drink, and a lot of the poets became more interested in the bottle than they were in conversations about life and literature. Then, unbeknownst to me, one of the waitresses got caught trying to sell liquor to a cop in plain-clothes, so they put a cop on the premises every night, and there he sat in his uniform, and it put a pall on the place. I could have given him twenty-five dollars and he would have gone away, but I didn't know enough. The place had been jammed every night, but in a month's time it was empty, and we closed. We'd been running a year."

Gordon stood up, cigar in mouth, and stretched. "I've got to get down to the club. There are some orders coming in, and my day porter is sick. The old Charles on Sixth Avenue serves a pretty good lunch." Ten minutes later he reappeared, housed in a dark suit and a lively tie. He walked to Park Avenue and found a cab.

"I was out of work for a while," Gordon said. "Then I put in six weeks running a place for a mob underling named Frankie Starch. He wasn't doing any business in the place he had, and he asked me to come in as a partner at thirty-five dollars a week. I changed the name of the place to the Village Fair Coffee House, and all the same poets and painters appeared, but it wasn't the same, because Starch and his friends were always around. I couldn't handle them. They were a tough bunch, and Starch kept referring to the poets as 'creeps.' I was eating in an all-night cafeteria after work one night and one of his hunkies found me and said, 'Frankie wants to see you.' Oh, boy, I thought. But all he wanted was to fire me, which he did. The last time I saw him, years ago, he was running a newsstand on Sixth Avenue and Third Street. I'd saved a hundred and fifty dollars, and I borrowed another fifty from a friend at Columbia, and in February of 1934 I found another basement place, at 1 Charles Street. Jack Delaney, the Village pub keeper, had had it one time, and I rented it for twenty-five dollars a month. It didn't have a stick of furniture, but I knew Frances Bell, from Provincetown. She had a place up there called the White Whale, and she had another one in an old blacksmith shop on Barrow Street. It had brick walls and belly stoves and it was so cold that winter—the temperature hit twenty below in New York—you couldn't pick up the silver. She gave me a bunch of barrels—big ones to stretch planks between for tables, and smaller ones to sit on—and I gave her a due bill for seventy-five dollars. I can't remember why, but I called the place the Village Vanguard, and a lot of the old crowd, including Gasparro and Maggie Egri and such, came back. After a year or so we moved, not losing a night's business, to the present Vanguard. It had been a speak called the Triangle Gardens. It was bigger—I could only seat forty or fifty at the old place—and it seemed to me that moving there would be like growing up. Then the damnedest thing happened, and it really shook me up. I got arrested and spent a night in jail. Someone had written obscene graffiti on the men's-room wall, and there is a crazy New York ordinance that holds a cabaret owner responsible for such things. I had to go to court in a paddy wagon, and when the judge heard from the cop why I'd been arrested and that I'd spent the night in jail, *he* was astonished and dismissed the case. But I've never forgotten the experience. There must be twenty coats of paint on the bathroom walls at the club, and the only things I don't wash off or paint over are scribblings like the one I found the other day: 'Roland Kirk is a nice cat.' "

Gordon ordered a Scotch-and-soda at the Charles, which is spacious and plush and emblazoned with paintings of nudes. He settled back and waved his hands in front of him. "This place always reminds me of one of my worst disasters—a fancy ice-cream parlor I opened in 1955 on Fifty-eighth Street near the Paris Theatre. My partner was Michael Field, and we called it Maxfield. The name was almost the only good thing about it. Michael had been a pianist before he got into his cooking school and his cookbooks, and he was a friend from the old days. The idea for the place was mine, and Michael was crazy about it. I wanted a place that would maybe cost ten thousand and that *looked* genuine, but he wanted it to *be* genuine. So we put in a mosaic floor, like the one in the men's room in Penn Station. We found an old Mazda-bulb sign for outside. All the tables and the counter top were marble. I think it took fourteen men to lift that counter into place. The chairs were old ice-cream-parlor chairs, the walls were red velvet and had hand-carved figures on the moldings, and the chandeliers were brass. It was a beautiful place, and it had beautiful food. Michael insisted we make our own ice cream, and he made all the desserts. I never saw so much cream in my life. But beauty is skin-deep, and underneath everything was wrong. We'd spent thousands and thousands and thousands. The floor alone cost thirty-five hundred and the sign twelve hundred, and all that marble was real. Those genuwine ice-cream-parlor chairs were so uncomfortable you couldn't sit in them for more than twenty minutes. We'd found these old glasses for the ice cream in a place down in the Bowery, but they were so heavy you could barely lift them, and they were so big they wouldn't fit into the dishwasher until we had special trays built. The prices were too high. People came around from Bergdorf's for a cup of coffee—*fresh* coffee, never more than twenty minutes old—and it would cost them twenty-five cents, and they'd hit the ceiling. We stayed open until one or two in the morning trying to catch the late crowd, but we didn't have a liquor license. And then the union started giving us trouble. It turned out that I had to run the place because Michael was so busy with his other interests, and at the time I had the Vanguard *and* the Blue Angel to worry about. I'd get to Maxfields at ten every morning absolutely pooped. I told Michael I couldn't put so much time in, and he said he couldn't spare any more, and shortly afterward he walked out and I never saw him again. The place is a Shelley's luncheonette now."

Gordon downed a second Scotch, neat, and ordered bay scallops. "My other great disaster took place ten years before, and the only difference was that it happened on *East* Fifty-eighth Street. Barney Josephson's Café Society Uptown had started doing poorly, and Herbert Jacoby and I bought it from him for seventy-five thousand, renamed it Le Directoire, tossed everything out, redecorated, and maybe spent another seventy thousand. At first it went like a house afire. We had Kay Thompson and the Williams Brothers, and there were literally lines around the block every night. But she left, and Abe Burrows came in, then Pearl Bailey, then Mata and Hari, and everything changed. We charged so much money that people got mad and stayed away, and the reason we charged so much was that when we redecorated we had somehow managed to reduce the seating capacity from three hundred and fifty to one hundred and thirty-six. Business got worse and worse, and finally, after eight months, we gave the place back to Barney for five thousand and got out. We'd poured everything from the Blue Angel into it, and it's a wonder that didn't fold, too."

Gordon speared some scallops with his fork and pushed them through his tartar sauce. "The food isn't bad in this old place. These are honest-to-God bay scallops, not the chopped-up haddock that you get most places. At the time of Le Directoire, Jacoby and I had already been in business five years at the Blue Angel, which was on Fifty-fifth between Third and Lexington. He had managed the Ruban Blue before that, but there was some sort of ruckus and he had walked out. He started coming down to the Vanguard to watch the acts, and we talked. He wanted to open a place, but he didn't have any money, and he asked me to come in as a partner. I put down five thousand, and he borrowed five thousand. It was a strange relationship. Jacoby had run places in Paris, and I guess he had more to do than anyone else with establishing the supper club over here. He's a man of taste and some background and he's also a snob, but I was just a downtown Village boy who got dressed up to go uptown. So at first I had to defer to him in many ways. He did the emceeing, at which he was good, and he did the booking, which tended to follow a delicate, almost esoteric line. The very first show included a French singer, Madame Claude Alphand, and an Ecuadorian baritone, who was terrible, and Sylvia Marlowe, the harpsichordist. The décor reflected Jacoby, too, with its gray velvet walls and rosettes and pink crystal chandeliers. And so did the food. We had a French chef, our own pastries, and Mme. Romaine, the omelette lady, came in every night to cook omelettes for supper. I don't know whether it was ego or what, but as time went on I started making booking suggestions, and it turned out that we tended to agree on most acts. We held auditions one afternoon a week, and eventually the Blue Angel had such a reputation that anyone who had worked there could get a job in any room in the country. In fact, there were acts who'd say they had worked with us when they hadn't, and we'd get verifying calls from bookers and club owners all over the country.

"It's hard to believe now some of the people who worked at the Blue Angel, the acts we helped start off—Josephine Premice, the dancer, and comedians like Kaye Ballard and Carol Burnett and Alice Pearce and Wally Cox and Orson Bean and Phyllis Diller and Shelley Berman. Woody Allen, too, who was so nervous when he started he shook like a leaf, and Nichols and May. There were dozens of singers. Some were established, like Mildred Bailey and Maxine Sullivan, but most were starters, like Andy Williams and the Inca Trio, which had that fantastic soprano, Yma Sumac, and Martha Wright and Pearl Bailey and Bobby Short and Harry Belafonte and Barbra Streisand. Jacoby doted on French acts, and there were nights at the Blue Angel when I never heard a word of English. Irene Bordoni was an oo-la-la French singer and Odette Myrtil was a French comedienne, and there was an amazing act, Les Mains d'Yves Joly, who used their fingers as puppets. There were a lot of English comedians, and one, Douglas Byng, was nerve-racking. He kept twitching his head and looking at his shoulder, as if some sort of bird was sitting there, and he talked so fast I couldn't understand a word. And, of course, there were a great

many people—and this is one of the sad things about show business—who performed and did nothing and disappeared. The
Blue Angel was a quality room, and we did a good business
until we began to feel the pressure from television, in the late
fifties. Business dropped off, as it did everywhere. Jacoby got
restless, anxious. He wanted to turn the place into a full-time
restaurant. We dickered, and I found some buyers from Chicago
who were interested in taking over his share, but he couldn't
make up his mind, and finally I bought him out for fifteen
thousand in cash and a twenty-thousand-dollar mortgage. I
changed the acts a little, bringing in Nipsy Russell and Clara
Ward, the gospel singer, and Max Morath, the ragtime pianist.
But everything looked musty and dusty to me. I couldn't stand
the rosettes on the walls, and the floor had got tacky. We were
doing fairly well, but the place needed new blood, a new face.
After a year or so I said the hell with it, and in the spring of
1964 I sold the works to the Living Room people. It was time
for me to go back downtown where I belonged. I'd been neglect-
ing the Vanguard and it wasn't doing well."

Gordon lit a cigar, and walked over to the Vanguard. It is in
the basement of a triangular, two-story building that faces
Seventh Avenue and is wedged between Eleventh Street and
Waverly Place. The door needs paint, and the awning is tat-
tered and worn. It's the sort of entranceway you could pass at an
amble and miss. Gordon went down narrow, steep stairs and
under a low arch that has probably cracked some of the most
distinguished heads in the world. The main room of the Vanguard is, like the building it is in, triangular, and is fifty or
sixty feet long. At its apex there is a small bandstand, and its
base is flanked by a coatroom and the bar. Behind the bar are
the washrooms and a small kitchen. Banquettes line the walls
of the main room, and there are a dozen tiny tables. The place
didn't look like the Hollywood version of an empty night club.
The chairs, instead of being stacked upside down on the tables,
were exactly where their last occupants had left them, and the

floor was littered with cigarette butts. It was cold, and the room smelled like a cave.

"I've got to get someone in here to clean up," Gordon said. "I never get spooked when I'm here alone, but I can't stand the cold." He turned on a small gas heater by the bandstand, and we went into the kitchen. It was clean and compact, with two big black stoves, a sink, a worktable, a small wooden desk, and a couple of chairs. Gordon sat down at his desk in his hat and coat and made a couple of telephone calls. "My office, my home, my palace," he said when he had finished. "This place has been like a love match to me. I've probably spent more time in it than anywhere else. I've even slept here, stretched out on a couple of tables. I've learned that if you're good to the Vanguard, the Vanguard will be good to you. And I learned that when we moved here. The entertainment then was pretty much catch-as-catch-can. Ivan Black had taken a job over at the Four Trees, which later became Café Society Downtown, and Eli Siegel replaced him as master of ceremonies. He never drank, so I had to pay him, and he recited Vachel Lindsay at the top of his voice. He wasn't everybody's favorite, but he kept things in hand. In between poetry readings I played a phonograph for dancing, and we had a lot of itinerant entertainers. They floated all over the village—operatic baritones, comedians, piano players—and they'd come in and perform and people threw money at them. On Christmas Eves the Almanac Singers would come in and everybody would join them singing. Pete Seeger and Woody Guthrie were in that group. I began to look for acts to put in, and what I wanted was something that would comment on the social and political scene. There was a girl who used to hang around at this time, and her name was Judy Tuvim, which is Hebrew for 'holiday.' She was answering telephones with Orson Welles's Mercury Theatre. She brought down Adolph Green, and he brought in Betty Comden, who was a student at N.Y.U. They were part of a group that had been rehearsing uptown called Six and Company, and I hired them for Sunday nights for twenty-five or thirty dollars. They did a lot of topical stuff, like our selling the Sixth Avenue 'L' to the Japs so that they could make bombs to blow up the Chinese with. They changed their name to the Revuers, and they were so good that the whole town started knocking at the Vanguard door. It got so crowded people had to sit on the floor. So they began performing six nights a week, and they were with me a year. I could have kept them five years, but they were offered more money by the Rainbow Room, and it was a step up for them. They spawned a lot of imitators, but none had that same fresh young quality, that quickness and sparkle. Folk singers started getting big, and Josh White and Leadbelly came in as a team, and I had Burl Ives and Richard Dyer Bennett and Pete Seeger. I also began hiring jazz groups, like a marvellous trio with Zutty Singleton and Eddie Heywood and Albert Nicholas. I had calpyso groups, and Professor Irwin Corey, the comic, first came in 1945. And, by God, he was back with me last week. By this time the Blue Angel was going strong, so we began trying out acts here first and then sending them uptown. That happened with Eartha Kitt and Pearl Bailey and Josephine Premice and Harry Belafonte. Eddie Heywood had brought Pearl Bailey to me, which was often the way I got my best acts, like Aretha Franklin, who was brought here by Major Holley, the bassist. Pearl was a band singer, but she was already doing her thing of switching from singing to talking in the middle of a number, and I encouraged her to do it. I had established a room that was free and easy, and I think *she* felt free and easy. Then somewhere in 1957 I switched almost completely to a jazz policy, even though I still had acts like the Kingston Trio and Mort Sahl and Nina Simone and Miriam Makeba and Lenny Bruce. I never *did* get completely used to Bruce. The four-letter words stuck to me like burrs, the way they still do when I find them on the printed page."

There was a banging at the street door. "That'll be the Coca-Cola man," Gordon said. "I have to let him in. The door upstairs never used to be locked, and people would wander in all afternoon—singers, comics, musicians, looking for jobs. But I got mugged on the stairs about a year and a half ago, so I keep it locked now." Gordon returned, and there was a tremendous *thump-thump-thump* as the delivery man eased his dolly down the stairs. Gordon paid him in cash and sat down.

"I probably have the smallest staff of any place this size in New York. My bartender has been with me twenty years, and there's my day porter. I have a couple of waiters who come and go, and my sister Sadye helps out. She'll be in in a while, so that I can go uptown for a nap. People sometimes ask me who decorated the place. The answer is nobody. It decorated itself. It hasn't changed much. The stage used to be where the bar is now, and a Refregier protégé did the original murals. I remember a horse playing a piano. But the walls crumbled, and the murals with them. People don't seem to care much about eating in basements, so the food end has never been very important. The most ambitious I ever got was when I hired a chef who said he'd studied cooking in Paris. I auditioned him by bringing five or six friends down, and he cooked a beautiful meal. I bought a whole bunch of those utensils for eating snails with and special bowls for onion soup. All that stuff is still packed away in here somewhere. His first night, fifty or so people ordered dinner. The orders kept coming into the kitchen, but nothing came out. The waiters stood around, and when the food was finally ready it was either overdone or underdone or cold. He didn't know what the hell he was doing, but when dinner was over, out he went into the room in his chef's garb, perspiring and covered with gravy stains, and said, 'Well, how was everything, folks?'

"The worst time for the Vanguard came in the early sixties. I had to sell our car and the little place we had built out on Fire Island. One of my girls was there visiting a friend last summer, and they went by our old house and the friend told her it's still called 'the Gordon house.' One of the axioms of the night-club business is that you have to have somebody to lean on for money. Like the man who lent me the fifty dollars to open the first Vanguard in 1934. He lent me ten thousand during the bad days in the sixties, and a week ago I paid him the last fifty dollars. I've never been much of a businessman, but we've taken in some money at times. When I could still afford Miles Davis, he'd bring in nine thousand a week. Money is a funny thing. A lot of musicians have borrowed from me—twenty-five, fifty, a hundred—and most of them pay it back. The ones who don't, though, will pay me, say, half, and then usually I don't see them for a long time. When they show up again, I think, He still owes me twenty bucks, but I don't say anything and he doesn't say anything, and after a while the unpaid money just seems to disappear, as though it had never existed. It's amazing how money can vanish like that. Business has picked up in the last year or so. The kids are coming in, and they aren't so different from the way we were in the late twenties. And I get a lot of blacks, so I only use strong black acts like Elvin Jones and Roland Kirk and Pharoah Saunders. And the Thad Jones–Mel Lewis big band is in its sixth year of Monday nights. They jam the place, they keep me going. A lot of people sit in, like Ray Charles, when he's around, and last week there were so many visiting musicians in this kitchen I could hardly get in the door. It's like the old jam sessions Harry Lim ran here one night a week in the forties. Of course, I'll never retire. How could I? I couldn't live on Social Security. When my present lease is up, I'll renew it for another ten years."

There were steps on the stairs. "That'll be Sadye now," Gordon said.

[1971]

Max Gordon has just celebrated his staying power (the Vanguard may be the oldest night club in the world) by publishing a remarkable autobiography called *Live at the Village Vanguard*. The dust jacket starts the book off just right. A sepia montage photograph shows Gordon standing in front of the Vanguard surrounded by a crowd of his performers. Some are playing instruments (John Coltraine, Miles Davis, Percy Heath, Gerry Mulligan), one is singing (Leadbelly), some are smiling wildly (Coleman Hawkins, Dexter Gordon, Keith Jarrett), some are looking supercilious (Woody Guthrie, Milt Jackson), and one is gazing into the middle distance (Dizzy Gillespie). No one is looking at Gordon. Inside, Gordon threads his way through his life, which must sometimes seem like a montage to him, in a highly original way. The book, which he wrote sheet by careful sheet over a period of seven years, is not a cascade of names (many of his graduates are not mentioned) but a series of sharp, funny dialogues between him and various interlocutors, some real and some distillations of people he has known. Gordon's literary dynamics are startling. He is gentle and poetic, he drones, he is almost ribald. He talks to Joe Glaser, the tough booking agent who made Louis Armstrong a millionaire:

> [Dinah Washington] came out of the dressing room into the spotlight and as the applause died down and she was about to go into her opening number, I noticed that she was wearing a blond wig. I couldn't believe it. . . . Nobody laughed, but that was only because of the innate good taste of the Village Vanguard audiences. I told Joe that I was so upset by this vision of a blond wig on Dinah Washington's head that I had to see him. . . .
>
> "A blond wig!" shouted Joe.
>
> "Yes, a blond wig!" I shouted back. "Here's a handsome black woman, a great singer, a star, and she comes out—I didn't believe my eyes—with a blond wig sitting on top of her head."
>
> "These *schwarzes* are nuts," said Joe. "She's got herself a new guy; that's what it is. Otherwise why should she put a blond wig on her head? She's got a new guy taking her money. Let me give you some advice, Max. Don't pay it any attention. Make believe you don't see it. She'll get over it. I know Dinah.
>
> "She'll dump this guy, whoever he is. And the blond wig will go away. As long as business holds up, what've you got to worry about? And, another thing, you think it's undignified, you think it's grotesque. But I'll bet you some fancy customers are quietly getting a kick out of the sight of a blond wig on a black broad."

And he talks to a customer he calls Jim:

"Like I'm telling you, if you'd signed them in the beginning when they came to you, all those acts, unknown, unemployed, raw, hungry acts—if you'd got a piece of the action right in the beginning—then, when they got to be stars, celebrities, you'd be on easy street today, collecting 10 percent of their paychecks and living like a king. Know what I mean?"

It was my friend Jim talking. I hadn't seen him in twenty years. He made a fortune in plastics. He used to be a regular when he was a student at N.Y.U. and Wally Cox was working at the Vanguard . . . I remember he was crazy about Wally Cox.

"Look at the names you found, or they found you— what'd it matter? . . . You turned 'em into stars! You made 'em famous! But what good did it do you? You didn't have a piece of the action.

"All right, you paid Wally peanuts. You thought you were getting a bargain. When he graduated from your joint and went on television, when he was cast as Mr. Peepers in that television series that ran for years, you were left out in the cold. Why? Because you didn't sign him up at the start, when he was still an unknown and needed you."

Jim had a way of worrying me.

"It wasn't so easy," I said to Jim.

Here is Gordon talking to Miles Davis:

Miles didn't coddle his audiences, or his boss either. "You talk, 'Man, this, man that!' " he once growled at me. "Don't talk to me like a black man. You're a white man and don't forget it."

I was in his house on West Seventy-seventh Street. Miles, neat, immaculate, in a tailored suit, dark glasses, asked me, "Did you go up to see my tailor like I told you?"

"Who can afford three hundred for a suit?"

"You're too goddamn cheap."

"If I was making the kind of money I'm paying you, I'd get myself one."

The Baroness Nica Koenigswarter, a Rothschild and an indefatigable aide-de-camp to jazz musicians, stops in at the Vanguard and talks to Gordon in the kitchen, which is furnished with towering stacks of Heineken's beer, a huge red sink, box after box of waiters' checks, a wall clock, photographs, and two dog-eared journals, one to record reservations and one to record the musicians signed up for the coming six months:

> "Darling," the Baroness was saying to me, "you can thank me that Thelonious was on time tonight. If I hadn't driven him down, he'd still be on Sixty-fifth Street waving for a cab. Cabs won't stop for him. They're afraid of him, a big black man gesturing wildly on the corner."

Gordon speculates on the failure of the Blue Angel:

> But there it was, happening all around me. I didn't see it, didn't want to see it—that a new generation of night prowlers didn't want to go to the kind of place the Blue Angel was. They didn't want to watch an act; they wanted to do their own act. They didn't want to sit glued to a chair in a nightclub. They wanted to do their "own thing," investigate the mystery of the night, listen to a little music, get up and dance maybe, or just sit and talk to the girl sitting next to them at the bar.

A week before *Live at the Village Vanguard* was published, Gordon had dinner at La Tulipe with his friend Jim, who was in town for a visit. La Tulipe is the small, first-class French restaurant that was opened on West Thirteenth Street a year and a half ago by John and Sally Darr, who are old acquaintances of Gordon's. Gordon was dressed in his winter uniform: a chocolate corduroy suit, a yellow flannel shirt, long johns, Wallabees, and a black fedora with its brim down. He has become about the size and shape of a Seckel pear. White hair curtains the back of his bare head, and bumperlike black-rimmed glasses shield the front. He walks slowly and sparingly, his feet making parentheses. When he puts on his overcoat and pulls down his black hat, he disappears. Gordon and Jim arrived at La Tulipe at six-thirty and sat down in the tiny bar by the front door. Jim has red hair and is twice the size of Gordon, and he idolizes him. "Max," he has said to Gordon, "you are one of the wonders of New York life." Gordon ordered a half bottle of Chablis, and introduced Jim to John Darr, a bespectacled former headmaster who looks like a former headmaster.

"It's cold in here," Gordon said to Jim. "I don't know, I have this cough and I haven't been feeling all that well lately. But I haven't had a cigar today and I'm not going to have one."

"You should give them up, Max," Jim said. "They'll stunt your growth."

Darr asked Gordon if he'd like to move to his table, and the two men followed him down a short hall and into the dining room, which is medium-sized and plum-colored. "It's cold in here, too," Gordon said. "It feels like the Vanguard before I turn on the gas heaters."

"Those heaters should have gone out with Hoover, Max," Jim said.

Gordon looked at the menu—and the prices—a long time, and shook his head. "And to think I used to eat Sally Darr's cooking free in her apartment." Gordon and Jim settled on tongue päté, sweetbreads (Gordon), red snapper steamed in paper (Jim), and an apricot soufflé. Gordon ordered a bottle of Spanna.

"Max, you wrote a book," Jim said, as if he were complimenting him on catching a huge fish. "When did you get time to write books? During intermission? Who's your ghost?"

"Me!" Gordon said, laughing. Then he leaned back and opened his eyes and mouth, making three big O's. He has a muscular baritone—a voice accustomed to elbowing its way through night clubs. "I started the book around the time Charlie Mingus published his autobiography, *Beneath the Underdog*. That was seven or eight years ago. In fact, I started it with Nel King, who did Mingus's book with him. She talked to me and wrote a chapter, and on the basis of that chapter she sold the book to Peggy Brooks at Coward-McCann. But when I read what she'd done I hated it. It wasn't me. So Peggy Brooks got Sy Krim, and he taped me and did a chapter, and it wasn't any better. Sy said, 'Max, you gotta write it yourself.' So I began to write. I'd get up at six or seven and have breakfast and write four or five hours. I had a wonderful time. I'd sit there and laugh and knock myself out. But I discovered I had to rewrite everything four times to make it sound like it was only written once. So I rewrote and rewrote—always in longhand on yellow legal pads—and eventually I got a little help from a free-lance editor named Judy Murphy. I kept trying to find a way to get my ideas across, and I hit on dialogues, sometimes with real people, sometimes with people based on real people. Some of the dialogues are fictional, but it's fiction borrowed directly from life. Life fiction, you might call it. And I wanted to make the book a New York book, which it is. It celebrates New York. When I got enough of it in what I considered decent shape, I sent a few chapters around—to Pete Hamill and Nat Hentoff— and the *Village Voice* ran excerpts from them. I got an agent, who wanted to do this and that. One of the thats was Double-day, which took six months to turn the book down. The manu-script went to Coward-McCann. Peggy Brooks had left, and I'd given my two-thousand-dollar advance to Nel King, who died. Coward-McCann turned it down. Then Marcia Markland at St. Martin's saw the chapters in the *Voice* and called me. I didn't pay any attention at first, but then I did, and we have a book. I'm surprised it came out so well. I really like the chapter on going to Russia with the Thad Jones–Mel Lewis band, and I like the chapters on Lenny Bruce and Richard Dyer-Bennet and the early days with Eli Siegel. People have told me they love the book. I hope they're telling the truth. I've also heard from people who aren't in the book, like Katie O'Brien, a Martha Graham dancer who worked for me forty-four years ago. She said the book was too short. But I never got to know a lot of the people who appeared at the Vanguard. Maybe they were scared of me, maybe I was scared of them. Maybe they were like John Coltrane, who was always surrounded by worshippers. I loved his music, but I never said four words to him."

Gordon picked at his sweetbreads, and Jim tore into his snap-per, which he said was superb. The dining room had filled up and warmed up, and Gordon said he was comfortable. Sally Darr, attractive in whites, came out of the kitchen to say hello to Max, and Max asked her who the famous comedian had been at one of the dinner parties he'd attended at her house. He said he'd been trying to think of his name for a week. Did he mean Danny Kaye, she asked. Gordon laughed, slapped the table, and made three O's. Mrs. Darr told the men to enjoy their dinner and said the soufflé would be ready in twenty minutes. Gordon told Jim that his life had changed since he'd last seen him. He said that he and his wife, Lorraine, were separated, and that his daughters, Deborah and Rebecca, were grownup and working. "I live alone in a one-bedroom at Fifth Avenue and Eleventh," Gordon said. "Lorraine and I have dinner every so often, and a couple of summers ago we rented a house out at Three Mile Harbor, on the Island. I have all these little habits that keep me company, and I don't know where they came from. When I get up in the morning, I have a glass of lemon juice and hot water, and half a grapefruit. Then I have two cups of coffee—one with cream and one with boiled milk, half and half. Sometimes I make a little oatmeal, too. I read the *Times* from cover to cover. I'm always reading a book. I don't like modern novels, but I just reread *War and Peace*. What a fantastic, beautiful book! I look at very little television—sometimes Phil Donahue or 'Good Morning America.' I think Donahue is honest. Later in the morning, I might take a nap. Then I have lunch. Sometimes I eat with someone in a restaurant, but not often. Generally, I eat at counters, because I'm alone and you have company at counters. I go to a little place and have steamed milk and honey, or to another place for fruit and cheese. If I want a glass of wine, I go to One Fifth Avenue. After lunch, I go to the Vanguard and put everything in order—phone calls and publicity and liquor orders and booking, and the like. The phone rings every couple of minutes. I've never been able to find anyone who would run the Vanguard the way I do, so I do it myself. Anyway, I'll never sell it. When and if the time comes, I'll give it away. After I've finished my business at the club, around five-thirty, I have another little nap, and go out for dinner—at Joe's, on MacDougal Street, or at Pirandello, on Washington Place. I'm an old face at both places, and that's what I like—to go to places where I'm known. On almost any street in the Village, which *is* a village, someone recognizes me. When I take a little walk Sunday afternoons, I'll stop at the Spring Street Bar and have a glass of wine or some espresso, and the man at the bar knows me and serves me espresso right there. If I go to Bradley's or the Cedar bar, it's the same—someone knows you and you feel like you're in a small town. After dinner, I go back to the Vanguard and stay until midnight. The old days, I used to walk out of here sweating and exhausted at 4 a.m. I don't have much of a social life anymore. I don't have the time, and I suppose it's different since Lorraine and I aren't together."

Gordon told Jim to eat all the apricot soufflé himself, and Jim did and said it was the best dessert he'd ever had. Jim asked Gordon how his sister Sadye was.

"Funny you should ask," Gordon said. "She gave me quite a scare this week. Sadye's two years younger than I am, and we're very close. She lives by herself up near the George Washington Bridge, but we talk almost every day. I worry about her being alone, because she's inclined to take falls, you know. Anyway, when I called her this past Tuesday the phone rang and rang: no answer. I called back every fifteen minutes for an hour, an hour and a half. The same. I called one more time. Still the same. I got panicky. I called her landlord, and asked him would he take a look for her in her apartment. He said, 'I have no key.' I said, 'You have no key? What do you mean you have no key? I never heard of a landlord who hasn't got a key!' I was getting excited, you see. I said, 'Please take a look in her window from the fire escape.' He did. He saw a light but couldn't see Sadye. I thought, Maybe she's lying on the floor and can't help herself. So I called 911, and they told me to call the 34th Precinct, where Sadye lives, and I did. Then I called Sadye again—and she answered. She just went out to shop and got talking to a neighbor at the market. I called the 34th Precinct back and said she just went to shop and was O.K. Sadye is a good girl. She is very intelligent, but, like all old-fashioned Jewish girls, she had little education and was kept in the home."

Gordon paid the check and said good night to Darr, and he and Jim walked the three blocks to the Vanguard. "Who's this Pat Metheny you have here tonight?" Jim asked when they reached the Vanguard door.

"I've been listening to his records off and on for two or three years, and at first I didn't like them," Gordon said. "It's taken me all that time to decide whether or not I wanted him in the place. Finally, he called me up, and I guess that helped me decide. He's just a kid, but he said he wanted to work at the Vanguard in the worst way. He said the Vanguard is where the vibes are—he used the word 'vibes.' He said the Vanguard was the place to be."

Gordon and Jim sat down at a table in the rear, and the music began. The band, which included Dewey Redman on tenor saxophone, Charlie Haden on bass, and Paul Motian on drums, started a fast blues. Metheny plays guitar. He uses a lot of amplifiers and sounds as if he were in Radio City Music Hall. Jim listened closely and looked over at Gordon. His arms were folded across his stomach, and his head was almost touching them.

"Max, you should be home in bed," Jim said, leaning over and touching one of Gordon's arms.

"What?" Gordon said, lifting his head. "I'm all right. I'm here. Metheny sounds pretty good. He sounds all right."

Two days later, Gordon's publisher gave an early-evening party at the Vanguard for Gordon's book. He paid for the booze and the music (a quintet led by the trumpeter Benny Bailey and including the tenor saxophonist Charlie Rouse), and the publisher supplied the food. A couple of hundred people came, and Gordon, circulating steadily, was invisible unless you were standing beside him. He was dressed in a stiff gray suit and a blue flannel shirt open at the neck. He said that this was the first time he'd worn the suit, even though he'd bought it four years before. John Wilcock, a founder of the *Village Voice*, said hello to him, and so did Stanton Wheeler, the Yale professor. Gordon said that Wheeler had taken him to the Yale Club bar, and that that was a sign of upward mobility. Jack Levine and his wife said hello. Gordon posed for a family photograph with Lorraine and their daughters. He had several glasses of champagne, which he doesn't like except at parties. During an intermission, Irwin Corey gave a speech from the bandstand, and called Gordon "a beacon." Betty Comden and Adolph Green said that their love for Gordon was "unbounded." The band returned, and Gordon, standing just in front, made Toscanini shushing gestures. Jim came up and put an arm around Gordon's shoulders. "Betty and Adolph almost made me cry, Jim," Gordon said. "What do you think of that?"

[1980]

II

Barney Josephson, who is sixty-nine, still cherishes and grows eloquent over what he wrought at Café Society Downtown and Café Society Uptown thirty-three years ago. His intent was simple and revolutionary: to present first-rate but generally unknown Negro and white talent to integrated audiences in honest, attractive surroundings. The performers at the clubs were as often as not discovered by Josephson or by the critic John Hammond, who provided the musical talent. Among the singers were Sarah Vaughan, Billie Holiday, Mildred Bailey, Lena Horne, Kenneth Spencer, Lucienne Boyer, Joe Turner, the Golden Gate Quartet, Patti Page, Josh White, Burl Ives, Big Bill Broonzy, Susan Reed, and Kay Starr. Among the comedians were Imogene Coca, Zero Mostel, Jimmy Savo, Jack Gilford, Jim Backus, Carol Channing, and Jim Copp. Among the dancers were the Kraft Sisters and Pearl Primus. And among the musicians were Frankie Newton, Red Allen, Bill Coleman, Teddy Wilson, Art Tatum, James P. Johnson, Albert Ammons, Meade

Lux Lewis, Pete Johnson, Edmond Hall, Lester Young, Sidney Catlett, John Kirby, Eddie Heywood, Vincente Gomez, Django Reinhardt, Hazel Scott, Mary Lou Williams, Cliff Jackson, and Ellis Larkins. The surroundings in which this galaxy revolved were remarkable. Café Society Downtown in Sheridan Square was in a comfortable, L-shaped basement (capacity two hundred and ten) decorated with funny murals by the likes of Adolf Dehn, Sam Berman, Ad Reinhardt, and Abe Birnbaum. The Uptown was on Fifty-eighth Street between Park and Lexington, in what is now the Fine Arts Theatre. It was an airy, two-story amphitheatre (capacity three hundred and fifty), with surrealistic murals by Anton Refregier. The bandstand was at the rear, and it was flanked by tiers of banquettes and tables that descended to a dance floor. A balcony with more tables ran along the back of the room. There were floor shows at both clubs at nine, twelve, and two, and a typical one at the Uptown included several numbers by Teddy Wilson's band (Joe Thomas, trumpet; Edmond Hall, clarinet; Benny Morton, trombone; John Williams, bass; Sidney Catlett, drums), one of them a flagwaver built around an invariably ingenious Catlett solo; half a dozen rushing, helter-skelter piano solos by Hazel Scott, who liked to jazz up Bach and "In a Country Garden"; Jimmy Savo's inimitable pantomime; and the loose-boned gospel songs and spirituals of the Golden Gate Quartet. In effect, three concerts, or recitals, were offered every night, and each was different. Between the shows, which lasted about an hour, one ate and danced—not to an intermission trio but to Wilson's great band. Both clubs were congenial, clean, and pressureless. One could sit at the bar, nursing a single beer, for an entire evening. And parents actually *sent* their children to them unchaperoned for such state occasions as birthday parties and graduation parties. The food was important. It was fancier at the Uptown, partly owing to the fact that this club brought in a different sort of trade and partly owing to Josephson's mysterious belief that "people at Downtown just didn't pay much attention to eating, because they were in a basement." (Vide Max

Gordon.) There was no cover charge in either club, and the minimum—a dollar or two—included food and/or drink. At the Uptown, the table d'hote dinner ranged from $2.25 (creamed chicken) to $4.75 (prime sirloin steak). The service made both eighteen-year-olds and seventy-year-olds comfortable. "Many of the people who came to my clubs were like Eleanor Roosevelt," Josephson has said. "She had never been in a nightclub in her life, and she never went to another one."

Josephson, who has kept to himself since the Café Society days, has owned a Village restaurant called The Cookery for the past seventeen years. Located on the northeast corner of Eighth Street and University Place, it is a spic-and-span place furnished with plain, wood-topped tables and an omelette bar and decorated with Refregier hangings and murals. The prices are reasonable, and both cheeseburgers and steak all' pizzaiola are on the menu. The Cookery has never had music, but recently Josephson announced that the pianist Mary Lou Williams would soon open there. One afternoon, Josephson talked about his new venture, and about what he had been doing during the past twenty years. Josephson was sitting at a table in the Cookery with his wife, Gloria. She is intense, wiry, and fast-moving; Josephson is easy-going. He wears glasses, his cheeks are pink, his hair is white, and he looks like the late Ed Wynn. He speaks softly and quickly, has a high Wynn giggle, and is an effortless monologist.

Mrs. Josephson departed, and Josephson began to talk. "I've had three other Cookerys uptown that were either unprofitable or were in buildings that were torn down. I live in the apartment house upstairs—right over the candy store, you could say, like the immigrants who roomed in the back of their shops and turned down the heat under their soup when the little bell out front rang and they had to go see who was in the store. "I can't get over having Mary Lou Williams working for me again. She was at the Downtown for five years, and although she was never an overpowering attraction, she had a devoted coterie. Her coming back happened in the damnedest way. A young

Jesuit named Peter O'Brien called me and said he had spent a lot of time recently with Mary Lou Williams, and could he come and see me? He did—in fact, he came several times—but he never mentioned just what he had on his mind. I found him a charming man, and if I were an important Catholic layman I'd tell the Pope to keep an eye on him. Then O'Brien appeared with Mary. I hadn't seen her for twenty years. From time to time she had called me, generally about someone she knew who was in trouble, but never about herself. Well, out it came: "If I could only work for you again, Barney'—in that funny, chuckling way she has—'the happiest days of my life were at the Downtown.' She wasn't interested in cash, she said. She just wanted to work, and—well—she'd been getting seventeen hundred plus a week when she finally left me. I thought about it and looked into it and found I didn't need a cabaret license as long as there were no more than three instruments, all stringed. She brought along a bassist, Michael Fleming, and they opened soon after. I can't get over watching my old Cookery patrons watching her, and I can't get over how many of my Café Society customers have come in.

"The way I first got into the night-club business was far stranger. My parents came over from Latvia in 1900, and I was born two years later in Trenton. There were already two girls and three boys. My father was a cobbler and my mother a seamstress. When I was eight or nine months old my father stepped on a rusty nail and gangrene set in, and it was fatal. My mother was left with six children and no money. She went to work for a ladies' tailor, and an Irish lady who had twelve or thirteen children of her own took care of me during the day. My oldest brother, David, worked in a shoe store, and my oldest sister in a sweatshop, making ladies' silk bathrobes. We lived in an apartment so small one of my sisters slept in a closet. But my mother was a very frugal woman, and in time she had enough money to buy a house. It had four floors and cost a thousand dollars. It even had a bathroom, and the bathroom had a copper tub that David painted white every spring. When I got out of

high school, David, who now had his own shoe business, told
me that since we already had two brothers who were lawyers
and I didn't look like medical material, I had better go into the
shoe business with him. He had a keen sense of style. If he
picked out a hundred pairs of shoes, they were *all* good. But he
always overbought. He showed a profit—but in inventory,
not cash. So along came the Depression, and there we were,
with all those Whitehouse & Hardy shoes and $75,000 in ac-
counts receivable. We went broke. My brother eventually
started up again, but I didn't want any more of being an owner,
so by the mid-thirties I was clerking in a shoe store in Atlantic
City. I made forty dollars a month, lived in a four-dollar room,
and ate my meals across the street in Bayliss's drugstore. But all
this time I had the notion of starting a nightclub in the back of
my head.

"When I worked for my brother, I used to go to the Marbridge
Building on Herald Square, where all the shoe manufacturers
showed their wares. I was an out-of-town buyer, so I was taken
out to nightclubs. I liked what I saw, at least from a business
point of view. A café restaurant has no inventory. The food
turns over every day and the liquor once a week. And it's a
cash business, or it was before credit cards and charge accounts.
I had been to Europe in the early thirties and had visited the
political cabarets, where there was very pointed satire. And I'd
seen Gypsy Rose Lee doing a political strip tease at fund-raising
affairs in New York for the Lincoln Brigade. I conceived the
idea of presenting some sort of satire and alternating it with
jazz music. But there was an even more important reason why
I wanted to start a club. My fondness for jazz often took me to
places like the Cotton Club in Harlem to hear Ethel Waters or
Duke Ellington. Well, the Negro patrons were seated at the
back in a segregated section—in a *Harlem* night club! And I'd
been to the Kit-Kat Club in the East Fifties, which had all-black
entertainment, plus black help, and yet not a Negro was ad-
mitted to the place. Until junior high I had gone to school with
nothing but other Jews and the Irish. The first day I walked

into class I saw a black boy sitting at a desk. The desk you picked became your desk for the year. Nobody had taken a desk near him, so I did, and we became great friends. And later I argued in a debate against military training in schools. I lost the debate, but afterward eight or ten boys got me in a corner and beat me up for what I'd said. So all those things were in my background, and New York in the mid-thirties echoed my feelings. It was the time of the labor organizers and the Ladies Garment Workers' show called *Pins and Needles* and the W.P.A. Art Movement and *The Cradle Will Rock*. I wanted a club where blacks and whites worked together behind the footlights and sat together out front. There wasn't, so far as I knew, a place like it in New York or in the country."

Two skinny, shy, dark-haired boys who turned out to be Josephson's sons, Edward and Louis, tumbled in the restaurant door and stopped at the table. They said they had taken the subway all the way from school on the upper West Side and hadn't got lost once. Josephson laughed. "Go and eat. Go and eat," he said. "Your mother's in the back.

"I made my decision early in 1938. I quit my job in Atlantic City and, with just $7.60 to my name, borrowed $6000 from two friends in Trenton. I had found a shuttered-up basement in Sheridan Square. The liquor license was $1200, the cabaret license $150, and the rent $200, and out the money began to go. And there was the decorating. I didn't want mirrors and draperies and velours. I wanted art. Sam Shaw, a painter and photographer, brought some of his W.P.A. Art friends in to do some murals—Adolf Dehn, William Gropper, Sam Berman, Gregor Duncan, and Abe Birnbaum. I paid them $200 each and gave them due bills of a like amount for food and liquor. Some of those due bills went on for years, too. I didn't tell them what to paint, only that the place would be called, in a tongue-in-cheek way, Café Society. Clare Boothe Luce had suggested it, through some mutual friends, and it fitted into my satirical scheme. A couple of girls on *Vogue* who had given me all sorts of ideas suggested we have a doorman but that he be dressed in a raggedy coat and white gloves with the fingertips out. They also suggested we find an Elsa Maxwell type who'd ride a scooter up and down the aisles. We did have the doorman for six or eight months, but we never found the right Elsa Maxwell. But the greatest help to me was John Hammond. He built my first band around the trumpet player Frankie Newton, and he brought in Albert Ammons and Meade Lux Lewis, the boogie-woogie pianists. And three weeks later he told me I had to have still another boogie-woogie pianist, Pete Johnson, but that Johnson only came with Joe Turner, the blues shouter. Jack Gilford was my first comedian. He'd been a stooge for Milton Berle at vaudeville houses like the Palace, where he was planted in the audience to shout insults at Berle onstage. John brought in the Golden Gate Quartet soon after, and they made the blood rush up my arms, which brought the goose pimples out when they sang—and here I was a disbeliever—'As they were driving the nails in His feet / You could hear the hammer ringing in Jerusalem's streets.' We opened on December 18, 1938. Village people came, and so did uptown types and the college kids. On Friday nights the place looked like Princeton, Yale, and Harvard rolled into one. It was a grand success, but I was losing money. I simply didn't know enough about this sort of merchandising. By the end of the first year I was $28,000 in the hole. It became a holding operation, paying out two hundred here and three hundred there to my creditors. I began to think that I had opened the club in the wrong part of town, that I should move uptown. I found a place on Fifty-eighth Street which had changed hands a lot and been burned out by some mugs trying to collect fire insurance. My press agent, Ivan Black, sent out a release saying that Café Society was so successful I was opening an uptown branch. Actually, I planned to dump the original club, but when people heard about the uptown club the crowd doubled downtown and I suddenly began making money. Café Society Uptown opened on October 8, 1940. A waiter I had stopped by to see me the other day, and he'd come across the menu for that night. It offered shrimps and oysters and clams, celery and olives, a couple of soups, a two-inch prime filet mignon with mushrooms, two vegetables, a choice of potatoes, and dessert. The price on the card was a dollar fifty! Uptown had cost me almost $30,000 to put in shape, all of it borrowed, but it started making money immediately, and by the end of that year I had paid off every cent."

The lights in the Cookery dimmed for the start of the dinner hour. Several groups of people came in, and Josephson excused himself to seat them. A headwaiter carried a huge poinsettia from the back of the restaurant and put it on one end of the omelette bar. Next to the bar was a brand-new grand piano. Josephson finished seating a family of five, then sat down. "That plant adds a little festivity to where Mary sits. She didn't want a Steinway, she wanted a Baldwin. I'm renting it, and if I decide to buy it the rent money goes toward the purchase." Josephson laughed. "I've got some accountant, and she's having fits over all this. "You bring this piano player in here and it's doing nothing but costing money,' she says to me. 'Thirty dollars for that plant and nineteen dollars for the piano tuner each time he comes, and now he's coming *twice* a week. Next thing, you'll be out of business, with all your music.'

"I moved the Downtown show to the Uptown when it opened, and brought new people in Downtown. Mary took Hazel Scott's place, and Ida Cox came in for Billie Holiday. Teddy Wilson went Uptown and Eddie Heywood came in Downtown. In time I had a steady floating company of musicians and comedians and dancers and singers that moved back and forth between the clubs and that worked on a nearly permanent basis. It was a new concept in night clubs, and it gave the performers a sense of security most of them had never had before. It also gave them time to try out new routines and ideas. Hazel Scott was with me for seven years and the boogie-woogie boys, as we called them, for over four. Billie and Lena Horne stayed a year, and so did Jack Gilford. Jimmy Savo, who hadn't worked for ten years, stayed for three. People like Suzy Reed and Josh White were in and out for years, and so was Mildred Bailey. I don't know how I had this in me, but I learned how to shape talent, how to bring a performer's best out. I even costumed them, and I'd find myself in Bergdorf's with some cute new little singer and saying to one of those gray-haired salesladies, 'I'd like this young lady gowned.' Lena Horne was one of my first projects. She had worked in the line at the Cotton Club, and I first heard her, at John Hammond's suggestion, when she was singing with Charlie Barnet's band at the Paramount. She was beautiful, stunning, but it was hard to tell whether she could really sing or not. But I hired her, and at her first rehearsal I noticed that all her movements and routines were done in Latin rhythms, which were very big then. It didn't look right. I asked her if she was a Negro, and she bristled and said yes. I told her she could pass for anything, and she blew up. 'I don't dig you,' she said, and I said, 'Lena, there are dozens of nice Jewish girls from Brooklyn doing the Latin routines. Let me present you as a Negro talent. There won't be another like you for ten or fifteen years.' I got her singing blues and things like 'Summertime,' but she didn't have any contact with the audience because she wasn't putting feeling and meaning into what she sang. She would close her eyes when she sang or look at the ceiling. So I said to her, 'I know about white people and the Negroes and that most Negroes cannot look white people in the eye. Is that why you never look at your audience? Don't be afraid of them.' I sat at a ringside table, and when she looked at the ceiling I'd make signals. And I went over the lyrics of her songs, pointing out their meanings. Finally, she got to the point when she sang a blues of making people stand up and shout.

"Suzy Reed was the first Joan Baez—a beautiful girl with long reddish hair and a simple, direct manner. I made her keep her hair straight, told her not to wear makeup, and dressed her in little-girl frocks. At her first rehearsal she came out with a hop, skip, and jump and said, 'This is a zither.' I shouted, 'That's it, that's it! Don't ever change a thing!' And when she skipped out there in front of the audience and said, 'This is a zither,' she had them. I don't know whether it was because nobody had ever seen a zither before or whether it was the peaches-and-cream way she said it. I got Josh White to sit on a high stool when he sang, and I dressed him in open-necked shirts. He was a terror with the girls, and when they saw that neck—all muscles and tendons—they wanted to bite it. Of course, there were people I missed and people I nearly missed. I missed out on Pearl Bailey altogether. She struck me as a bit of a Tom, and I never hired her, but I know now I was being over-sensitive. And I almost didn't get Pearl Primus, a great dancer. She brought some records to her audition, but she looked so awful I made an excuse about the phonograph being broken and asked her to come back another time. She started to cry. I excused myself and pretended to fuss over the phonograph. She put on a record, took one fantastic leap, and that was it. John Martin of the *Times* ranked her with Ted Shawn and Martha Graham. I had my share of busts, generally with singers who, though I'd give them months of vocal lessons, just couldn't sing. Sarah Vaughan didn't work out, but for different reasons. I kept her six months, but people couldn't understand her singing—all the strange twists and turns she did with her voice—and she still didn't know how to get herself up right. Carol Channing was a bust, too. She sang and did impersonations of society dowagers and her special number was supposed to be a take-off of Ethel Waters in *Cabin in the Sky*. It struck me the wrong way, and I asked her not to use it. She felt I'd cut the heart out of her act, and she went ahead and did it anyway, so I fired her. Jim Backus flopped. He had another man with him, and I think they had a radio show, but nobody listened to them at the club. I was beginning to learn that although performers fail at one thing it doesn't mean they aren't good at something else. So I was always very careful not to hurt people at my auditions, especially because I never forgot a story Bernie Bernard told me. He was a Hollywood agent who had booked vaudeville talent in the Midwest. Two men auditioned for him, and he told them their act wouldn't go. He looked at one of them and said, '*You* have some possibilities, but your partner is impossible.' The next day the one he had spoken to came back, very upset, and it turned out his partner had just hung himself. When I was convinced a performer had gifts, despite negative audience reactions, I stayed with him. Jack Gilford started slowly and he used to beg me to let him go, but I refused, and one night his time came. It was at the two-o'clock show. Ammons and Johnson and Lewis and Billie Holiday were doing a benefit somewhere, and Joe Turner hadn't showed up, so all we had were the band and Gilford. He asked me what in God's name he was supposed to do. I told him he had to go on. The place was only half full, but a table of six or eight people had just come in. I'd been in enough places where the last show would be cancelled under such circumstances, but anyway Gilford, who was also the master of ceremonies, introduced the band, and they did their production numbers. Then he said, 'I would now like to introduce Albert Ammons, but Albert Ammons isn't here.' He got a laugh. Then he sat down at the piano and went into his beautiful pantomime with his great rubber face and made you *believe* he was Albert Ammons, by his motions and by scrunching up the back of his neck so that it looked like Ammons's rolls of fat. Then he did Meade Lux Lewis. Sometimes Lewis would start to fall asleep when he was playing, and I'd have to get someone to poke him, so Jack sat there nodding and swaying, and it was perfect. He did Billie and Johnson and Joe Turner and his own act, and the next day I had a call from one of the latecomers. It was Jed Harris, the David Merrick of the time, and he wanted Gilford for a revue called *Meet the People* that he was bringing to New York from California. Gilford joined it, and it was a great success. His Broadway career had begun. And do you know what he does every year on December eighteenth, the anniversary of Downtown's opening? He sends me a telegram, wishing me well, and it doesn't matter where in the world he is.

"I also had a hand, in a roundabout way, in getting a girl named Betty Perske started. She was tall and thin and had a deep voice, and she used to hang around Downtown all the time by herself. I didn't care for single girls in the club, but I found out that she lived over on Barrow Street with her aunt, and I told my headwaiter to keep an eye on her. There was something special about her, and one night she told me she wanted to act. I said I'd arrange a meeting for her with Jack Shalitt, a talent scout for Howard Hughes. That was the last I saw of her. Time passed, and one evening Shalitt came in with a long face and asked me if I'd seen *Life* magazine that week. I had and I was delighted. There was a nine-page spread on Zero Mostel. I had hired Zero in the early days at the Downtown, when none of the uptown operators would touch him. Shalitt said, 'No, no, I don't mean that. I mean the girl on the cover. We didn't get her, we missed her.' I didn't recognize the girl or her name. Shalitt said she was Betty Perske. She *had* gone to Shalitt, and he'd sent pictures of her to Hughes. He wasn't impressed, and when Mrs. Howard Hawks saw them on his desk one evening at a dinner party and asked if she could show them to *her* Howard, Hughes said fine, and Hawks signed her and changed her name to Lauren Bacall."

It was eight o'clock, and Mary Lou Williams sat down at the piano. She was in a dark blue gown and her hair was parted on one side, débutante fashion. She looked around in a bemused way, rubbed her hands together, said something to her bassist, and started "My Blue Heaven." Her playing was sure and inventive and utterly relaxed. There was no microphone, but her long, graceful melodic lines moved easily through the room. "Yesterdays" went by, and it was followed by a rocking boogie-woogie number and a fast "Blue Skies." Josephson was smiling and his cheeks were flushed. "She's playing better now than she did thirty years ago," he said. The set ended; Miss Williams greeted Josephson and sat down with Peter O'Brien.

"I got along very well with my performers, and they with me," Josephson said. "I always paid people at scale or better, and the highest salary I paid was thirty-five hundred a week. I also managed a lot of my performers for free when they went out to Hollywood and such. But no matter how well we got on, surprising things happened. I had an iron law at both clubs that there was to be no marijuana. When Billie Holiday was with me she'd get in a cab between shows and drive through Central Park, smoking. One night she came back and I could tell by her eyes that she was really high. She finished her first number and I guess she didn't like the way the audience reacted. Performers often wear just gowns and slippers, no underwear, and at the end of the song Billie turned her back to the audience, bent over, flipped up her gown, and walked off the floor." Josephson laughed. "I asked her backstage what in heaven's name she thought she was doing, and she just mumbled and slammed the dressing-room door.

"It had become the custom by the time Eddie Heywood came into the Downtown for the bandleader to double as m.c. Heywood stammered. He told me he was afraid people would laugh at him, and I told him not to worry. The first night was pretty bad, the next night better, and in a week there was only a trace. It must have had something to do with the intimacy of a microphone, and possibly also my confidence in him. Anyway, a couple of weeks later he explained that he was classified 4-F because of his stammering and that he was due for a medical review and could he quit emceeing for a few days until his stammer returned? He did, his 4-F status was renewed, and that night he announced shows again. One of the most surprising things also happened during the war, but it was at the Uptown. Jimmy Savo had a marvellous silent act in which he'd stop at a ringside table and pick up a customer's pack of cigarettes—this when cigarettes were so scarce. He'd take out a cigarette and, breaking it in two, light one half and put the other half in his pocket—all the while bowing and smiling to the owner of the cigarettes. Then he'd move to another table, still carrying the pack, and offer each of the people a cigarette, and keep this up until the cigarettes were gone. He'd return the empty pack to its owner, again bowing and scraping. He was in the middle of his act when a British sailor jumped up and grabbed a microphone and announced in a Cockney accent that he was going to sing a famous British Navy song about the time a British sailor floored 'that black nigger Jack Johnson.' Big Sid Catlett was sitting up there on the bandstand with his arms folded, and suddenly he picked up his drumsticks and began this tremendous thundering. The rest of the band joined in and the sailor was drowned out. The place was packed with servicemen, and they were outraged that one of them had been insulted, and there was nearly a riot. Afterward, I told the sailor that the word 'nigger' was not appreciated at Café Society Uptown, and he said he never knew there was anything insulting about the word and that he had black friends all over the world. It's a wonder more things didn't happen in those days. Like the time John Hammond and his wife came for dinner at the Uptown with Paul Robeson. Robeson and Mrs. Hammond danced. The headwaiter told me that the people at table forty-one would like to see me. There were two couples at the table, and one of the men said, 'Do you allow niggers to dance with white women in this place?' 'Sir,' I replied, 'we do not use that word in here. Furthermore, there is a law in this state against discrimination, and we abide by it. But it's still a democracy and you have a right not to like what you see.' 'Well, we don't like it at all,' he said. They walked out, but I made sure they paid their bill in full, even though they had just begun their shrimp cocktails."

Mary Lou Williams was playing again, and Josephson turned to watch her. Five minutes went by, and he said, "In the late forties, with both clubs going full steam, my life turned inside out. My brother Leon, who was working for me, was subpoenaed by the Un-American Activities Committee, which was headed by J. Parnell Thomas, the gent who later served time for misusing government funds. Leon was an avowed Communist and he refused to answer any questions, on the ground that the Committee was an illegal tribunal. He was cited for contempt, tried, and found guilty. His case was appealed to the Supreme Court, which refused to hear it, and he served ten months in prison. I think he may have been the first person to go to jail for contempt of the Committee. It was front-page stuff, and since no one knew who Leon Josephson was, he was always mentioned in the papers as the brother of Barney Josephson, the owner of Café Society Uptown and Café Society Downtown. The Hearst press—Pegler and Kilgallen and Lee Mortimer and Winchell—took off, and the innuendo, the guilt-by-association, began. Pegler devoted a column to Leon implying that he was a drug addict, and the last line was 'And there is much to be said about his brother Barney.' Just that, no more. So I was the brother of a Communist drug addict, I allowed Negroes in my clubs, I had introduced inflammatory songs like 'Strange Fruit' and 'The House I Live In,' and on and on. It ruined my clubs. Three weeks after the first uproar, business at the Uptown dropped 45 percent. I was determined not to give in to such viciousness, and I kept going for almost a year. But I had already lost $90,000, so I sold both clubs, and by 1950 I was out of the nightclub business and flat broke. I've only been into the Uptown once since it's become the Fine Arts Theatre, and that was to see 'Riffifi.' But all I could see were Teddy Wilson and Jimmy Savo.

"Part of the reason I started a place like the Cookery was that I could be unknown, anonymous, and that's the way it's been. But this morning I ran into one of my old neighborhood customers, a lovely lady who has been eating here since we opened. She stopped me outside the supermarket and said, 'Mr. Josephson, you have made our world, our city a little bigger and a little better by bringing Mary Lou Williams into the Cookery, and I thank you.' That made me feel marvellous."

[1971]

III

Part of the success of Bradley's, which occupies the ground floor of a brick-faced brownstone on University Place between Tenth and Eleventh Streets, is its benign mysteriousness, its avoidance of being categorized. "How can you get tired of a place when you don't know what it is?" one of its oldest customers has asked. "Every time you go in, you think you're going to find out. But you don't. So you go back again." Some of Bradley's customers think of it as a bar. They never get past the sixth or seventh bar stool (the bar is to the right of the door, and it runs about thirty feet), and can tell you little of the rest of the place. Some customers consider it a unique jazz club, where, seven nights a week from ten o'clock on, they can hear such pianists as Teddy Wilson, Tommy Flanagan, Hank Jones, and Joanne Brackeen. Other customers, particularly older locals, think of it as a restaurant where they can eat a peaceful early dinner and be home in time for the seven-o'clock news. Still others, taking the food and the music largely for granted, consider it a semiprivate club, where on bleak evenings they can generally find a friend to talk to or, failing that, the proprietor himself, a quite famous Village person named Bradley Cunningham. Three of these club members recently talked about Bradley's. The first, a retired magazine editor, lives a block or two away. "Bradley's is a haven—figuratively and literally," he said. "One night, I beat two guys to the door who I'm sure were going to mug me. Bradley runs a clean house, a good house. The waitresses are friendly, the food is friendly, and there's always somebody to talk to. It attracts people who are not bores. I like the music—Tommy Flanagan best of all. The music just ripples off him. If anyone gets obstreperous in the place, God help him. The other evening, some guy who'd been drinking a lot brandished a gun, and Bradley threw him the length of the bar and into the street. He ran over him like a tank." The second club member is a feminist writer who lives in Murray Hill. "I'd never think of going to Elaine's by myself, but I've been in Bradley's alone many times," she said. "It's like a family there, a strange family—a family that can be a combination of writers and business types and muscians and neighborhood people, and even uptown people. Bradley runs a very good place. It's never been corny, and he doesn't tolerate silly business with

drunks or people getting out of hand. He always keeps the place
at an interesting level. Bradley first had a following when he
tended bar at Chumley's, and when he moved to the 55 Bar people followed him. Then, when he opened Bradley's, they followed him there. He's attractive to both women and men, but
he's hard to talk to and he's a hard person to know. He's very
bright and he's very moral. If he cares about you, he's loyal to
the death. He very rarely entertains at home. That's what Bradley's is for him—a living room to entertain his friends and himself in." The third club member is a painter who lives on
Twenty-second Street. He likes to go to Bradley's and listen
to the conversations at the bar: "One night, these two high-
powered New York types were sitting there trying to one-up
each other. One said, 'I went to camp with Bobby'—meaning
Bobby Kennedy. The other said, 'Bobby and I were in the same
graduating class at Harvard.' The saxophonist Al Cohn was
standing there, and he said, 'I met Babe Ruth once.' I asked
Cohn what Ruth had said to him, and Cohn replied, 'Hiya, kid.'"

Bradley resembles a djinni. He is wide-shouldered, thick-
chested, long-armed, rock-fisted, and tall, and he seems to swell
as he talks to you. His head is covered with wavy, graying hair,
and his eyes are green and deep-set. His face is craggy and
handsome. He has a Kirk Douglas smile. He barely fits in his
office, a tiny room off a passageway that runs from the dining
room to the boxy, gleaming kitchen. The office has a small For-
mica-topped desk built into one wall, two desk chairs, a knee-
high filing cabinet, and a narrow barred window with an air-
conditioner in it. A big plastic container next to the window
holds the waitresses' work shoes. A primping mirror hangs on
the wall, and there are photographs of jazz musicians and singers. One day he sat in his office and talked. He had just had his
lunch at the bar—two fried eggs over, bacon, and hashed-brown
potatoes. He likes to talk, and he speaks in a universal, nonde-
nominational drawl full of silences and stretched, see-through
words. His laugh is robust and explosive. He lit a cigarette, and
said: "Our menu hasn't changed essentially since we opened,

thirteen years ago, so I've just hired my friend Miriam Ungerer, who writes about food and is married to Wilfrid Sheed. She's going to upgrade the menu—cue us in to the food explosion that's been going on out there. I've never been as interested in food as I should be. The first place I owned—the 55 Bar, at 55 Christopher Street—didn't have any at all. It was and is a drinking place that offers alcohol, cigarettes, and a jukebox. You'd have thought from the look of it that I threw a hand grenade inside and we were open. Actually, I put a billiard lamp over the table in the Hawaiian Room, which is a booth at the back of the place—the *only* booth—and I put Reynolds Wrap with holes punched in it over the other light fixtures. I replaced the twenty-eight-inch television set with a jukebox, because I didn't feel it would be consonant with the kind of place I had in mind to have neighborhood guys sitting around with a beer in hand watching *On the Waterfront*. In fact, I had a big list of people I didn't want in there. The people who worked for me weren't going to be subjected to the nonsense I'd been subjected to when I was a bartender. The 55 opened the night of the blackout in November of 1965, and we did a hundred and eighty-five dollars of business, which wasn't bad. The 55 eventually made a lot of money, and it could still be making money, but I haven't paid much attention to it in years. It got very raffish, even riffraffish. So I've sold it, and we're just waiting for the State Liquor Authority to O.K. the sale. When the 55 was on its feet, I began looking at a bar on University Place called the Stirrup. It was full of Naugahyde banquettes with aluminum trim, and the walls, which were varnished white pine, were covered with English hunting scenes. The place had a cheap blonde look. But there was something about it I liked very much, and in June of 1969 Jerry McGruddy and I took it over. We paid thirty-five thousand, and put fifteen more into it. McGruddy had been involved in Casey's, on West Tenth Street. Casey's was a beautiful jet-setty place, with good French food, that had been started by my friend K. C. Li. He was a Flying Tiger, and later he was in the tungsten business, and he had put a quarter of a million dollars into the restaurant. He and McGruddy parted company, and McGruddy was looking for something else. We replaced the banquettes with tables. We stripped the pine panelling, and stained it mahogany. It was my notion to put the mirror over the bar, and it was McGruddy's to call the place Bradley's. Everybody, including me, thought it was a bad idea, but I acquiesced as a consequence of my vanity, which is just below the surface." Bradley laughed, and went into the bar to get a Coke.

When he got back, he lit a cigarette. "We opened, and nothing happened. The help was getting paid, but we were scraping bottom. I used to stand out on the sidewalk and say to myself, 'There are eight million people in this city, and, please, all I need is forty of them.' The next spring, I went to Portugal for a couple of weeks to visit friends. David Sharpe, who had worked for me at the 55, had opened a place called Godot's, in Praia da Luz. I was in there talking to him one evening and I wasn't getting much response, and suddenly I realized why. He was doing exactly what I had been doing for months in New York—looking at the goddam front door and waiting for customers to walk in. Then my friend Danny Dod, who had come to Bradley's as bartender from the 55, called me in Portugal and told me I'd better get back—things were getting busy. *New York* had run a little piece with a photograph of Woody Allen and me at the bar. I came back, and we *were* busy, but the food wasn't together yet and we lost it. Then we hired Afortunado Perez as our chef. He's Puerto Rican—a Nuyorican, as the Puerto Ricans call people who emigrate to New York. He was the second cook at the Renaissance, on East Forty-ninth Street, and we offered him more money. He's been with us almost ten years, and he's hardworking and loyal. Then McGruddy suggested we hire a piano player. They'd had one at Casey's, and it had helped attract people. I play a little piano, so I put in an electric piano I'd bought from Roy Kral for $350, and the first person to play it was Dave Frishberg. Joe Zawinul, of Weather Report, came in later that year, and he started in full speed ahead—lighting a stick of incense and playing all this fast, heavy stuff during dinner. I told him none of this would do, and we had some words. But he settled down, and later we became pretty good friends. In fact, most of my friendships have started that way— clear the air first, then look around and see where you are. By 1972, the place had taken off. We were paying our bills, and even taking out a stipend. So McGruddy and I sat down and talked over a buy-out arrangement, which would give each partner first chance to buy out the other for an agreed-upon sum of money. We discussed the amount, and it all drifted off and we never put anything on paper. Then John Kadesch, a bartender and my day manager, and Timothy Duffy, who had worked for me and was a bartender at the Buffalo Roadhouse, told me that McGruddy was talking about selling them his share of the business. McGruddy wasn't satisfied with the price we had discussed, and they were willing to pay him more. I suggested to Kadesch and Duffy that I was shocked by the news. I told McGruddy that I was disappointed in him. I stared at the wall for a while. I saw a couple of lawyers who didn't have any ideas; then someone put me onto a restaurant lawyer that Elaine Kaufman had used. Kadesch and Duffy gave McGruddy a thousand dollars down, and he took off. They started behaving like partners—ordering drinks on the house, and such. I told them they had absolutely no say in anything, because they were not on the board of directors and couldn't be unless they were voted on by me. There was a Mexican standoff, which I watched with a certain relish. They sued me in State Supreme Court. The case became bogged down in technicalities, and the stock reverted to McGruddy. He came in for lunch, and I told *him* he no longer had any say in the business. He sued me in District Court, and we settled out of court, and I bought his stock. My landlady had put the building Bradley's is in on the market, and other wolves were gathering. With my sister's help, I bought the building, and now we're as safe as a church."

Bradley said goodbye to his day cook, to his waitresses, and to Tommy Derecas, his manager. He walked to his apartment, where he lives with his wife, Wendy, and their son, Jed. The apartment is on the south side of Sheridan Square. Once or twice a block, he greeted someone he knew. On the way, he talked about his new sobriety. 'I started drinking heavily in California after the Second World War. I was depressed. I read Proust for a week or two instead of looking for work, which I hate to do. Drinking can get to be a debilitating hobby. It can get to be a full-time job, which is what it was by the time I finally quit. I was drinking around the clock. I'd hang out at Bradley's all night with the piano players, and I'd sleep off and on all day. I thought I was having the time of my life, but I wasn't going anywhere. I was on the roller coaster, and I was bored with it. I knew I was bored, but couldn't seem to get off. I was never one of those drinkers who carom off the wall. I'd be smashed and no one would know it. I had also gotten enormous. I had outgrown Brooks Brothers and had to buy my clothes at the baby-elephant shop. My son Jed, who's six, told a schoolmate, 'My father is older than your father, and he's as big as a refrigerator.' In November of 1981, I went to St. Mary's Rehabilitation Center, in Minneapolis. They search your luggage for pills or whatever, and put you on Librium the first few days. You are assigned to a group, which meets twice a day, and it's no holds barred. You also have three lectures a day, and you have to write a paper on why you are there, what kind of person you are. Most people write pretty bland things. I tried to be as tough as I could on myself, but it wasn't easy. The next thing was Family Week. A member of your family visits, and there is a brutal confrontation in which you give your version of your drinking and the family member gives his. There were some pretty red faces. I got back here just before Christmas. It's a very gradual thing. They told me I wouldn't be completely right for five years. I'm still not doing too well at filling up my life. I may go to Bradley's once or twice a day, but the Greek, as Tommy Derecas calls himself, is a workaholic. I leased a Saab Turbo, and I'll run down to the Bowery to buy some bar stools, or somewhere else to pick up candleholders.

Nice days, I drive up to the Palisades to hit golf balls. Every Monday evening, I go to my FACT meeting. That's the Family Alcoholism Consultants Team. It's a structured professional therapy group, and we talk about the past week and what might come."

Bradley lives in a loft about the same size as Bradley's At its east end are a bedroom, a bathroom, and a walk-in closet that serves as a dressing room. The main room, which is two stories high and has a balcony on one side, starts with a galley kitchen and dining area, moves past the front door and an upright piano (once at Bradley's), encloses a living area that includes a couple of desks (one is Jed's), an Eames chair that belonged to the late alto saxophonist Paul Desmond (Desmond bequeathed his concert grand to Bradley's, and there it sits, a beautiful whale, between the bar and the dining room), a television set, and some sofas and chairs, and ends at Roy Kral's electric piano and the door to Jed's room, which looks like F. A. O. Schwarz. The loft has a concrete floor, part of it painted beige and part of it covered with a biege carpet. The walls are off-white. The room is lined with windows, and flights of pigeons comb past them into the low sky. Bradley likes nothing better than strolling from his bedroom to the electric piano and back, a round trip he estimates at 180 feet. "I love this apartment, and I love New York City," he said. "I can look up Seventh Avenue from my windows. I can look out into Christopher Park. I can look down West Fourth Street and Grove Street and Christopher Street. One Thanksgiving evening, Wendy called me to the window, and the traffic was backed way up Seventh Avenue—people trying to get to the Holland Tunnel, or, as Wendy aptly put it, 'Underneath the river and through the ghetto to Grandmother's house we go.' I can look out and everybody is carrying on busy as hell, and I can hear that murmur, that undercurrent, that goes on all the time in New York. New York is *power*, yet at the center of that power is a certain amount of calm. When I step outside, I love to see the red lights turn green, especially in the rain. And when Con Edison is digging, and they put up all those lights, it knocks me out. You can do what you want in New York. You can start a business and people will let you live. In a small town, if they don't like you they'll figure a way to keep you out. In New York, you take people one by one. You learn what the city is when you come back after a vacation. It's a shock. You have to tighten your reflexes, tighten your act. You have to regalvanize yourself into the city's tempo. You've got to rally, as one of my bartenders used to say."

Bradley sat down abruptly at the upright piano by the door and went into Thelonious Monk's "Crepuscule with Nellie," following it with Monk's "Ruby, My Dear." He has been play-ing the piano since he was a teen-ager, and he is a good modern chordal pianist. He has had countless impromptu early-morning lessons from the likes of Jimmy Rowles and Cedar Walton. While he played, he shouted, "I guess I'm glad I'm not an itinerant piano player, but it sure would be a fine way to travel to Japan and Europe and Australia!" He started "Shall We Dance?" and sang it in a pleasant light baritone. Before he fin-ished, the telephone rang, and it was his sister Nancy, calling from California. He talked four or five minutes, hung up, and poured himself a glass of iced tea.

"I was born four years after Nancy, on September 9, 1925, in Chicago, which I left almost immediately, and didn't get back to until last December, when I was on my way home from St. Mary's Rehab. My mother was Gretchen Dau, and she was from Galveston, Texas. She was born in 1890, and had three younger sisters and a younger brother. Their father, Fred Dau, was a clipper-ship captain from Hamburg. He was a good old guy who lived to be eighty-eight. We called him Opa, and Grandma Oma. My mother was a charming chick. She had blue eyes and blond hair, and tended to be a little overweight. She didn't drink and she didn't smoke, and she had a good sense of humor. She had a very strong sense of justice, and the vocabu-lary to go with it. She was never obscene, but there were always a lot of 'bastards' and 'sons of bitches' flying around. She liked men, and men liked her, because she could talk about anything.

She married my father, Charles Bradley Cunningham, in 1919, and they were divorced when I was still a little kid. He was from Buffalo, and was a pilot in the First World War. He never got overseas. He was in the insurance business, but he had a tendency to become involved in things like selling subterranean real estate in Florida. I think Gretchen divested herself of him when he got the notion of taking arms down to Central America in a yacht he had bought and bringing back rum, it being Prohibition time. Anyway, there was a shipwreck that threw everything into a different motion. The last time I saw him, I was six or seven. We lived in Altadena, California—2756 Highland Avenue—and my father had a Studebaker convertible with about thirty-eight cylinders. It was tan, with green pinstripes, and it made this huge *vroom vroom vroom* when he stepped on the gas. One day, he took me to the Annandale Golf Club, and we had a terrific time. At the end of the afternoon, he told me he was leaving us. That broke me up so much that I wasn't able to talk about it without weeping until six months ago. He wrote me a couple of times during the war, telling me to be tough, and he died not long after. Many years later, I asked my Aunt Helen Pritchard—one of my mother's sisters—what he was like, and she surprised me. Here was this seventy-five-year-old lady with concrete-gray hair, and she said, 'I was the first to go out with him, and through me he met Gretchen, and that bitch—he never had eyes for anyone else.' She died the winter before last, in her eighties, in Killeen, Texas.

"When I was two and a half or three and Nancy was seven, we were put in the Bon Avon School, in San Antonio, Texas. After a year or so, we joined Gretchen in New York. She was always in government or politics. At the time, she was a friend of John Raskob, who was chairman of the Democratic National Committee. Later, she was in charge of the women's part of the D.N.C., and she was a director of the League of Women Voters for four or five years. She was also a member of the woman-suffrage movement. But I don't think she ever had the power she felt she deserved. We lived at the Ritz-Carlton, at Madison

Avenue and Forty-sixth Street. I remember shrimp cocktail
served in blue cut glass, and throwing snowballs down on the
people on Madison Avenue, and riding a tricycle up and down
the corridors. I remember being taken to Central Park by a
wonderful Irish cat named Alan. He was the chauffeur of a
friend of my mother's. I also remember going with a Mrs. Fin-
negan, whom we hated. We called her Mrs. Vinegar. I went to
a nursery school, and the apartment was always full of people
like Hiram Johnson, a senator from California, and Claude
Bowers, who was the Ambassador to Spain, and William Mc-
Adoo, another senator from California, and Rabbi Stephen Wise,
an early Zionist. Then we moved to Altadena. We were in the
foothills of the San Gabriel Mountains, just below the Mt. Wilson Observatory, which had the world's largest telescope before
the Mt. Palomar mirror was ground. Roosevelt came to power,
and Gretchen went to Washington to work in the N.R.A. Aunt
Helen came, with her daughter Jacquelyn, to take care of
Nancy and me. I was put in the Trailfinder's School, which was
run by an early conservationist named Harry James. It was
strictly male, and everyone wore a uniform—corduroy shorts
or knickers. I was terribly unhappy. You know—deserted
again. There was a Hopi chief's son in the school, and one day
when I was feeling low he said, 'Hey, Brad, you feel bad?' Sym-
pathy, I thought, but all he wanted was to divert my attention
while somebody else held a magnifying glass up to my neck in
the sunlight. One summer, I went to Yosemite with some wil-
derness-prone people from across the street named Adams. Another summer, I visited Daus in Galveston and Houston. Oma
would say, 'If you don't behave, I won't give you the *kruste*,'
which means 'bread crust.' It was the only hangover from the
German days I ever saw in my family. My mother materialized
for a summer and rented the Sunset Hotel in Laguna Beach
with two or three other people. Laguna was beautiful then. It
was like the Mediterranean—nothing but white stucco walls
and red tile roofs. I went to a public school in Pasadena, and on
to Eliot Junior High, in Altadena, where I began to get in trou-

ble. I'd skip school and hitch to Santa Anita. They put me in a
private school near Caltech, and I got in a fight and was asked
to leave. I went to the Cathedral High School, a Catholic school,
in Los Angeles, where I lasted two or three months. It was full
of Mexican and Irish kids, and was the toughest school I was
ever in. After that, I was put in the Bonita Vista High School,
in Chula Vista, on the way to San Diego. I left there in the
ninth grade—this would be around 1940—and joined my
mother in Needham, Massachusetts. She had just remarried.
My stepfather was from San Francisco, and his name was
Frederick William Witt. He worked in the Treasury Department. They were married at the Ritz-Carlton in Boston. I went
to a school in Wellesley, then to one in Providence. Then my
folks moved to Washington, D.C., to a nice pad at Thirty-first
and R, near Dumbarton Oaks, and I was asked to go along. I
went to Western High, and didn't do too well at my studies.
What happened was I went to bed one night five feet nine
inches and woke up six feet two, and when the basketball coach
said to me in September 'Cunningham, are you coming out for
basketball?' I was puffing and told him 'No, I don't have the
energy'—which was true. I just sat around and played Benny
Goodman records and was clumsy. I was passing a sugar bowl
when I was introduced to some senator and I stood up and
dropped it and shook hands with him. I finished my prepara-
tory-school career at Millard Prep, on Connecticut Avenue. It
was a mill full of Army brats prepping for West Point. I took
the West Point exam and did surprisingly well in English and
history but not too well in math. So I went to Haverford College, and loved it. I played left tackle on the football team. By
this time, it was 1943, and I was about to get drafted. Because
I didn't want to get lost in the Army, I enlisted in the Marines,
and by December of that year I was at Parris Island."

Wendy and Jed came in, home from school. They are vigor-
ous and attractive. Wendy has long brown hair, sharp wide-set
hazel eyes, and a good smile. Her shoulders are broad, and her

waist is trim. She has a big, direct way of talking, Jed, as tall as an Indian club, is her spit and image. His hair is light, and he was wearing a Yankee jacket, a blue button-down shirt, a navy-blue-and-red clip-on tie, and navy-blue corduroy pants. His eyes are as wide apart as Wendy's. Bradley nodded at everyone and sat down at the electric piano and played "Easy Living." Jed washed his hands and got his Sonic Fazer from his room and zapped Bradley from behind a sofa. Bradley played on. Wendy gave Jed a glass of milk and some Fig Newtons. Jed brandished a wooden American flag he had made in wood-working class, and sat down. He took a half-moon bite out of a Fig Newton and drank his milk. Then he got out his snow walker—an eighteen-inch-high replica of the towering war machines that walk across the opening sequences of *The Empire Strikes Back*. He made the snow walker go half the length of the room, and it moved, and even looked, like Bradley. Jed climbed the ladder that leads to the balcony in the living room, and rescued a ball that he had kicked up there last night. Bradley announced that he was going out to buy some Coke and the *Village Voice*.

Wendy sat down at the kitchen table and lit a cigarette. "Bradley's a lovable bully," she said. "He's a manipulative man. He used to edit my grammar when we were arguing. He's got excessive charm when he wants something. He's witty. He'll flirt his way out of things. He's kind to people he respects, but he can be terribly critical of people—particularly women. He can't cope with certain things—death, for one. If someone he's fond of is ill and dying, he'll just shut it out. He'll cop out. We have respect for each other's intelligence. I'm not as well read as he is, and I never will be, but he learns as much from me as I learn from him. Bradley demands a good deal. There's a lot of cacophony and eighth notes and blaring colors when he's around. He's at the piano, he's on the telephone, he has both TV sets going. He travels with noise. I met him at Bradley's when I went to work there as a waitress, a month after the place opened. I'd just come off a bad short marriage. I come from Cochituate, about fifteen miles west of Boston, where I was born, in 1946. My parents live in Florida now, but they were hardworking folks. My father was a house painter, and my mother did secretarial work. I went to a two-year college in Illinois. Then I came to New York. I was Wendy the waitress at Bradley's for three years. Then Bradley fired me, and I moved in with him. We were married in December of 1975, at St. Luke in the Fields. Jackie Cain and Roy Kral were the witnesses, and Alec Wilder gave me away. Jed was born in 1976. This place was a mess when I moved in. I've scraped and sanded and repainted. I've built a big storage space behind Jed's room which Bradley calls 'the garage.' It's what I do best. Things have improved considerably since Bradley quit drinking. I used to feel like a single woman with a kid and a tenant who paid a very good rent. I finally gave him an ultimatum—quit or Jed and I leave—and that is what got him off to St. Mary's Rehab."

Bradley returned, riffled through the *Voice* and said that he was going to run up to the 9 W Golf Range and hit a couple of buckets of balls. He got his Saab out of a garage a block or two away and drove up Twelfth Avenue to the Fifties, where he turned onto the West Side Highway. He is a careful, vociferous driver, and he opened up on the drive. The Marines were still on his mind. "After boot camp, I went to combat-intelligence school at Camp Lejeune. Then it was through the Panama Canal to Hawaii to the Eighth Marines on Tinian Island. We landed the day after the invasion. I was a scout who shuttled back and forth between headquarters and frontline observation posts. Just before the island was secured, I watched the Japanese soldiers throw themselves off the cliffs into the sea. I was asked if I wanted to go to Japanese-language school, and I said yes. It was eight hours a day for ten weeks on Saipan. We learned conversational Japanese and also some *kanji*, which is ideographic writing, and *katakana*, which is phonetic spelling. In April of 1945, we landed on Okinawa; then we were assigned to the floating reserves on a troop ship in the South China Sea. One day, the Red Cross or somebody dumped a whole bunch of books down on us jarheads from a higher deck, and the only one left after the scramble was a fat volume of Mr. Leo Tolstoy named *War and Peace*, which is how I got acquainted with him. We went back to Okinawa after the Battle of Naha, and my job was to talk Japanese soldiers out of the bunkers and caves they were holed up in and interrogate them. A lot of them were simply shot by the Americans, but when we did get to question a prisoner he'd generally tell us everything. Captured G.I.s were only supposed to give their name, rank, and serial number, but the Japanese had never been told anything similar, because they were never expected to be captured. My great contribution to the war was questioning an officer and finding out about a huge cave filled with snipers—several hundred of them. Finding out about that cave saved a lot of lives, and I'm proud of that. When Okinawa was secured, we went back to Saipan to get ready for the landing on Japan itself. Then they dropped the bomb, and the war ended. We landed at Nagasaki, and it was just as devastating as everybody said. We eventually moved to Misumi, thirty-five miles away, and they sent all the confiscated weapons to us and we dumped them offshore in the Ryukyu Trench, which is about twenty thousand feet deep. I stayed in Japan until February of 1946, when I had enough points to come home. I loved Japan and I liked the Japanese. By the time I left, I could speak fairly well, but I still had trouble understanding when I was spoken to. So what I would do was construct these elaborate and complicated sentences that would require only a yes-or-no answer."

Bradley swept across the George Washington Bridge and onto the Palisades Interstate Parkway. The Hudson was afternoon gray, and the sun hit Bradley right in the eyes until he turned onto the parkway, where it dodged through the trees on his left. "I went back to Haverford, but after a term or two I got antsy and asked for a leave of absence. My mother was living in Georgetown, and she told me I couldn't sit around there. I went to Coral Gables, Florida, where I had a cousin. I drove a truck in Miami, and met a girl there, and we got married—in the summer of 1947. She was a student at the University of Miami. Then I enrolled in the School of Foreign Service at Georgetown University, and we moved to Washington. She worked as a secretary, and I worked part time in the House mailroom—and we split. I did a year or so at the foreign-service school, and took off for California, where my sister Nancy was. I lived in Laguna Beach, which was as beautiful as ever. I'd work like a son of a bitch as a carpenter all day at three dollars an hour and drink all night. One night, this guy who worked at the Sandpiper, where I hung out, said, 'Why don't you work behind the stick?'—which means tend bar. 'You can go to the beach by day and make money by night.' So I did. I moved over to a really neat placed called Christian's Hut. It had Hawaiian music and Polynesian décor, and the help wore Hawaiian shirts. It was part of a chain that had been started by a brother of the cameraman on *Mutiny on the Bounty*. The Pitcairn Island sequences had been filmed on Catalina Island, and when the picture was finished this brother bought the set and opened the first Christian's Hut in it. A girl named Jean Packard came in to play piano. She was a good pianist with a great sense of inner harmonies. We got married in Tijuana after a bullfight. Then I decided to come to New York. It was 1956. I had worked behind the stick at the Brussels and the White House Café in Laguna Beach. I was a good bartender, but I was a little ashamed of the work. So I landed a job at Grey Advertising producing radio commercials, but by the time I knew what I was doing they had fired me. I ended up behind the stick at Nob Hill, at Forty-fourth and Second. Then I went to Stefan's, on Christopher Street. George Darcy owned Nob Hill, and he gave me a reference that went like this: 'He has a good appearance, he's a good bartender, it's beneath him to steal, and he's never lost a fight.' I have a reputation for being tough, but I'm not a tough guy. I don't have a taste for it. Situations come up that simply have to be taken care of, like the wrong people coming into Bradley's when you've asked them to stay away. Ray Santini bought Chumley's, on Barrow Street. It had been an old newspaperman's hangout. I worked behind the stick, and I managed the place. It was a beautiful little dugout bar. I was there a couple of years. After the No Name Bar and the Corner Bistro, I opened the 55. Jean and I split while I was at the No Name. But what does it all matter? Every once in a while, Wendy's parents ask her, 'When is Bradley going to get a job?' "

[1982]

IN THE
WILDERNESS

~~

The number of jazz musicians in this country who piece out their lives in the shadows and shoals of show business has always been surprising. They play in roadhouses and motel lounges. They play in country inns and small hotels. They appear in seafood restaurants in ocean resorts and in steak houses in suburban shopping centers. They play in band shells on yellow summer evenings. They sit in, gloriously, with famous bands on one-night stands when the third trumpeter fails to show. They play wedding receptions and country-club dances and bar mitzvahs, and they turn up at intense Saturday-night parties given by small-town businessmen who clap them on the back and request "Ain't She Sweet," and then sing along. Occasionally, they venture into the big cities and appear for a week in obscure nightclubs. But more often they take almost permanent gigs in South Orange and Rochester and Albany. There is a spate of reasons for their perennial ghostliness: The spirit may be willing but the flesh weak; their talents, though sure, are small; they may be bound by domineering spouses or ailing mothers; they may abhor traveling; they may be among those rare performers who are sated by the enthusiasms of a small house in a Syracuse bar on a February night. Whatever the reasons, these musicians form a heroic legion. They work long hours in seedy and/or pretentious places for minimum money. They make sporadic recordings on unknown labels. They play for benefits but are refused loans at the bank. They pass their lives pumping up their egos. Some of them sink into sadness and bitterness and dissolution, but by and large they remain a hardy, ingenious group who subsist by charitably keeping the music alive in Danville and Worcester and Ish Peming.

One of the most steadfast of these common-grass musicians is Marie Marcus, a Boston-born pianist who has spent most of her forty-year career on Cape Cod and in Miami Beach. She is a household name on the Cape, where she lives. Short, round, talkative, and accessible, she plays very good Fats Waller piano, and keeps her ego alongside her sugar and tea bags. She lives in a tiny gray cottage with blue shutters in a part of Harwich where the houses shoulder one another and where a Stop & Shop and a Howard Johnson's are around the corner. The house, compact and spotless, has a living room, a kitchen, a bedroom, and a bathroom. The living room looks as if it could be packed up and moved in minutes. It contains a sofa and an armchair, a stereo, a television, a sewing machine, a piano, and a corner wardrobe. The walls are bare except for photographs of her grandchildren and an autographed picture of Oscar Peterson. One afternoon, the front door and both windows were open, and a smart Cape Cod breeze was funneling through. Marie Marcus was on the phone. She was wearing a voluminous housedress, and her blond hair was piled on top of her head. She hung up and perched like a pigeon at one end of the sofa. "That was my mother," she said. Her voice is high, and the edges of her Boston accent have been rubbed smooth. "She's worried because I killed a spider in here last night that looked after I'd sprayed it like it might be a black widow. It probably wasn't, because you don't hear much about black widows on the Cape, but she's all bothered about it. She hates the Cape anyway, and she and my stepfather, Lou Martin, are moving back to Boston next week. He's a fine man, and he plays ragtime. They just celebrated their twenty-fifth, but they're young in action. Then, my mother has always been young-minded. She married my father, whose name was Dougherty, when she was sixteen or seventeen, and she was a live wire, full of pep and energy. She sang in the church choir, and she played piano by ear. And she and my father were great ballroom dancers. They were on the dance floor two or three nights a week at the Totem Pole or Nutting's-on-the-Charles or Loew's State Ballroom. She taught my son Bill, who's a jazz piano player, how to ballroom dance, and he was amazed. He'd never heard of dancing like that. The house where I grew up, in Roxbury—the ghetto is there now—was always full of music, and it was always full of people, too. My mother and father lived in an attic apartment in the house, which was big and old and was owned by my grandmother. She was a fantastic woman who lived to be ninety-three, a woman of the old-fashioned Irish stock, and she ran the roost, which also numbered my uncle and my four aunts. They weren't that much older than I was, and after my grandfather died—I was just three—she raised them all. I was an only child, and for seventeen years I was an only grandchild and an only niece, so in one way I was spoiled. But it was a very religious Catholic household, and those were still the seen-and-not-heard days. So I never seemed to get the kind of affection that my four children give me now. My father was a plumber, and a good one, and he worked at the Charlestown Navy Yard. He was considerate to me and saw to it that I had all the piano lessons and education I needed. But he had a drinking problem that finally drove him and my mother apart. He couldn't help himself, and, of course, there was no AA then. On top of that, drinking was considered a sin, and not a sickness. The poor man died when I was in my late twenties. He was coming home from work on payday, and three men jumped him, and that was it. They never found out who did it. But the music in the house is what's stayed with me. One of my aunts, Mrs. Parnell, would have been a great jazz piano player, but she gave it up when she married. My mother had a player piano and all those rolls by Fats Waller and James P. Johnson, and there were always musicians from Boston in the house. People like Joe Sullivan—not the Chicago jazz pianist Joe Sullivan—who was good in the ragtime style, and Billy Paine, who was a fine singer. It was all an influence on me, and when I was about four I got up on the piano stool and played a whole number. I started lessons, when I was eight or nine, with Miss Teitelbaum, who was a wonderful musician and teacher. We used to kid her about being a nice Jewish lady from Ireland, which she was. I studied with her four years, and when I was thirteen I gave a recital at Judson Hall, in Boston. I continued my music at the New England Conservatory and attended Roxbury Memorial High at the same time. But my career began elsewhere. When I was fourteen or fifteen, I got a job playing piano once a week on a children's radio show, 'Bill Toomey's Stars of Tomorrow.' I accompanied the other kids, and I also had my own solo spot. Then I was hired by Big Brother Bob Emery, who had the most famous children's radio program in New England. He was a strict, smart man and a radio pioneer who'd been on the first Boston station, WGI. I had become a pretty fair tap dancer, and for a while I didn't know whether I wanted to dance or play piano. When I played and danced for a week one summer at a Chinese restaurant in Boston called the Mahjong, I asked the orchestra leader, Jimmy Gallagher, whether he thought I should be a dancer or a pianist, and he told me I had something special on the piano and that there were girl dancers under every stone, and that made up my mind. When I graduated from high school, Bob Emery got a call to do a radio show in New York, and he asked me to go with him. It was nineteen thirty-two, and I was just eighteen. We were supposed to stay at the Royalton, on West Forty-fourth Street, but somehow I got turned around and ended up at the Claridge, which wasn't far away. Emery was in a state of shock when he found me. He told me my mother would have his head, which she would have. So I moved to the Royalton, and I met Robert Benchley, who lived there. He was a friend of Emery's, and he was a delightful man. I had lunch with him several times, and I was fascinated with his witty sayings. I started with Emery at WEAF for Humphrey's Remedies. The show was sort of philosophical, with poetry readings, and I played background music. Then we went over to WNEW, which we helped open, and finally we ended with a children's program on WOR. My mother and father came up from Boston not long after I was in New York, and we took an apartment at the Hildona, over on Forty-fifth Street, between Eighth and Ninth Avenues. I loved the movies, and I went to every show in New York, but I was bored with all the spare time I had. A friend of Emery's owned a bar and grill on Amsterdam Avenue that had a Hawaiian trio, and he hired me as the intermission pianist. After a while, the boss and some of the waiters asked me to go to Tillie's Chicken Shack, in Harlem. It was a fried-chicken place, and Bob Howard, who sounded just like Fats Waller, was on piano. We went up there quite often, and one night Fats himself came in. I remember the whole room lighted up. He played, and then Howard persuaded me to play, even though I was scared to death. Fats listened, and when I'd finished he pointed to his heart and said, 'For a white gal, you sure got it there.' I was amazed, but I guess he was, too, since practically the only women who were playing jazz then were Mary Lou Williams and Lil Armstrong, and they were still working mainly out West. We got to talking, and I told him that I would like to further my education in jazz and did he know a good teacher? He looked at me and said, 'How about me?' I thought he was putting me on, but he wasn't. He had a small office, with two pianos, in the Brill Building, at 1619 Broadway, and during the next year or so, when he wasn't on the road or making records, he'd call me up and say, 'Come on down and let's play some piano.' You couldn't exactly call them lessons. We'd play duets, and then he'd play and have me listen carefully to the things he did. He'd tell me, 'When you're playing jazz, remember the rhythm, remember the rhythm. Make the number of notes count. Tell a story, and get that feeling across to the people. Please the people by making it come from here.' He was very serious when we were working together, and I was grateful for every minute. And I could never get over his reach on the keyboard. He had stubby hands, but he could span way over a tenth, which gave him that great left hand."

Marie Marcus got up and went into the kitchen to get a glass of water. She sat down again and laughed. She is a pretty woman with a prominent nose, a high forehead, and a long face. It is a cheerful New England face, and it is also a child's birthday-party face. "I never make excuses about my weight," she said. "I love to eat, and that's it. I've been fighting the battle of the bulge for ten years. I have a sign on my icebox door: 'Marie Marcus is a big fat slob,' and one of these days I'm going to pay attention to it. I did try Weight Watchers a while ago. You have to be weighed every time you go, in front of a whole bunch of women, and you get embarrassed. But a couple of jobs came up, and I couldn't fit it in anymore. Now I've started the water diet. Eight glasses a day and just meat and fish. The trouble is I can't stand water. I did take off forty-five pounds in 1969, but I put it right back on in a year. So I know my health is in jeopardy, and that's a constant elbow in my side. You tend to let yourself go, living alone. My second husband, Bill Marcus, died seven years ago. He had perfect health, but he had a heart attack and died right on the bandstand. He was a trumpet player, a society-band trumpet player, who worked for Meyer Davis and the Lanins and Ruby Newman. We had just bought the big house next door, and this place—I wouldn't even say what my mother calls it—was the garage. He was a lawyer, graduated from BU, and he had hung out a sign and was starting to practice again, and he had fixed this up as his office, which accounts for the linoleum floor and the paneling. After he passed, I moved in here, and now my three aunts and my uncle live next door. So I use this place for sleeping and eating, and it's all I need." She took a sip of water and made a face.

"My next job was at a speakeasy on Eighth Avenue owned by Dutch Schulz. I worked from ten-thirty till seven in the morning, and then did my radio show late in the afternoon. I was in a little room next to the saloon-type bar, and I was treated beautifully. I built up a following of fans who would come in and scat-sing new phrases they'd heard uptown, where they'd take me on my day off. We'd go to the Savoy Ballroom to hear Chick Webb and Ella Fitzgerald, and it was one of the experiences of my life. Another was being at Benny Goodman's famous opening at the Paramount. I'd heard an early Goodman band in Boston, and something about it told me that this was the coming music. I was at the Paramount for the first show—the ten-o'clock morning show—and I couldn't believe what happened. That music just carried everybody away, and people started dancing in the aisles and on their seats. Somebody grabbed me, and there I was, dancing away like crazy. The quartet in particular knocked me out, and although I wouldn't wait for St. Peter today, I stayed through three or four shows that morning. From Dutch Schulz's place I moved over to the Venetian Palace, which I think was owned by Frank Costello. It was scary there. Kids were naïve in those days, and I was the most naïve of all. I didn't drink or smoke, and I'd been taught all my life that sex was a dirty word. One night the bosses sent me and this little red-headed singer to play at a private party in a hotel, and when I got there I couldn't find any piano, and I began to realize I was in a strange situation. So I up and said to the hoods who were there, 'If you force me to do anything, it'll be like your kid sister.' They took one look at my Boston Irish face and sent me back to the club. But I never saw the singer again. The Venetian didn't last long, and after a couple of jobs in between I finally made it to Fifty-second Street, to the Swing Club. It was paradise. Stuff Smith and Jonah Jones were working next door, and Art Tatum was across the street, and Billie

Holiday was two doors away. I learned and I learned, not so much from piano players as from horn players and singers. It was a fantastic time in New York; there was so much good music.

"In 1937, I got married the first time. I married a native New York boy named Jack Brown. He was a singer and an m.c., and he ran shows at a couple of Chinese restaurants on Broadway in the Forties. We got a job together at Barkley's, in Brooklyn, and we moved out there. In 1938, my son Jackie was born, and I had to go back to work two weeks later, because my husband had had a nervous breakdown. He was in a hospital in Brooklyn and then in a sanitarium, where he was for quite a while. Things were never quite the same after that, and eventually we drifted apart and separated, and he died several years later. I raised Jackie, with help from my mother and my aunts, from the time he was fifteen months. I stayed on at Barkley's, and I also worked at the Embassy Club, where I had my own band, and where there were big plans to make a star out of me. But my agent decided I was bushed and that first I should go up to the Coonamessett Club, in Falmouth, on the Cape, where the work would be light and I'd get a rest. It was 1942, and the war had just started. I came by train and I got off at Falmouth, and a hostess from the club met me. It was the dead of winter, and I looked around and thought, My God, I'm in the wilderness. But within a week my love affair with the Cape began, and I never did get back to New York. The Coonamessett, which is gone now, was a huge place, with a bowling alley and ballrooms and restaurants, and the work was anything but light. The day after I arrived was St. Patrick's, and the whole of Camp Edwards came over. I was at the Coonamessett or over at Camp Edwards, where I became a sort of mother confessor to the wounded boys, during most of the war. I was working at the Panama Club, in Hyannis, on V-J Day. It was a high-class steak pub and the number one club on the Cape. It's gone now, too. In fact, I seem to turn most of the places I've worked in up here into parking fields. It was at the Panama Club that I met Bill Marcus, and we were married just after the war. We started going to Florida for the winter, and my two girls, Mary and Barbara, were born there. We worked every winter in Miami Beach and every summer on the Cape until 1961. After that, we stayed up here all year. It was in Miami that I really got deeply into Dixieland for the first time. I joined Preacher Rollo and the Five Saints—Preacher was a drummer named Rollo Layan—and I was with them five or six years, and we were a big hit. We worked every hotel in Miami Beach and had a national radio hookup five days a week and a recording contract with M-G-M. We were on Steve Allen's 'Tonight Show' and the 'Dave Garroway Show' and Arthur Godfrey's program. But it was very hard work. I didn't finish until three or four in the morning, and I had to take several different buses going home and then be up at seven to get the kids off to school. My Dixie experience has continued ever since. In the fifties, I toured the Midwest with Wild Bill Davison, and I worked for George Wein in Boston. I got $108 and I worked seven nights a week, and when I asked him for a day off he said, 'Fine, but I'll have to dock your pay.' So I quit."

Marie Marcus took a sip of water and made another face. She looked at her hands and flexed them slowly. "I have arthritis. I can't even bend this finger. A doctor fan told me to keep playing and to keep squeezing two little rubber balls he gave me." The telephone rang, and she talked briefly. "That was my friend Mildred. She calls me every day. She lives near here, with her husband, in a great big house that looks over the water and has an Olympic-size indoor swimming pool. I love to swim, and I always have the whole pool to myself. Up and down, up and down, and nobody to bother me. I love golf, too. I was a very good woman golfer. I played in the low eighties when I was at the Coonamessett, and they used to talk to me about going in tournaments. But I've been too busy running all over the Cape and working in every place imaginable. I play full-time summers and maybe two or three nights a week during the off season, when I sometimes do a little teaching to fill in the chinks. Since I've settled here, I've worked the Nauset Inn, in Orleans,

which is now the Olde Inn. I played duets there with a wonderful piano player, Leo Grimes, who's at the Ritz in Boston now.
He's self-taught, and he told me once that he can't help himself,
that he thinks about music twenty-four hours a day—on the
street, when he eats, when he dreams, when he gets up in the
morning, all the time figuring out new things to play. In 1963,
after the Nauset Inn, I formed a partnership with Carl German—he pronounces it 'Germane'—which is still going on.
He's a bass player and a singer, and we sing duets. I have a little Bonnie Baker voice, and I sing only with him, because I
get very nervous by myself. Carl commutes from Mattapoisett,
where he lives, and it's an hour and a half each way. We worked
the winter of 1963 at Mildred's Chowder House, in Hyannis, and
the summer in Mashpee, at Ellie's Drift Inn, which is now
called On the Rocks. It was the same two places in 1964 and
1965, and then we went into the Windjammer Lounge, in Hyannis, where we built up a terrific following. We worked the
Windjammer the next four years, with a side job at the Orleans
Inn. In 1970, we were at the Gateway Yacht Club, in West Yar-
mouth, and at La Coquille, in Dennis, and we did the Lighthouse Inn, the Sandbar, and Deacon's Perch. The winter of
1971, I was with Bobby Hackett at the Gateway, which was a
ball, and during the summer Carl and I were at the Hereford
House, in Dennisport. And this summer it's the Charcoal Pit, in
Chatham."

Marie Marcus looked at her watch. "I'm going over to Mildred's and take a swim, and then I have to get dressed for our
Sunday afternoon concert at the Olde Inn. It's with my Dixieland band, which was formed seven years ago. We work eight
or nine months of the year, at least once a week, at clubs and
private parties and at outdoor concerts. The last outdoor concert we gave it rained, and the electric piano I was playing got
wet and I had to stop. Every time I touched the keys I got a
shock. Everybody in the band has day jobs, except for Alan
Pratt, our drummer, and me. Jim Blackmore, our cornetist, de-
signs heating systems for houses and such all over the Cape, and

Paul Nossiter, who plays clarinet and sings and is our m.c., is a teacher at the Sea Pines School, in Brewster. Our trombonist, Charlie Tourjée, teaches at the Dennis-Yarmouth Regional High School, and Jimmy Cullum, the bassist, runs a music store, Musictronics, in Orleans. We hit at four and play until seven-thirty, when I have to get to my regular job."

It was a little after four, and the band was deep in a medium-tempo version of "Pee Wee's Blues." It was set up in a big bay window at one end of a high, raftered room. A dance floor in front of the bandstand was surrounded by tables with red-checked tablecloths. Half the tables were already full. The band finished the blues, moved easily through Louis Armstrong's "Swing That Music," and started the rarely heard verse of "After You've Gone." The band sounded trim and compact and unhurried. Its ensembles revolved slowly and surely, and its solos were brief and to the point. It had a nice sense of dynamics and kept its volume at the conversation level. Blackmore is a gentle, sweet cornet player, cast in the mold of his friend Bobby Hackett, and Tourjée, who is free of the harrumphing approach that afflicts most white Dixieland trombonists, suggests Jack Jenney and even Benny Morton. Nossiter is a fluent clarinetist who favors the chalumeau register. Marie Marcus looked very different now. She was wearing a smart blue overblouse and a long black skirt, and she had vanished into her music. Her mouth moved continually while she played, as if she were spelling out difficult words to herself, and her head went through an endless series of dips, nods, and snaps. Her shoulders rolled, and her feet swung back and forth, back and forth—a little girl sitting on a porch railing and eating a cone. At first, her style seems a simple mélange of chunky chords and brief connective runs, but on closer examination it is a repository of the jazz piano playing of the thirties and forties. In her left hand, she uses Waller oompahs and Teddy Wilson tenths and quick, stabbing Nat Cole punctuations, and her right hand works through short Tatum runs and dense Bob Zurke chords and spacious Jess Stacy intervals. Her melodic lines are short and often affecting, and they duck and bob and weave through complicated chordal patterns that are occasionally lightened by single-note figures. She is a driving pianist, but she never hurries, and her solos have a serene, homey texture, as if she were crocheting them. Her solos meet the listener exactly halfway. She does not bother with dynamics, and she rarely pauses between phrases. The "Satanic Blues" followed "After You've Gone," gave way to Jelly Roll Morton's "Doctor Jazz," and it was intermission time.

Marie Marcus sat down, dabbed her brow, and ordered a diet Coke. A swarm of admirers appeared, and she was alternately patted, squeezed, kissed, and poked. They included Roland Sears, a sometime drummer, photographer, painter, electronics expert, and disk jockey, who runs a funny weekly jazz program for the Orleans station, WVLC; Heinie Greer, a retired New York lawyer and banjoist, who lives in Dennis and spends most of his evenings faithfully touring the jazz spots on the Cape; Bobby Hackett, who lives in Chatham, and who told Marie Marcus it was high time they made a record together; and Alec Wilder, who had just flown over from Nantucket for a few days' visit. "That felt pretty good," Marie Marcus said. "And I'm in a good mood. The mood I'm in and what I'm thinking about directly affect my music. It's gotten to the point where if I play something in a certain way, people can tell right off what's in my mind. When I do a ballad, I try and interpret the story that the composer gets across in the lyrics. And I'm more melody-conscious than chord-conscious. The melody runs along the back of my mind, and I listen and try to fit pretty chords to it. There are certain tunes I associate with certain people, and when I play them I see their faces before me. They might be old fans who always request that particular tune, or musicians like Bobby Hackett. I'll play 'Memories of You' alone at night in my house and I'll see Bobby in my mind. Playing is always a question of trying to project the right feeling, the feeling of the heart. Sometimes, when you get warmed up, it's a carried-away feel-

ing, and you come up with things that surprise even you—
phrases that you *know* you've never played before. This will
happen mostly with a good audience—generally a concert audience and not a noisy nightclub crowd. A good audience is like
food to me. It sparkles my imagination, and I can run twice as
fast. And playing with my band does that, too. I don't like to
play alone, the way I am now down at the Charcoal Pit. I don't
even have Carl German; the boss let him go, because he said
there wasn't enough business. Anyway, the room is big and
cold, and I don't feel like anyone when I'm working in there."

Paul Nossiter made an announcement to the effect that Bobby
Hackett and the clarinetist Joe Muranyi would sit in for the
next set, and the band went back to work. There were now a
cornet and a trumpet, and Nossiter switched to soprano saxophone. The first tune was a medium version of "Struttin' with
Some Barbecue." The dance floor filled up rapidly, and Marie
Marcus was lost from sight for a moment. When the dancers
parted, she looked radiant. Her face was shining and her mouth
was going.

[1972]

BRIGHT UNISON
CLARINETS

~~~

The harder the pianist and arranger Claude Thornhill tried to make a commercial success of his big band, the more musical and original it became. The band flourished just before and just after the Second World War, and Thornhill thought of it as a "ballad" band; that is, it played a lot of slow tunes, many of them with vocals. But Thornhill's ballads, with their unique ensemble voicings (three or four clarinets, a saxophone or two, two French horns, a tuba, and various intermarriages between these instruments and the trumpets and trombones), were more like tone poems than like dance-band arrangements. Somewhere along the line, Thornhill decided he wanted his sections to play without vibrato; the blocks of sound they produced were smooth, rectangular, and weightless. These sounds glided along above the rhythm section, which was always discreet, and they suggested Debussy, and even Berlioz. They spoke of deep velvet, of Matisse reds, of melancholy without tears. It was always October in Thornhill's slow numbers. In the late forties, his ballads tended to get slower and slower, until, as the Thornhill arranger Bill Borden has pointed out, they got "so slow you couldn't even walk to them—unless you were in a funeral procession." At the same time, Thornhill went along with the jazz fashion of the postwar period—bebop. The arranger Gil Evans, who joined Borden in the band in 1941 (and who died, at the age of seventy-five, in March of this year), began writing tight, leaping, arcane bop arrangements in 1946, and they were no more danceable than the ballad numbers. But they were brilliant works—the first fresh big-band inventions to come along since the great Ellington concertos of 1939–42. The best of Thornhill fed, directly and indirectly, the entire non-hot side of jazz— Miles Davis and Gerry Mulligan and the Modern Jazz Quartet. The Thornhill band, an ensemble band, was as maneuverable as a chamber group, and it used improvisation largely to offset its late-Victorian sounds. It owed much to Duke Ellington, yet it also showed how Ellington, had he wished to, could have moved into the bebop era.

Thornhill's career meandered for a long time. An only child, he was born in 1909 in Terre Haute, Indiana. His mother had German blood, and his father, whom he disliked, had English blood. Artie Shaw, who for a time was Thornhill's closest friend, has described the Thornhills as "American Gothic," and not the sort of people you dropped in on. Thornhill's mother said at his funeral, "I miss my Claudie. He brung us fame." Thornhill started playing piano around the age of ten, and he ran away from home when he was fourteen. He got a job on a riverboat, in a band led by Heavy Elder. Then he turned up in a Midwest group called the Kentucky Colonels. He and Shaw met briefly at that time, and in the late twenties Shaw got him a job with Austin Wylie's band in Cleveland. The two men had moved to New York by the early thirties. Thornhill worked for Hal Kemp, Don Voorhees, Freddy Martin, Jacques Renard, and Paul Whiteman. In 1934, he passed through Benny Goodman's first big band, and in 1935 he was in the all-star group that Ray Noble took into the Rainbow Room. He went from Noble to André Kostelanetz's radio show, and in 1938 he gave up New York for Hollywood. (Thornhill apparently learned a good deal about tonal color from the way Kostelanetz used strings and horns.)

Artie Shaw has said this about Thornhill's early days: "Austin Wylie already had a piano player when I brought Claude into the band, but I had persuaded Wylie that he needed two pianists. We played at the Golden Pheasant, next to the old Hotel Winton, where Claude and I roomed. He had a great musical ear but not much time—in a jazz sense. He practiced things like 'Danse Nègre' for hours. He had studied for a while at the Cincinnati Conservatory. He was also listening to stride piano. I'd take him to Harlem, after we moved to New York, to hear Willie the Lion Smith, and he loved that. We both did some arranging with Wylie. One day, we started to run down a new arrangement Claude had brought in. We played the intro and the first chorus—probably sweet saxophones and muted trumpets—and then nothing seemed to happen. The rhythm section was still playing, but there wasn't any other sound. Then we realized that Claude was over there at the piano *singing*. He had written in a vocal for himself, even though he wasn't much of a singer. He was a funny-looking gent, with that potato nose and round Germanic face, and we all broke up. It wasn't easy for him to express himself. He was like Basie in that respect. He hid inside himself. But he was more guileful than he appeared, because he generally got what he wanted. This was particularly true when he joined my Navy band, in 1942. I was a C.P.O., and I was responsible for band discipline, but Claude and I couldn't arrive at a modus vivendi. After all, we had been close a long time, and it wasn't easy being thrust into what amounted to a master-servant relationship. He would miss muster or bed check or rehearsals, and resentment began to build on both sides. He was already a heavy drinker, and that didn't help. He made it known that he wanted his own band, so I talked to Admiral Calhoun, and they gave him one before we left Hawaii for the Pacific Islands. Our relationship was never quite the same, and I didn't see much of Claude after that."

There was a second side to Thornhill's New York career in

the thirties. He recorded with every sort of jazz group. Perhaps it was just larking for him, or perhaps he really wanted to be a good jazz pianist. He recorded a dozen numbers in 1934 with the rambunctious trumpeter and singer Louis Prima, and he was on the first sides that Benny Goodman made with his new big band. The following year, he showed up on Glenn Miller's first big-band recordings and on a session organized by the Casa Loma Band arranger Gene Gifford. He recorded with a pickup group that included Bud Freeman, Bunny Berigan, and Cozy Cole. In 1937, he arranged, and played on, the singer Maxine Sullivan's famous recording of "Loch Lomond." Before he went West, he did two dates with Billie Holiday. He even takes a fine sixteen-bar single-note solo on her version of "Forget If You Can."

Not long before he died, Gil Evans recalled how Thornhill happened to move to the Coast: "In the late thirties, Skinnay Ennis, the drummer and a very popular vocalist with Hal Kemp, decided to go out on his own. He took over the band I had at the Rendezvous Room in Balboa, and I stayed on as an arranger. He asked me who the best vocal arranger was, and I said Claude Thornhill. Claude came out and rented a house in West Los Angeles, and we both wrote arrangements for Skinnay's band. Claude was already a fine arranger. Very quick. He had done a lot of arranging in New York. Then, one day, he said that he was going to cash in an insurance policy and that he couldn't decide whether to take the proceeds and go to Tahiti or go back to New York and organize his own band. He went to New York. He brought his band out to the Rendezvous in 1939, and Bill Borden was the arranger. I have a fixed image in mind from this time of Claude with his cigarette holder and his eternal cup of coffee. They were his badges. So were his Adler Elevator shoes. While he was at the Rendezvous, he took his band out to Catalina Island to hear Benny Goodman and Eddie Sauter, who had just joined Goodman. He rented an open fishing boat, and the water was very rough. Everybody was, like, whoof. Except for Claude, who sat there smoking his cigarette and drinking his coffee."

The trumpeter and arranger Rusty Dedrick joined Thornhill the same year as Evans. "I went with the band just before it opened at the Glen Island Casino, and I left early in 1942," he said not long ago. "I rejoined in 1946 and stayed until 1947. There was never much money; we did it for love of the music. Claude was an enigma. He was extremely shy, and it was difficult for him to be a front man. He had had some psychiatric therapy after the war—possibly even electric-shock treatments, which tend to affect the memory. He knew the book by heart, but he would forget names. He'd announce a singer's first name but not her last, unless one of us shouted it to him. He was a funny man, but his humor was off the wall. He had written a silly poem about one of the islands in the Pacific, and he'd recite it to audiences apropos of nothing. The band was so of a piece that musicians visiting Glen Island would say, 'Hey, I love this band, but I wouldn't want to be on it. You must rehearse all the time.' But we didn't. We had those certain sounds—the bright unison clarinets and the low French-horn/tuba sounds—and we had them down perfectly. Sometimes we played new arrangements the first time on the stand."

Gil Evans again: "I drove across the country from California, and I arrived at the casino in the evening, just before the band hit. I was told that Claude was sick and I would have to take his place. Well, he wasn't. It was one of his practical jokes. When he was with Freddy Martin in the thirties, he arranged to have a series of insulting telegrams sent to Martin from various parts of the country—one every couple of nights. They all said in different ways how awful Martin's band was, and Claude would watch Martin read these things and get mad as hell, and Claude would laugh and laugh—later. But he wasn't much at taking jokes. Once, I set an alarm clock to go off on the bandstand just as he was playing his tinkly piano on 'Autumn Nocturne.' He didn't think it was very funny. He rented a house in Pelham when we were at the casino, and I stayed with him. He'd practice classical exercises on the piano every night until four or five in the morning. His time was something, and so was his touch. I've never heard anyone get a better sound on a piano than he did. And his ear was infallible. When someone in one of the sections went out of tune, Claude would lead the musician through his part and play the correct notes to get him back on pitch. He'd achieve the no-vibrato effect he wanted in the sections by telling the musicians to play with a vibrato; then he'd make them take it down until there was no vibrato. He wasn't really a jazz piano player. He had heard Bix Beiderbecke when he was young, and the two of them had spent an evening together drinking gin. Afterward, Claude put brackets on the wall in his room and hung the empty gin bottle there. What he wanted in his band was that ballad style with the clarinet lead, then alto saxophone and two tenors, and finally the French horns—all pitched an octave below Glenn Miller's reed section. When the band started to run through my arrangement of Charlie Parker's 'Anthropology,' I saw Claude up in the balcony making faces. He was a night owl, and he finally came to my room at three or four one morning and told me he didn't want to play bebop anymore. Claude wasn't really mysterious. He just liked people to think he was. He had one habit, though, that I never understood. He loved to buy clothes. He had closets of new clothes in his house in Pelham, and he had a basement room full of new clothes in a building on West Fifty-fifth Street that he had an apartment in. But he almost never wore them."

In October of 1947, the Thornhill band recorded Gil Evans's arrangement of "Robbins Nest," written by Sir Charles Thompson and Illinois Jacquet for the disk jockey Freddy Robbins. The recording immediately catches you. A sustained, vibratoless single note, played by a combination of saxophones and horns, is held over a medium tempo for two measures, dips a tone, rises quickly against a soft, offbeat brass burst, falls again, and gives way to Thornhill playing the melody with spare, legato Basie-like single notes. This daring, complex introduction lasts just six measures, and is a classic instance of how the Thornhill band almost completely circumvented the big-band clichés of riffs, call-and-response patterns, and empty counterpoint. It made originality sound comfortable and complexity sound simple. A little reed figure binds the end of Thornhill's first eight bars, and at the end of his second eight the reeds appear again and slip into organ chords, which carry Thornhill, still noodling the melody, through the bridge of tune. Then the reeds and horns assume the melody for the final eight bars of the first chorus. The clarinettist Danny Polo plays a variation of the melody for sixteen bars, and during the second eight is backed by oh-so-soft counterpoint between the reeds and the brass. A tenor saxophonist, playing melody, takes over on the bridge and is echoed by Polo. Then the whole band spins trickily through what sounds like a transcribed bebop solo. There is a brief Thornhill piano interlude, and the band returns for eight bars of melody and a kind of variation of the opening six measures, and it is over. There is a lot of fast and subtle rhythmic footwork on the recording, and Thornhill's use of dynamics is exhilarating. Yet everything is *quiet*.

Musicians loved the Thornhill band. The French-horn player Sandy Sigelstein has said, "I met Gil Evans in the service, and I ran into him in Los Angeles in 1946, when I was with Martha Graham. I was strictly a legitimate player. Gil said they needed a horn, so I joined. Then I discovered I couldn't play four-four time, and I was humiliated. But the challenge was on, and eventually I learned. The camaraderie in that band through music was out of this world. Claude was always good to me, but he was mysterious. He would never call out the next number. Instead, he would noodle around, giving little hints, until we figured out what he had in mind. He knew how to underplay on the piano and at the same time lead with it. That band was like a concert. Several horn players from the Cleveland Orchestra came one night, and so did all the dance-band people. Being in the Thornhill band was an experience that has been with me all my life."

There was never any extra money. The tubist Bill Barber said not long ago, "I had been in classical work before I went with the Thornhill band, in 1947. I was only with them ten months. The big-band business had begun to crumble, and the last to be hired were the first to be fired, which meant me. I don't think the band wanted me to leave, because they loved that soft tuba carpet underneath. Claude was a fine musician, but he was a little tight with money. I had a friend who left Benny Goodman because he was so excited about playing with Thornhill, and he estimated that during the year he stayed with Thornhill he lost two or three thousand dollars."

Here is what the arranger Bill Borden said about Thornhill recently: "I don't know whether Claude was shy or diffident. He was often indecisive. If you asked him to made a decision, he would do the equivalent of shuffling his feet—unless it was something he felt strongly about or something that had to do with music. He was also decisive if someone did something behind his back that he didn't care for. He wasn't above jokes. He'd do this shtick of pretending not to understand. Or he'd break into ragtime piano if a new arrangement had a section that seemed too square. Mostly, he let our arrangements alone, although he'd cut things he didn't like. When I joined the band, in December of 1939, it hadn't settled into a groove. Sometimes it sounded like Jimmie Lunceford, sometimes like Bob Crosby. Claude said he had started out with sixty arrangements, but I suspect it was fewer than that. I suggested he get Gil Evans, who wasn't happy with Skinnay Ennis. The band became a kind of lab for Gil. He super-imposed bebop arrangements on the band in the late forties. Claude never mastered bop on the piano. He sounded a little like he was playing eighteenth-century drawing-room music when he tried. He was a forceful pianist, but he did those tinkling things on 'Snowfall' and 'Autumn Nocturne' because he felt that was what people liked. I never felt that the second band was as good as the first. It could cut the arrangements, but Louis Mucci was never the lead trumpeter that Conrad Gozzo was, and Danny Polo couldn't match Irving Fazola, who had the most beautiful sound I've ever heard on a clarinet. For what it's worth, Claude used to say that his favorite band was Guy Lombardo's. Toward the end of his life, he limped along with a kind of society band, but he had been rehearsing a new big band when he died. In fact, he was supposed to open in Atlantic City the next night."

During the fifties and early sixties, Thornhill took small bands on the road, playing either society-band music or stripped-down versions of his old book. The trombonist and writer Mike Zwerin worked for Thornhill in 1958. He writes in his autobiography, *Close Enough for Jazz:*

> Arrangements written for full sections were being played by only one trombone, two trumpets, four saxophones, a now guitarless rhythm section plus the essential French horn. We worked country clubs, American Legion halls and high-school gymnasiums in provincial towns where Claude Thornhill was still a name. Referring to more successful "ghost bands"—Sam Donahue and the Tommy Dorsey Orchestra, Ray McKinley and the Glenn Miller Orchestra—Claude once said to me after a particularly grungy affair: "I guess you have to be dead to make it these days."
>
> But he kept his dignity as his audience dwindled. His hair was always combed, his suits pressed, his face shaven, his bow-tie straight. I marvel at how much control that must have involved, considering the skid he was on. He knew he had been something special. It had taken imagination, taste, talent ad courage to play Charlie Parker's "Anthropology" at fancy hotels and supper clubs when people had paid to hear a band that had won two *Billboard* magazine polls in the "sweet band" category.

A few years earlier, when Thornhill was between bands, he worked for Tony Bennett. "Claude was with me as musical director and pianist for eight weeks in Vegas in the mid-fifties," Bennett said recently. "My drummer, Billy Exiner, who had been in Claude's second band, suggested him. Claude's attitude was that it was all a vacation, that we shouldn't worry about anything. We were kids and he was the veteran, and he'd teach us what he knew. He was a sweet man. But he didn't care for pretension. A big old-time movie star was on the bill with us. She was a prima donna, and she'd carry on and yell at her chorus girls during rehearsals. She did only one number, and it was called 'Dungaree Doll.' Claude couldn't get over her behavior, and whenever I ran into him backstage or coming around a corner he'd sing 'Dungaree Doll,' and laugh."

By the sixties, Thornhill and his wife were living in New Jersey, and Artie Shaw had an apartment in New York. Shaw recalled recently, "The night Claude died, in the summer of 1965, I got a phone call at three in the morning from Claude's wife, I hadn't talked to him in a long while. She said Claude had told her I was his best friend, and then she said that he had just had a heart attack and died. She said he had spent the day in his garden and had told her it had been one of the best days he had ever had. Later, I found out that Claude had been paying frequent visits to my mother, who lived in New York. He had made her promise never to tell me about the visits, and, of course, he never did, either."

[1988]

CHANTING WITH
BUSTER

~~

When Jimmy Rowles at last began his brave invasion of New York City, a little over a year ago, perhaps a hundred people took note. But this was hardly surprising. Rowles's previous visits to the city, in the forties and fifties, had been brief and in the semi-visible guises of accompanist for Evelyn Knight and Peggy Lee and of big-band pianist for Benny Goodman and Woody Herman. The rest of his career had been spent around Los Angeles, in a variety of equally subaqueous roles that included studio work, fleeting nightclub appearances, countless recordings for other people, and coaching singers and non-singers, one of whom was Marilyn Monroe. "The studio sent me over to this sumptuous office on the lot where she was supposed to be," he said recently, "and when I got there the blinds were drawn and the place looked empty. Then I saw this form asleep on the sofa. I didn't know what to do, so I sat down in a chair and lit a cigarette and dug it all. 'Here I am,' I thought, 'sitting alone in the dark with the most beautiful woman in the world.' Then I got nervous. So I cleared my throat several times and she woke up." In January of last year, Johnny Mercer brought Rowles with him as his accompanist for his Town Hall concert, and five months later, Rowles took a two-week gig at Michael's Pub and concurrently appeared in the Newport Jazz Festival-New York. Perhaps a hundred more people took note, and one of them was Barney Josephson who has brought Rowles into the Cookery for a seven-week engagement that sets one Rowles record and nearly breaks another: It is the longest solo stint he has had outside Los Angeles, and the second-longest he has had anywhere.

One night, a half-hour before his first set, Rowles was sitting by himself at a table near the piano. He does not stand out in crowds. Compact and medium-sized, he is gray-haired and be-spectacled and clerkly looking. His face is chipped and worn, and he has a low, gravelly voice. His mod California clothes, instead of accenting him, almost extinguish him. "It was a little strange in here at first," he said. "I felt like I was playing in a cafeteria, what with all the dish sounds and steady talking. And I don't think I ever played in a club without a bandstand, with the piano right down on the floor in the middle of the tables. A bandstand gives you a little defense, a little privilege. But I'm getting used to it, and Buster Williams, the bass player who'll be with me until Tommy Bryant takes over, is a big help. A lot of the tunes I play he doesn't know, but he's got awful ears. He grabs the structure and chords of a new tune after the first chorus, and he doesn't forget it if I play it a couple of nights later. But *my* ears have been giving me trouble. They've been stuffed up ever since I got off the plane, like as if I caught a little cold out there and carried it east with me. I've been think-ing more and more lately that its time for me to be doing some-thing like this. I'm fifty-five years old, and it won't be that much longer before I get away, like all my friends seem to be doing. This past year, Ben Webster, Don Fagerquist, and Frank Beach all passed. And a couple of weeks ago it was Bobby Tim-mons, who was only in his thirties. So I figure it's time to play the way I want to play, time to see if I can make a go of it out-side the studios and accompanying people." Rowles paused, and waved to a waitress. "Honey, get me a vodka-tonic, please. My wife, Dorothy, was all for the move, and that means everything to me, because she's smart musically and every other way. Lord! The other night, I found myself staring at the back of some woman's legs because they looked exactly like Dorothy's. That's how much I miss her already. We met in '36. She was going to a high school on one side of Spokane, where we were both born, and I was going to one on the other side, and we met at a dance I was playing at her school. When I went down to L.A. the first time, in 1940, I asked her to wait a year, and if it worked out I'd send for her and we'd get married. It did and we did, and it's been thirty-two years. She's been my life's blood. Of course, it wouldn't be right if we didn't fight at least once a week. She's thrown me out of the house as much as two weeks at a time. Once, when I came back, she was gone, and there was a note: 'Try and straighten up. And feed the animals.' She stayed away two weeks, and I didn't find out until later that she was just around the corner.

"We've got three kids, and they're *all* musical. Several years ago, my older daughter—her name is Stacy—saw a trumpet up in the attic which Frank Beach had given me. Chuck Peterson, the high-note man with Tommy Dorsey, had taught me a little trumpet when we were in Skinnay Ennis's band in the Army. Stacy said 'How do you play it?' and I showed her the scales. And last year, when she was eighteen, she won first prize at a big-band contest, and then she played at the Monterey Festival, and was hugged and kissed by Dizzy Gillespie and Clark Terry. And my younger daughter, Stephanie, who we call Zip, is into the flute. So I asked Arthur Gleghorn, a great English flute player who works in the studios out there, would he come by and play for us. We laid in plenty of vodka, and his old lady brought him over and he sat by our pool and played for hours— Ravel and Debussy—and it was fantastic. My son, Gary, plays organ and guitar. He's thirty-one. He began to break away from me when he was fourteen. I couldn't tell him where the sun rose, he knew so much. But he came around in his early twenties. He's a car genius, and he stops by and gives my arm a squeeze and works on my car, and everything is fine.

"Uh-oh. It's five after eight. Time to work." Rowles took a small blue box out of his pocket. It had the words "Tacky-Finger" on the lid. With careful, ritualistic movements, he dipped the ends of his fingers into the waxlike substance in the box and then massaged them. "I saw a teller in a bank put this stuff on before she counted a pile of bills, and now I can't live without it. It keeps my fingers from slipping off the keys into my lap. Before, I used to rub them under any old table to get them tacky, and later I'd have to wash the keyboard." Rowles went to the piano, picked up the bench, and put it behind the cash register, near the front door. He replaced it with a Cookery chair. In one motion, he sat down, leaned over, poised his fingers a second over the keyboard, and sank into a very slow "Mood Indigo." He moved in a gentle, circular fashion, as if he were leafing through a stamp album, and he punctuated his felicitous phrases by pointing his right toe at the ceiling. It lasted close to ten minutes, and was followed by an equally long and introverted version of "Prelude to a Kiss." Rowles's engine steadied, and the tempo went up in "I Can't Get Started." A light seemed to go on within the tune, and one could see the outline of its pleasant bones. A ruminative "Skylark" came next, and Rowles closed the set with a candent version of Fats Waller's "Jitterbug Waltz."

He remained at the piano half a minute, and, letting his hands hang loose, vibrated them vigorously, like a swimmer loosening his muscles. "I've got to go downstairs and chant with Buster," he said. "I'll be back in ten minutes." Jazz musicians, like poets, are prone to inscrutable remarks; here is what Rowles had told a friend about Thelonious Monk: "I went into this restaurant in Tokyo six or seven years ago, when I was on a tour, and there was Monk standing at the bar. He was wearing one of his funny hats, and the whole time he revolved slowly, his hands raised and fluttering like moths around his head. When he came face to face with the bar, he'd stop, take a drink, then start spinning again. I'd seen him before, of course, but I'd never talked to him, so I introduced myself. I made a couple of attempts at conversation. Silence. Then he said, 'You got any kids?' I told him I had a son who was twenty-four, and I was about to mention Stacy and Zip when he said, 'He's too old. Get rid of him.' And he never said another word." And here is what Rowles said one night at Michael's Pub when he was asked how he was. "Oh, I feel more like I do now than when I first came in."

Rowles's playing is extraordinarily intense, and it demands exactly as much as it offers. Every tune is multi-layered, and, except for those rare times when he tires and repeats certain phrases, it has no soft spots. His singular harmonic sense governs his attack. He uses strange, flatted chords that seem to leave his phrases suspended and unresolved. They are questioning chords. His delicate runs have the same upturned, searching air. They begin in odd places, and while a run is moving buoyantly up the keyboard it suddenly breaks off, there is a pause, and the run resumes, descending through the very notes just played, as if Rowles were trying to knit the two parts. The melody slopes along in the middle distance, and his immaculate time is a further stabilizer. His touch is almost Tatum-light, and even his rushes of hard, no-nonsense single notes in fast numbers have no clamor or urgency. His chords and broken, winding runs suggest a hesitant, puzzled attitude, a continual where-do-I-go-from-here approach. But this is only a delightful illusion, a polite way of not overwhelming the listener.

Rowles reappeared. "I chant with Buster a lot," he said. "He's into the Buddhist thing, and chanting keeps him cool. 'Nam Myoho Renge Kyo' we go, over and over, in unison. I don't know what it means, but it makes you feel like you're doing your rosary. It makes you less conscious of yourself, and I always get in my own way during the first set every night. My playing is a matter of concentration, a matter of intensity. A jumble of things flash constantly through my mind, like people's faces and what I'm going to play in the channel, and all the while the melody is with me subconsciously. I have that, and I have the chords. They're the carpet, and my playing is like dancing on that carpet. I learned how to accompany singers and horn players by listening to the backgrounds that arrangers like Sy Oliver and Duke Ellington and Mary Lou Williams wrote for their soloists. Particularly Mary Lou when she was with Andy Kirk. In fact, I want to meet her while I'm here. It's unbelievable how much I owe that woman. It's unbelievable how much I owe a lot of people. Like Donald Brown, a Blackfoot Indian from Montana, who got me going in the right direction when I was a kid. He played tenor. When I first knew him, I was deep into Guy Lombardo. He was my favorite band, and I loved his piano player Freddy Kreitzer. Brown heard me doing some Lombardo tune at the piano in the gym at Gonzaga University, where I went for a year and a half, and he said, 'Ace, what are you doin' that for? You should be listening to the Benny Goodman Trio.' He took me downtown to a record store, and when I heard Teddy Wilson in the Trio, that was it. It changed my whole life. Brown had absolute pitch and radar ears. If I played a Wilson or Tatum record and asked him about certain cords, he'd tell me to slow the turntable down, which you could do on those old windup Victrolas, and he'd spell out every note. Another person I'll always owe is Ben Webster. I met him late in 1939, in Seattle, where I was studying law—or at least my family thought I was—at the University of Washington. My real father, whose name was Hunter, passed when I was three months old, and I was raised by my mother and a stepfather, who adopted me and gave me his name. My mother had studied guitar, and she played the piano real well by ear, but he was in the rug business and wasn't musical at all, except when he'd come home with some cronies at two in the morning and get me up to play the piano while they sang gems like 'Ace in the Hole.' Anyway, Ben had just joined Duke Ellington, and I knew Ben was *the* man. He introduced me around to all the musicians, and when I was twenty-one and legally free, I dumped the law thing for good and took off for L.A. I played with Slim and Slam. Slim was into his crazy vooterini talk then, and he played the piano with the backs of his hands as well as the regular way. Then I played intermission piano for Art Tatum. Man, I was smothered I was so scared. I couldn't believe his hands. They were stubby, but they stretched like cobras when he wanted to reach a tenth or more. And the way they moved, he didn't look like he was playing at all. I'd ask him how he did such-and-such, and he'd show me. But if I mentioned his fantastic touch, all he'd say was 'Oh, I don't know' and start talking about Westerns or baseball. Once, I hung out with him for three days and three nights, and sometimes he'd play seven or eight hours at a stretch. Dorothy and I were married by then, and when I got home she was so mad she Art-Tatumed me right out of the house for a week. I never travel without Art; I have six cassettes of him over in my hotel room. I worked with the Spirits of Rhythm, too. Teddy Bunn was in the group and so was Leo Watson. And I worked with Lee and Lester Young. Lester was the coolest man I ever met. He wasn't Pres to us but Bubba, after some nephews who called him Uncle Bubba. He had his own language. He'd turn to me on the bandstand and say, 'Startled doe. Two o'clock,' which meant if you looked into the audience at where two o'clock was you'd see this pretty chick with big eyes. 'Bob Crosby's in the house' meant a cop had just come in, and 'Bing and Bob' meant the fuzz were all over the place. When I first knew him, he said, 'There's a gray boy at the bar who is looking for you.' 'What's a gray boy?' I said. 'Man, *you're* a gray boy,' he said, smiling with those green teeth he had then, 'and I'm an Oxford gray.'

"And everything that was good was 'bulging.' It was a telescoping of a phrase that had started out 'I've got eyes for that,' which meant 'I like that,' and became 'I've got great big eyes for that,' and then 'I've got bulging eyes for that.' But if he didn't like something or somebody, all he did was puff out his cheeks—no words at all, just balloon cheeks."

It was nine-thirty, and Rowles applied more Tacky-Finger, then went back to the piano. He began an intense study of

"Willow Weep for Me," an immovable song that ultimately bowed to his relentlessly polite exploration. He seemed to tunnel right through "The Man I Love," circumventing its singsong, steplike melody. "My Buddy," its melody decked out with embellishments, and properly played as a waltz, followed. It gave way to "Miss Brown to You," which he sang in a pleasant, husky voice. Freddie Hubbard's "Down Under," Billy Strayhorn's "Lush Life," and an ancient tune called "In the Middle of a Kiss" came next, and he closed with a rocking, medium-tempo rendition of Duke Ellington's "Cottontail" which included a witty paraphrase of Ben Webster's famous solo.

Rowles put a fat, leather-bound loose-leaf book on his table, and went to get a fresh vodka-tonic. "I call that *My Book*," he said when he returned. "It has all the tunes in it I play—maybe a thousand or so." The neatly typed titles were arranged by letter and by category. There were no fewer than seventy waltzes, among them "My Mom," "Dancing with Tears," "Millicent," "Charade," and "Many Happy Returns." The letter "I" began: "It's Like Reaching for the Moon," "I Was Doing All Right," "It Don't Mean a Thing," "It All Depends on You," "I'll See You in My Dreams," "I'll Never Be the Same," and "I'll Remember April." And the letter "S" started out: "Suppertime," "Some Saturday," "Solitaire," "Something," and "Skylark." "Ive written some of my own songs and lyrics in the last couple of years. Just off-the-wall stuff. There's one about tennis, a game I love and think of as physical chess. And there's one about Monk, and one about Fred Astaire, and a thing about missionaries called 'Behind the Faith.' " He started to sing softly, "I loved the Matto Grosso/All the wild Indians in it/ Shooting food with spears/ And shrinking heads." And he went on, "Just imagine their reaction/ When a missionary shows up/ And tries to tell them how to live/ As if they didn't know already.

"Ben Webster and I used to play a lot of golf in the fifties, when he lived on the Coast," he said. "We'd tee up, and all these fancy types would be waiting their turn, mumbling under their breath about that big black guy who was holding them up. Ben would have one of his little hats on the back of his head, and he'd stand there before the ball, his big front sticking out, and talk to himself: 'Now, Ben, do it just like when you were in the Masters. Keep your head down, and not too many Wheaties.' And he'd take a terrific swing—pouf!—and the ball would dribble ten feet. We only saw each other on the tees and greens, but we laughed our way around the whole course. Then last summer I got a feeling, a notion. I hadn't seen him for years, and something told me it was time to get over to Copenhagen, where he was living. After I worked the Newport Festival here, I went to Europe with Carmen McRae. She gave me a week off, and I got up to Copenhagen and stayed on Ben's couch. He wasn't in good shape. He was drinking a lot and his legs hurt him, and he was enormous. He never wore anything the whole time but his shorts, and he'd sit in a little swivel chair and talk about 'the Judge,' which is what he called Milt Hinton. Ben was a Jekyll-and-Hyde. He was a sensitive cat, and when he wasn't drinking he was soft-spoken and polite and as gentle as cream. But after two drinks, forget it. Benny Carter was the only man he'd listen to when he was like that. If Ben was roaring around and Carter happened to be there, he'd say, 'Cut it out, Ben. Go sit down and behave yourself,' and Ben would. Ben used to say of Carter, "There's a man who can bake a cake as light as a feather and whip any man.' One night in Copenhagen, we put Ben to bed—there were always people flowing in and out—and went out to see the sights. I got back late, and there was Ben stretched out on the marble floor like a gingerbread man. I still don't know how I got him into bed again. When I had to leave to meet Carmen, Ben hung out the window, still in his shorts, his huge shoulders and chest bare, and waved and waved and kept saying, 'Come back, S.H.,' which is what we called each other. 'Come back and see me soon.' Ten days later, the cable came saying that he had got off."

[1974]

WHATEVER HAPPENED
TO MEL POWELL?

~~

There are two Mel Powells. One played brilliant piano and wrote brilliant arrangements for the Benny Goodman band of 1941 and 1942—and then, after several years of backing and filling, gave up jazz altogether. The other is the quietly famous composer (school of Milton Babbitt, Elliott Carter, Pierre Boulez, Luciano Berio) and professor of composition at the California Institute of the Arts. The two communicate easily—unlike the older and younger selves of the same person who meet in Max Beerbohm's drawings—and last fall they met again briefly. This occurred when Powell accepted an invitation to play on a two-week jazz cruise, and, after six months of heavy, restorative practicing, performed beautifully in seven concerts with the likes of Dizzy Gillespie, Ruby Braff, Dick Hyman, Tal Farlow, Bob Wilber, and the late Buddy Rich. Powell talked about the cruise not long ago when he was in town for the New York première of his Woodwind Quintet. He was staying with Madelin Gilpatric, an old friend, on Park Avenue. She supplies him with comfortable quarters and a housekeeper who appears at the appointed hour with breakfast or lunch or tea. "I agreed to go on a jazz cruise six months before it took place," he said. "I had not played much jazz for a long time, and my fingers had turned to spaghetti. I forced myself to go to the piano every day, and by the time of the cruise I was ready. In fact, I probably played with more exuberance than anyone else because I hadn't been playing. What surprised me was that I could play fast tempos, and what didn't surprise me was that I didn't have the endurance I used to have. Playing for ten straight hours was nothing in the Goodman days. Now, of course, my fingers are spaghetti again, but they're not so bad that I can't get off a little Bach or Beethoven in my classes."

Why Powell quit jazz for the world of formal music is not as puzzling as it once appeared. He was eighteen when he joined Goodman, but he had already had a dozen years of serious classical training on the piano, had studied theory with a Juilliard professor, and had written chamber music. One morning, he had this to say about his crossing-over: "I have decided that when I retire I will think through my decision to leave jazz— with the help of Freud and Jung. At the moment, I suspect it was this: I had done what I felt I had to do in jazz. I had decided it did not hold the deepest interest for me musically. And I had decided that it was a young man's music, even a black music. Also, the endless repetition of material in the Goodman band—playing the same tunes day after day and night after night—got to me. That repetition tended to kill spontaneity, which is the heart of jazz and which can give a lifetime's nourishment."

Like many consummate teachers, Powel is a marvellous talker. He has a Paul Robeson voice—big stones roll around in it. He speaks in a careful, orotund, mock-facetious way, surrounding himself with the sonority and the small jokes that are the academic's defense against philistinism. Powell is over six feet, and has narrow shoulders—a tall building seen from the sidewalk. He has large blue eyes, a large, soft, settled face, and a wide smile. He still wears his hair, now largely white, in a pompadour; the effect, above his high forehead, is of a thunder-head coming over a mountain. He has difficulty getting in and out of chairs, and he walks slowly, with a cane. "I have mus-cular dystrophy," he said. "It hit about five year ago, I was on my way to play tennis when I stopped to buy a paper and sud-denly found myself flat on my back. There are forty varieties of the disease, and mine affects my quadriceps, which are the lifting muscles in the front of the thighs. There is no pain, and I do what I do—only a little more pensively. I have to plot things. Self-pity comes because I can no longer play tennis. I had, of course, long since given up baseball. I grew up in a building on 161st Street in the Bronx that overlooked right field at Yankee Stadium. I used to go up on our roof and sell peanuts to the spectators during the games. In fact, so many people went up there to watch games that Jacob Ruppert raised the right-field wall and blocked us out. But we had the satisfaction of having players like Lefty Gomez and Tony Lazzeri live in our building. I became friendly with Bill Dickey, the great Yankee catcher, and he coached me. I played first base for a dollar a game for a team sponsored by Garcia Grande cigars. We played in the sandlot across from the stadium. Then, one day, the shortstop rifled a ball at me and I caught it on my right thumb—I was a lefty—and the thumb got beaten up. There was a family conference about whether I would play baseball or play the piano. The piano won.

"I was born Melvin Epstein, in 1923—February 12th, which meant I never had to go to school on my birthday. The name Melvin was impossible and I didn't find Epstein a beautiful sonic structure. I changed my name to Mel Powell just before I joined Benny Goodman. The Powell was borrowed from a Polish uncle on my father's side who had written some songs and changed his name from Poljanowsky. My mother's maiden name was Mildred Mark, and my father was Milton Epstein. They were both from Russia, and I always like to think of my mother as having come from Minsk and my father from Pinsk, al-though they probably didn't. My mother was deeply devoted to her father, who lived with us. He was from Prussia, a man of God, a Talmudic scholar, a true patriarch. Reaching for the butter before he did was out of the question. My mother, in her way, was a matriarch. She was dour and severely Orthodox. She was said to have been a great beauty in the Lillian Russell mode, and as such she met the Jewish ideal of female beauty. She was almost completely nonintegrated into American life. But my father took to this country as though it had been custom-designed for him. He had been a professional boxer who used the name Kid Dougherty, but he was knocked out too often and gave it up. He went into the jewelry business and was very successful until 1929. Then he became a traveling salesman, and one of the reigning professional bridge players. He was always off to bridge clubs in Tulsa or Houston. He had embraced the world of credit and frivolity, and once, when I was with Benny Goodman, he called me and said he needed $500. I was delighted to help him, and he arrived in a Cadillac with a liveried chauffeur. I asked why, if he was so broke, he didn't use the subway. He said, 'Where is this, the subway?' He also said that when he owed his chauffeur enough money he drove and the chauffeur sat in the back. He and my mother eventually got a divorce, and he married someone younger than I was and had two children, whom I have never met. He died nine or ten years ago. I have an older sister, Elinor Lenz, who lives in Westwood, in Los Angeles, and is retired from U.C.L.A. I tend to be cavalier about sociology and politics, but they are her life. I also had a brilliant brother, Lloyd, who died when he was twenty-one. To this day, we feel pain when we speak of him.

"In 1934 or 1935, my family moved downtown to 865 West End Avenue, at 102nd Street. Lloyd was a jazz aficionado, and it was around this time that he got me interested in the music. I remember our sitting in our beds, blankets up to our necks, listening to remote broadcasts of the big bands. I went to De Witt Clinton High School and on to City College when getting into City College was an achievement—when Bertrand Russell was teaching there, and giving lectures on free love. He immediately got my philosophical support. I majored in French literature, for reasons I no longer understand. I had studied piano for years with a severe German lady named Sara Barg. My grandfather, in one of his dazzling Turkish-bazaar arrangements, taught her nephews Hebrew in exchange. She was not above slapping your hands with a ruler—not so much for poor fingering as for poor preparation. I won third prize in a city-wide competition for young pianists, and it was bruited about in the family that the judges must have been anti-Semitic because I had not won first prize. Walter Damrosch, who commanded limitless musical vistas in New York at the time, recommended that I go to Germany and study. But other currents were flowing through me.

"The first jazz group I ever saw was the Benny Goodman band at the Paramount Theatre on Broadway. I was thirteen. Lloyd and I sat in the first row, and the movie with the show was *Maid of Salem*. We saw it five times. I had never heard anything so ecstatic as this music, and yet so gleaming and crystalline in its precision. Teddy Wilson's pianism in particular astonished me. And when Lionel Hampton lost one of his mallets and it flew off the stage and landed in my lap it was almost too much. At the time, I was preparing Beethoven's first Sonata in F Minor for Miss Barg, and at my next lesson I took the liberty of varying a passage, and Miss Barg said, 'Melvin, what are you doing?' I said, 'I'm improvising,' and she slapped me with the ruler.

"There were a bunch of kids in my neighborhood who played stickball and had a little band. Their piano player came down with a cold once, and I was asked to fill in. The band had a job at a Polish wedding, and it paid three dollars. The first tune was 'Goody Goody,' and I did what I could, which meant reading it off, ticktock, ticktock. They didn't use me again. But in that group was a man who became a kind of mentor to me. He played cornet and a little piano. His name was Heggie, and he was in his twenties and he was tiny. He made me listen to Art Hodes and Jess Stacy and Bix Beiderbeck's 'I'm Coming Virginia,' and then to Earl Hines and Fats Waller. Heggie was a purist. He didn't tolerate Benny Goodman; Pee Wee Russell was his clarinettist. He'd cart me around to places like Nick's, where we heard Sidney Bechet and Zutty Singleton and Bobby Hackett. I started playing jazz piano, and I thought I was pretty good. I stayed up later and later, I began peeling off from C.C.N.Y., and I never graduated. Anyway, I asked to sit in one night at Nick's. Heggie was at the bar, and there was a black man sitting about fourteen inches from my left elbow. When I finished, he leaned over and said, You're going to be a real one.' Well, it was Art Tatum, and after he had spoken to me he sat down and played. I was never nervous about performing after that. Nick hired me to work with Brad Gowans and Pee Wee and Eddie Condon. At the urging of George Simon, the jazz writer, I auditioned for Benny Goodman one afternoon, then sat in with the band the same night at Madison Square Garden. I guess Benny was impressed, because he hired me. I followed the pianist Johnny Guarnieri in the band, and Benny paid me $500 a week, which was very good money then. My contribution to my family suddenly became significant, because the Depression had hit them seriously. I liked to think that I behaved like a Harriman or a Rockefeller when Benny and I negotiated, and that he had the impression I came from an affluent family. Actually, part of the reason he paid me so well was that I handled both the big- and the small-band work, and I began contributing arrangements. I was ecstatic for the first eight or nine months with the band. Imagine working at age eighteen with the likes of Sidney Catlett and Cootie Williams and Billy Butterfield and Benny, and imagine what it felt like to be on that stage at the Paramount when it rose into view at the start of each show! Catlett was a particular delight. He had delicacy as powerful as a bomb. The comfort his support gave you!

"Benny was always a little paternal with me, even the last time I saw him four or five years ago. I live in Los Angeles, and he called early one morning from the Ambassador Hotel and invited me for breakfast. He always stayed there, even though it had seen better days. I had a lecture to give, but I postponed it, because I hadn't seen him in a long time. I arrived with my walking stick, and he was very solicitous and told me I should swim every day. I told him that when I first worked for him he had been about thirty and I had thought of him as an old man, but that now we were just about the same age. He said, 'Wait a minute, sonny'—which is what he always called me—'I've discovered there's a big difference between seventy-two and seventy-two and a half.' You were never sure where Benny's mind was. Backstage at the Paramount in the early days of bebop, George Simon asked Benny what he thought of Dizzy, meaning Dizzy Gillespie, and Benny said, 'What's Dizzy?' I adored traveling with the band, but I began to tire musically after a year or so. So I quit late in the summer of 1942 and came back to New York. I prepared myself to spend what looked like the rest of my life in the service. I went for my physical with Charlie Christian, who had t.b. and God knows what else. When he was deferred, he said, 'Mel, you know why I'm 4-F? It's because I wear glasses.'

"I was drafted and sent to Fort Dix and went through basic. Then I got word from Glenn Miller that he wanted me for his Army Air Forces band. It was enormous, and had a string section and some fine players—Ray McKinley on drums, Carmen Mastren on guitar, Peanuts Hucko on clarinet, Bernie Privin and Zeke Zarchy on trumpets, and the singer Johnny Desmond. Miller was a Midwesterner like Benny, but he was from a very different background. He was a lot more austere, and he was fussy about both musical articulation and personal things. Sometimes we'd rehearse nine hours a day. But he was like a fan with his jazz players. About this time, my musical schizophrenia was taking hold. I began to write some string trios and brass-quintet pieces. It was a marvellous opportunity, because there were straight players in the band, and when I would write a new piece they'd get together and play it. The band was on its way by ship to the Pacific theatre when they dropped the bomb on Japan. We were in mid-ocean, and they turned the boat around. Ray McKinley had taken over after Glenn disappeared on that flight from England to Paris. He flew in a seven-seater, a C-45, I think, and Ray, Johnny Desmond, and I were supposed to go, too. But Glenn, who hated flying, said that since the weather was bad wouldn't it be better to keep the plane light and maneuverable? So he took off with the pilot and we followed later in a C-47, which is the old DC-3. What happened to Glenn's plane was a complete mystery until a year or two ago when a retired R.A.F. bombardier said he remembered seeing a plane like Glenn's go down over the Channel at about the time Glenn disappeared. The R.A.F. plane was on its way back from an aborted bombing run and it jettisoned the bombs it had over the Channel. The R.A.F. bombardier guessed that the smaller plane, which was low over the water, was hit by one of the bombs, and that somehow mention of the incident had got left out of the flight log."

No jazz musician of comparable stature has had such a short career as Powell. It lasted about five years, and the amount of time Powell actually spent improvising can probably be counted in hours. His playing therefore never had a chance to go stale, to fall into mannerisms and preconceived patterns. His style drew on Teddy Wilson, Art Tatum, Jess Stacy, and Billy Kyle, all descendants of Earl Hines. Powell was never a copyist; he celebrated his idols with little exuberances—a Jess Stacy tremolo, a tumbling, on-the-beat single-note Kyle passage, a nifty, complex, zigzag ascending Wilson run—then went his inimitable way. His touch was oblique and dancing. Powell's fast solos steamed. His single-note lines, decorated with little tremolos, flashed. His chords jumped three steps at a time. His accented notes, sounding every three or four measures, pressed the momentum. His slow solos were delicate and exploratory. He would examine every facet of the original melody in a leisurely, behind-the-beat Billie Holiday manner, turning it this way and that, holding it to the light, testing its beauty and strength.

Then he would draw new melodies from it, embellish them once or twice if he liked them enough, and move on. He had a superb sense of dynamics. His climactic chords were delivered in shouts, his runs in whispers, his single-note figures as conversation.

It was one o'clock, and Madelin Gilpatric's housekeeper, a small blond woman with tightly swept-back hair, appeared with a tray of soup and sandwiches and coffee. Powell gave a deep "aaah," laughed, and thanked her, saying that if home were like this he would never leave it. Then he pushed himself up from his armchair, seized his cane, and moved slowly across the room to a window. Bent slightly to one side, he moved like a sailing ship just under way. He lit a cigarette and apologized, and, returning to his chair, turned his back to it and fell, his arms braking his descent.

"I was fairly well committed to composition after the war," Powell said. "But first I got a call from M-G-M on the Coast asking if I'd be interested in a staff job. It seemed silly to me— writing backup stuff for Mario Lanza, and such. But Lenny Hayton and André Previn were out there, and they told me, 'Come on out. We'll have a ball.' I went for a year, and it was awful. Writing a glissando when the mouse ran up the clock. I had married the actress Martha Scott in 1946. We had met on a bond-selling tour before I went into the service. She's from Missouri, near Kansas City. She was Emily in *Our Town*—on the stage and in the film, which got her an Oscar nomination. During the past ten years, she's become an accomplished producer, although she still acts in movies. She and Henry Fonda and Bob Ryan founded a repertory theatre called the Plumstead Playhouse. We have two daughters. Mary, who's the older, is a musician. She's a singer and songwriter who is probably too refined to be successful. Kati is a struggling actress. Martha has a son from a previous marriage—Carleton Scott Alsop. He's a very successful stage manager. There isn't a straight man among us.

"From Hollywood, I went directly to Yale. I had submitted a

composition to Paul Hindemith, who was in residence there, and he accepted me. My notoriety was good for my ego when I was standing in those long lines waiting to register. I'd hear whispers: 'Do you know who that is? Mel Powell. He played with Benny Goodman.' None of this impressed Hindemith. He found out quickly that I was a glib writer, and he didn't let me get away with it. He'd give me an exercise in which I had to write two-part counterpoint using whole notes against whole notes. I was reminded of Miss Barg. She paid less attention to finger dexterity than to musical content. She'd say to me: 'No, you must not *show* the subdominant, Melvin. You must *express* it.' Hindemith had the greatest pedagogical mind I've ever been in contact with. My style of teaching derives from him. He wouldn't tolerate cafeteria talk. Our work was as serious as if we were surgeons in a lab. Once, a student brought in a piece of work, and Hindemith, in his German accent, said, 'Vot is dis?'—pointing to a passage. The student said, 'I felt that—' Hindemith interrupted him, and said, 'I didn't ask how you feel. Dot is for your doctor.' He didn't try to charm you when he taught, and he didn't admire mere beauty of sound. He'd say that Ravel had a little French dressing, that Stravinsky had a little Russian dressing. When he heard my 'Filigree Setting,' a string quartet written in 1959, he said, 'I see you haf gone over to der enemy.' I said, 'No, I learned that from you.' He replied, 'I do not teach interesting noises.' When Stravinsky gave the Norton lectures at Harvard, he spoke in French. When Hindemith gave them, he spoke in English, as difficult as it was for him. He was short, and he may well have had some of that brusque Napoleonic temperament. Pierre Boulez, who is a foot shorter than I am, reminded me the other day that all good contemporary composers have been short—Schoenberg, Stravinsky, Bartók, Babbitt. I said there was at least one exception.

"During the early fifties, I still had one leg in the jazz world. I did occasional gigs with Benny Goodman, and I made recordings for John Hammond. But most of that had petered out by the time I taught my first course at Yale, in 1957 or 1958. It was called 'Late Renaissance Polyphony,' and I knew enough to stay about a week ahead of my students. Eventually, I taught myself to lecture without a syllabus or notes. The amount of preparation it took was unbelievable—sometimes I spent five days on one lecture. But this kind of showoff stuff has its advantages. It keeps you flexible and allows you to constantly rethink things. I loved Yale, partly because of the intellectual life and partly because it was the sort of place where the great literary scholar W. K. Wimsatt and I could lunch together off and on for a year at George and Harry's and not know each other's name. I was Hindemith's assistant for three or four years, and when he left I became chairman of the Composition Department. I also became a full professor.

"Then, in the mid-sixties, Aaron Copland recommended me to Herbert Blau and Robert Corrigan, who were in the process of founding the California Institute of the Arts. They wanted to start a place where artists of every sort would be integrated, where playwrights and dancers and actors and poets and painters would all lunch together. They wanted me to start the music school. I wasn't sure I could do it. I had never administered anything, and it would be a severe change, quite uprooting. Kingman Brewster was the head of Yale, and when I told him what I was thinking of doing he looked at me as if I were mad. 'All they have out there is carnivals,' he said. But this gathering of artists was very attractive to me, and I accepted. There were the inevitable growing pains: terrific conflicts between the faculty and the trustees, mostly left-right things, and before I knew it I had been appointed provost of the institute, a job that I held from 1972 to 1976. Then I rebelled. I said I hadn't moved out there to worry about faculty-student ratios. I resigned and appointed myself to the faculty and forbade myself ever to attend another committee meeting. We have between 700 and 800 students, and a hundred and thirty of them are in the school of music. We are the least academic of academic institutions. I teach a course called 'The Musics of Modernism,' and I have five or six graduate students in composition. I think it is crucial for composers to be taught by a composer. I also think it is crucial for a professor to cease teaching when it becomes a drudgery. I don't see it happening to me. Here I am at sixty-four, delighted to be working every day with bright young people of twenty, watching them experience the pleasures of discovery.

"I'm supposed to belong to the highly intellectual group of American composers which includes Babbitt and Carter. I like being thought of not as atonal but as nontonal. My music tends not to be long, and I tend to avoid the feverish expressivity of those of my colleagues who are even more influenced by the Europeans than I am. I like to think I have thinned out the self-pity—the whining quality I hear in their music. I try to keep the surface of my music dry. I am a slow worker—two pieces a year is very good for me. There is always the preposterous disproportion between the physicality of doing notation and the actual reality of the music. It's a kind of temporal dislocation. You are slowly writing down notes that will be played off in seconds. Before I put down the first of the many drafts I do of a piece, I try to do what Mozart is supposed to have been able to do—see an entire composition in a flash. I learned from Hindemith to have a godlike view of what you are about to do. Obviously, this view will not be greatly detailed. It will not include every C-sharp. Here is the first sketch of my 1982 String Quartet. It was the sketch I pinned to my lampshade as I went ahead with the work." Powell picked up a pencil from the coffee table in front of him, and rapidly drew this:

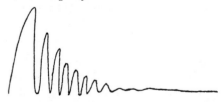

"What this means is that the piece begins with a great degree of complexity that is gradually resolved, like a haircut. You have to think through your whole structure. I would not dare to attempt writing a piece, small or large, without the knowledge of where it is going to end. I once heard a story about Charlie Chaplin asking Stravinsky at a gathering on the Coast, 'How do you know when to end a composition?,' to which Stravinsky said, 'Before I begin.'

"Composing is like the experiment with the ape. A banana is put outside his cage just beyond his reach. But a stick has been left in the cage, and eventually the ape sees the stick and uses it to reach the banana. You have to find the stick. When I worked under Hindemith, we were never allowed to touch a piano when we composed. Any instrumentalist who composes will perforce hear that instrument in his inner ear before he writes. Listen to the triad at the beginning of Stravinsky's 'Symphony of Psalms.' Nobody but a pianist sitting at his piano would write something like that. What has been particularly exciting for me recently in my music is working out the implications of what Schoenberg introduced in 1908 when he created nontonality. Not the problem of pitch but the problem of *time*. Up until now, Schoenberg's discoveries have largely been superimposed on a Brahmsian rhythmic structure. What we should be looking for is the analogy in time. We need a nontonal music that is also a nonperiodic music. There is a hierarchy in tonality—C major is boss. But in nontonality all pitches are equal, in principle. In the same way, tonality belongs to a two by two, singsong world. Rhythmic pulsing is its heart. This is inappropriate for nontonal music, which should be non-pulse. Finding out how to make it so is exciting. When I improvise, on the other hand, I live dangerously. I absolutely focus on the instant. I often find that I'm not thinking, beyond falling into certain patterns which may be dictated by finger convenience. Sometimes, when I play an Art Tatum run or a Mel Powell run, it is a signal that Powell is out of ideas, but he'll be back. He's flowing, but getting ready to fly. I used to hear this in Chopin. These are just breathing spells, and we're damn glad, we pianists, that they are there."

Powell laughed. "Who knows? Maybe I'll give up music and

become a painter. In the late seventies, I was asked to give a lecture on modern music to some painters at CalArts, and I drew a graphic analogue to the structure of a Schoenberg piece I was going to discuss. I enjoyed doing it so much that in time I started doing watercolors. I found that I loved ordering color. I also found that it gave me instant gratification. I could put a beautiful red on the paper and see it winking at me, while I might have to wait five years to hear the notes I had just written down. We began to hang these watercolors in the house, and one day Keith Holzman, who used to be the head of Nonesuch Records, was visiting and looked at one and said, 'This would make a lovely cover for your new album.' He asked me if I happened to know the artist, and I said I knew him very well."

[1987]

BOB'S
YOUR UNCLE

~~

George Shearing doesn't like his listeners to get too close. During the first part of his career—in England, where he was born, in 1919—he hid behind the styles of other pianists. He was considered England's Meade Lux Lewis, England's Art Tatum, England's Teddy Wilson. In the second part of his career, which began in the late forties, just after he settled in his country, he disappeared inside his smooth, famous quintet (vibraphone, guitar, piano, bass, and drums), emerging occasionally for a solo chorus but in general restricting himself to sixteen or twenty-four bars. The disguises he has used in the third part of his career, which started in the late seventies, when he gave up his quintet, are his most refined. He now works in a duo with a bassist (the Canadian Neil Swainson), but he is no more accessible than he ever was. He has long been thought of as a jazz pianist, but he is apt these days to play Kurt Weill's "Mack the Knife" at a very slow tempo, clothing it with thick Bartók chords. Or he will play the "Moonlight" Sonata straight for sixteen or twenty bars (he is an excellent classical pianist), and then, in the same tempo and using Beethoven harmonies, slip

seamlessly into Cole Porter's "Night and Day," staying with it
à la Beethoven for a chorus or so before easing back into the
sonata. He will play Porter's "Do I Love You" in Mozart fashion, and his own "Lullaby of Birdland" as a Bach fugue. Or he
will do a sorrowing, almost chanting rendition of Jobim's "How
Insensitive," and give Alec Wilder's "While We're Young" a
full-scale ballad treatment, filling it with substitute chords and
Art Tatum decorations. (There are signs, though, that his de-
fenses are crumbling. This year he released an out-and-out jazz
album, "Breakin' Out," and his recent performances at the Café
Carlyle, where he holds forth every January and February,
have been swinging and direct.) What is always present is a
superlative pianist, who can play Mozart with a feathery cor-
rectness, then improvise with swinging abandon. Shearing has
a beautiful touch, which falls somewhere between the sparkle of
Nat Cole and the buoyancy of Art Tatum. His jazzlike playing
is colored by Teddy Wilson and Hank Jones and Erroll Garner
and Bud Powell, but he does not have a style in the conven-
tional sense. He has perfected a unique *sound*, a kind of handsome aural presence, made up of his airborne tone; his wit (he
has a pleasant, slightly foggy tenor, and he puts words to "I
Can't Get Started" which go, "When I first met Benny G., He
said, 'Hi, Teddy,' to me"); his extraordinary harmonic sense;
and his refusal to use pianistic clichés. Shearing recently talked
about his playing in his apartment, which is in the East Eighties:

"When I sit down at the piano, I make sure my stool is in
front of middle C," he said. "Then I know I have three Cs on
my left and four on my right. I have my seven octaves, and I
know just where I am and where I can go. I've heard too many
players slog the piano. I feel sorry for an instrument that is
brutally treated. I love tone production—connecting my notes
so that they sing, instead of coming out clump-clump-clump.
When you improvise, in addition to your tone production you
must have a musical atmosphere in your head—a musical cli-
mate. You must have compounds of scales and arpeggios to fit
the chords you improvise on. Sometimes as I improvise I hear

a horn in my head, or an alto or a tenor saxophone, or a flugel-
horn. On a slow ballad, I hear Hank Jones, who is so good he
should be deported. The gift of improvisation is being able to
weave from one chord to another. It's a question of immediately
getting what's in your mind into your fingers. If you could ex-
plain it, which I can't, all the surprise and spontaneity and
unexpectedness would disappear.

"I no longer wish to work all the time. My ears get tired. I
want to play bridge with my wife, Ellie. I want to work on my
VersaBraille computer. I want to build up my compact-disk
library. I want to do more disk-jockeying. I want to ride my
tandem bike. Eventually, I probably won't play in public anymore, but I'll certainly play here."

During the past eight or nine years, Shearing and his bassist
have frequently joined forces with the singer-composer-instru-
mentalist Mel Tormé and his drummer, Donny Osborne, and
they have developed an effortless and engaging act. Shearing
accompanies Tormé's singing, Tormé plays piano with Shearing, Shearing sings by himself and with Tormé, Tormé plays
drums with Shearing. Tormé has said this about Shearing:

"I call George the Master. He is a blissful, constant surprise
musically. When we do two performances in an evening of
songs like 'Star Dust' and 'Dream Dancing,' each version George
plays is a spontaneous and exquisite work of art. He's got a
marvelous facility for inventing substitute chords in great songs.
A lot of pianists use substitute chords simply to call attention
to themselves, but George does it to enhance and embellish the
song. Add to that the incredible warehouse in his brain of classical music and of popular songs that no one else has ever heard
of. He's a lovely man, and the only time I have seen him
irascible is when people around him don't do their job right.
The last time we worked together, he played a solo number in
which he got softer and softer, creating a hypnotic delicacy and
quietude. When he was almost beneath hearing, the sound man

suddenly turned up the volume, wrecking everything. George made his feelings plain after the show."

Shearing has also worked often with Marian McPartland, his old friend and compatriot. She said the other day, "I first heard George in 1948 or 1949, at a club called the Silhouette, in Evanston, Illinois. He had his original quintet, with Denzil Best on drums and Marjorie Hyams on vibes and Chuck Wayne on guitar and John Levy on bass. It was, of course, a mixed group, and whenever George was asked about it he'd say, 'I don't know what color they are. I'm blind.' Without question, he's a genius. Every time I hear him or play with him, I rediscover how much music of all kinds he's absorbed. And he writes wonderful music—tunes like 'Lullaby of Birdland' and 'Conception,' which has a bebop melodic line as good as any Charlie Parker wrote. And there's 'Changin' with the Times,' and 'Bop's Your Uncle,' which is a play on the old English expression 'Bob's your uncle,' which means everything is O.K. He loves to joke around and laugh. I've played with him, and he'll put you on the spot by suddenly changing keys or going into a different style. And his puns are famous. It's hard to think of him as blind, because he constantly challenges himself. Sometimes I'm embarrassed to be around him and hear him talk about all the things he's doing outside of music. We've confided in each other at different times. George knows things about me that no one else does, and I probably know secrets about him."

Shearing lives with his wife in a comfortable, modern apartment. It has a sunken living room with yellow walls, an oatmeal wall-to-wall carpet, a fireplace, a Bösendorfer grand piano, an Eames chair, a wall of Braille books, and a marble head of Shearing by Ben Deane. Shearing's workroom, just off the foyer, contains two side-by-side unright pianos, his Braille word processor, all kinds of sound equipment, and a reclining chair that vibrates, massages your back, and plays tapes of birds singing in a ruined English abbey. Ellie Shearing is an excellent cook, and her sit-in kitchen has a six-burner electric stove and a plate warmer built into a wall. Shearing has a portable floor-to-ceiling temperature-controlled wine cellar in one corner, and in it are Château Lafite-Rothschild, Acacia Chardonnay, Fetzer Zinfandel, and Beaulieu Vineyard's Georges de Latour Private Reserve. (Shearing still marvels at the time he invited the jazz producer and oenophile George Wein to dinner and gave him, as a test, a decanted bottle of the Georges de Latour, vintage 1970. Wein took two sips and named the vineyard, the wine, and the year.) The apartment also has a stately dining room and a bedroom. Shearing moves around a lot, and when Ellie Shearing rings the lunch bell he travels the fifty feet or so from the living room to the kitchen in about three seconds. He also likes to lie flat in his Eames chair and talk, his hands crossed on his stomach. This is what he said one afternoon not long ago:

"Blindness is more of a nuisance than a handicap. People say they forget I'm blind, and that's the best compliment they can pay me. I have no desire to live a single day in an undignified way. I was born blind, and when I was a kid in London I used to go everywhere by myself. I went on the road with my quintet for ten years with guide dogs. It was one of the most enlightening experiences of my life. Maybe I'm a devout coward on the road, but I like my hotel rooms if possible to have the bathroom on the left, two chairs with a table between them, and a closet and bureau on the right. I can distinguish light and dark, and I like the window to be in front of me when I enter. An empty room is full of acoustics. In a full room, like this, sound dies. I have to snap my fingers in a full room that I don't know to find out when I'm approaching a wall or a bookcase. This is called facial vision. The movement of air is important. I can tell where people are around me simply by the way they displace the air. I think of sound as the vibration of air, and I think of color—I really don't know what color looks like—as the vibration of light. I used to travel by myself in New York taxis, but I don't much anymore, because you never know where you will end up. In general, getting around New York is wonderful, because of the grid pattern and the sharp corners. It's harder to lose your sight during your life than to be born blind. If you nurse the impairment, though, you'll be a pathetic blind man rather than a productive one. A sense of humor never hurts. Once, Ellie and I were waiting for a table in a local restaurant. It was very crowded, and a waitress carrying a huge tray of empty dishes tried to squeeze between Ellie and me. I didn't know what was happening, and I had my arm through Ellie's. The waitress said, 'Hey, what's the matter with you? Are you blind?' I said, 'As a matter of fact, I am.' Ellie said she will never forget the expression on the woman's face."

Shearing laughed, and his laughter loosened his imposing looks. He has a beaky nose, a high forehead, and grayish hair. He tilts his head up slightly when he is listening. Shearing stopped talking, sat up, stood, and, turning, went quickly up the living-room steps, across the foyer, and into his workroom. He talked as he went. "I've started writing some memoirs," he said, "and I'd like to read aloud what I've done. I've finished the first chapter, and begun the second." He sat down at his VersaBraille machine and began to read, his fingers moving over a Braille tape. Here is some of what he read:

"It appears that at the age of three I made gallant but improper attempts at producing music. I used to hit the piano with a hammer. The Shillington Street School, where I went, was in Battersea, in southwest London. The area was known as the Latchmere, so called because of a well-known pub, which benefitted from the same handle. This was just one of many pubs dotted around the neighborhood in case the inhabitants got thirsty. And, regrettably, they did. On numerous occasions, children would be heard crying outside pubs while adults inside were doing their level best to get to be the way I was born. It is with sadness that I relate the fact that my mother was a serious contestant. My mother, however, did her very best to keep these miseries at a minimum after I was born. Almost everything was purchased by the Y.P. method (Yours Perhaps). The installment collector was known as the tallyman. He would appear every week to collect his money. More often than not, he would be greeted with a friendly 'I'll see you next week.' This rather unpleasant task was often foisted upon one of us kids. In which case, it would be 'Mum will see you next week.' Purchases would be made far in excess of what would seem necessary, so that we could have collateral to borrow money to buy more, to have collateral to borrow, and so on.

"Dad was a coal man. This meant that his job was to carry as heavy a load as possible from his horse and cart to a private home or a place of business. He would leave home at about 6 a.m. and return about the same hour p.m. He worked for the same firm for three months short of fifty years and received the equivalent of twelve dollars a week. He got to retire on a handsome pension of a dollar a week. Like all working-class Englishmen, he was very proud. In my teens, when I thought of changing jobs, my dad would say, 'Why do you want to do that, son? The boss has been good to you.' I could never understand why paying me my hard-earned salary was being good to me. But through all this seeming consideration of management Dad was a very strong Labour man. He used to take me to the park on Sunday afternoons to hear some guy speaking in favor of Labour and, at times, for or against Communism. When no such oratory was to be found, we would witness part of a cricket match. Of course, we were never late home for afternoon tea, which would consist of watercress sandwiches and wonderful cake made by my mother.

"Were I more adept at putting things in their proper order, I would have saved some of the sweetness of the foregoing lines to lessen the depression of some of those to come. I remember the sound of rats scampering across the linoleum floor and the sound of my dad's boot trying to hit and kill them. I remember women begging their husbands not to get in a fight outside a pub when they had had too much to drink.

"Let's take a brief glimpse at my mother's life. Dad was earning a poverty-line salary. Mother had nine kids to raise, so she took care of the family during the day and cleaned railway trains at night. It's no wonder she tried to abort me—the youngest of the family. And no wonder I became blind in the process. Although she tried drowning her sorrows in drink, I feel that she really had a guilty conscience about my position and did her very best to repent.

"To this day, I am grateful that blind children were required to spend four years in residential school between the ages of twelve and sixteen. Linden Lodge was the name of the school I attended. Although it could not be counted among the twenty most beautiful residences in England, we had wonderful grounds, with a lawn, flowers, tennis courts for the staff, football and cricket fields, and all the things a little boy from Battersea didn't know existed. Cricket and football were played in the open air only by the partly sighted children. We blind kids played handball by using a football with a bell on it. Cricket was played inside by using a fair-sized balloon with a bell on it."

Shearing got up and went back into the living room and sat in his Eames chair. "That's all I've written so far," he said. He crossed his hands on his stomach. "I learned my Bach and Liszt and studied music theory at the Lodge. When I graduated, I went straight to work in a pub. A year or so later, I joined Claude Bampton's All-Blind Band. It was sponsored by the Royal National Institute for the Blind, and had been put together under the aegis of the bandleader Jack Hylton. There were fifteen of us, and we played Jimmie Lunceford and Benny Carter and Duke Ellington. We carried our own rostrum, and six grand pianos for the finale. Our suits were from Hawes & Curtis, on Savile Row. None of the bands of top condition would have dreamed of surrounding themselves with such glamour. Our leader was sighted, and he used a huge baton, which went swish, swish and told us what was what. Our music had been transcribed into Braille. We played all the major theatres in England and Scotland, and the tour lasted almost a year. I had my first contact with jazz in that band. Someone would pick up the new Armstrong or Berigan or Tatum record and say, 'Here's the new sender'—a good musician being known at the time as a solid sender. Through the band, I met Leonard Feather, who lived in London, and he helped me get recording dates and radio broadcasts. In 1941, I married my first wife, Trixie. I'd met her in an air-raid shelter where I used to play four-handed piano with the song plugger I was rooming with. Trixie and I had a daughter, Wendy, who now lives in North Hollywood. I had three or four jobs at once during the war—in theatres, supper clubs, jazz clubs. I had my own little band, and I also worked for the bandleader Ambrose. I toured a lot with Stéphane Grappelli, who spent the war in London. My mother was bombed out three times. We were Cockneys, and Cockneys tell jokes all the time. Here's one: This bloke says to his wife, 'Come on, Liza, the siren just went off.' She says, 'Hold it, Alf. I'm looking for my teeth.' And he says, 'Never mind that. They're dropping bombs, not sandwiches.' Around this time, I heard a recording of me speaking, and that told me I should do something about my Cockney accent. One time, I came home from school and my mother asked me what I had studied and I said, 'Six pieces of suet.' Or that's what she thought I had said. When she saw the teacher next, she asked her why we had been studying suet, and the teacher said the subject was 'Seek peace and pursue it.' Ellie tells me that when we visit London I revert to my old accent, and that if we stayed long enough she wouldn't understand a word I said. And when I see Grappelli I start talking like him: 'Stéphane, we go eat now.' I saved some money during the war, and in 1946 I visited New York. American musicians like Mel Powell and Glenn Miller had told me in England that I would kill them over here. I wasn't sure. Why would they want England's Teddy Wilson when they had the genuine article? But I liked New York so much I came back for good the next year.

"My first job was at the Onyx Club, on Fifty-second Street. I was the intermission pianist for Sarah Vaughan. I would be announced—'Ladies and gentlemen, from England the new and exciting pianist George Shearing'—and somebody would yell,

'Where's Sarah?' Then I spelled Ella Fitzgerald at the Three Deuces. She had Hank Jones and Ray Brown and Charlie Smith with her. When Hank took a night off, I played for Ella. I began to be asked to sit in on the Street, and Charlie Parker took me for walks between shows. Leonard Feather had moved to New York, and he introduced me to people and arranged gigs for me. In 1948, I played the old Clique Club, at Forty-ninth Street and Broadway, with Buddy De Franco on clarinet and John Levy and Denzil Best on bass and drums. We broke up after the engagement, and Leonard suggested I keep Best and Levy and add Marjorie Hyams on vibraphone and Chuck Wayne on guitar. I did some arrangements. Marjorie did some. We used a unison-octave voicing, like Glenn Miller's reed section. Our first New York gig was at Café Society Downtown, for $695 a week. We did the Blue Note in Chicago, and then the Embers and Birdland in New York—and the quintet took off. It lasted twenty-nine years, and a lot of wonderful musicians passed through—Cal Tjader and Gary Burton on vibes, Joe Pass and Toots Thielemans on guitar, Ralph Pena and Al McKibbon on bass, Charli Persip on drums. Toward the end, we traveled in a twenty-six-foot motor home with nine airplane seats and a couch and a refrigerator. On our last big tour, in the seventies, we did fifty-six concerts in sixty-three days, and I think that's what finally did me in."

Ellie Shearing brought in a tea tray and sat down. "Is that tea, Ellie?" Shearing asked. She said yes, and he made appreciative noises and said he would like a sugar and a half and enough milk to color his tea. "When I first came to this country," he said, "I couldn't believe what you got in a restaurant when you ordered tea. A cup of water that had never come to a boil and a tea bag sitting in the saucer. I'd tell the waitress, 'The water was good for my indigestion, now please bring me some tea.'" Shearing drank his tea quickly and excused himself, saying he wanted to get on with the next chapter of his memoirs. Ellie Shearing reminded him that they were supposed to have dinner at the Harvard Club with an old friend. She is trim and pretty and full of laughter. She has a long face, a wide smile, and auburn hair, tightly swept back. Her voice is big and carries easily around the apartment's corners. She is a quick, energetic talker.

"I marvel at the differences between George's and my background—at the fact that we ever came together," she said. "I was born in Harvey, Illinois, on August 22, 1932. My father was a Lutheran minister who had the same church—the first church he was given—for fifty-two years. His name was Rudolf Geffert, and he was born in Reed City, Michigan, the oldest of nine children. His father and his father's father were Lutheran ministers. He was short and dark and quiet, with a dry sense of humor. He did the Chicago *Tribune* crossword puzzle at breakfast, and he liked to translate Hebrew and Greek into English just for fun. I had three older brothers, and my mother did most of the raising of the children. Her name was Meta Hackbarth. She was little and always overweight, and she was a good plain cook. I was grown before I learned that all food wasn't fried and gray. She was well liked by the congregation, even though she had no patience for small-mindedness. She was born in Wausau, Wisconsin, and raised on a farm, and she hated it. To get away, she went to a normal school and became a teacher. After high school, I spent two years at Thornton Junior College and three at DePauw University. I was a piano major and a voice minor. I graduated in 1955, and my first job was writing radio commercials at WSBT, in South Bend. My second job was running a radio talk show in Niles, Michigan. Then I taught choir at a junior high school in East Grand Rapids. The next summer, I got into summer stock in New England through my old high-school speech teacher, Mae Sexauer. My mother was livid when she found out: her only daughter going on the wicked stage. She told me that I would bring shame on the family, that she'd disown me. But she eventually came to see me. After summer stock, I got a little apartment in New York, on Thirteenth Street between Avenues A and B, and I taught mu-

sic in a high school out in Levittown. I worked one summer in
'Around the World in Eighty Days' at Jones Beach, and I was
in 'To Broadway with Love,' a spectacle that ran at the Texas
Pavilion during the 1964 World's Fair. I had been doing choral
work around town, and I auditioned for Norman Luboff and
was his alto soloist for three years. In 1967, Norman told me I
should go to Hollywood and work in the studios, and I did that
for four years. I kept body and soul together by teaching reme-
dial reading in the Hollywood public schools. One of my students was a ten-year-old who had lived in communes all over
the West. He could shoot, skin a deer, and make deerskin clothes,
but he couldn't tell an 'A' from a 'B.' Within six months, he was
reading at third-grade level. I told him I looked forward to
teaching him the next year, and he said, 'I'm sorry, Miss Geffert, but my parents are moving again, and I don't know where
I'll be.'

"I met George in 1971, at a Christmas party at his place in
San Francisco. He was married, and I was dating someone reg-
ularly. We didn't see each other again for two years. By that
time, George was divorced from Trixie, and we began house-
keeping. We were married in 1984, in my dad's church. One of
my brothers, who's a minister, performed the ceremony. When
George and I started living together, I had been alone for a long
time. I had to learn not to leave doors half open, not to kick my
boots off in the middle of the room, not to not put things back
after I had used them. George is very independent. He does not
expect to be waited on. He's very sensitive, both emotionally
and physically. His fingers are so delicate that he can feel dust
on a table. Living with George can be difficult—sometimes on
the road we're together twenty-four hours a day—but he's my
best friend, and he's great fun."

[1987]

HERR
PROFESSOR

~

The Arkansas pianist Walter Norris passes through New York once or twice a year. He has lived in West Berlin since 1977, and since 1984 has been a guest professor at the Hochschule der Künste, where he teaches piano improvisation. Before that, he was the pianist for the Sender Freies Berlin, a radio studio orchestra. "My friend Rolf Ericson, the Swedish trumpeter, told me about the job with the S.F.B.," he said when he was here not long ago. "I wanted to go back to Europe, where I had been just twice. I knew it would change me and my playing. I knew the job would include improvising as well as playing everything that was put in front of me. I knew the pay was good. I also knew I would have a first-rate concert grand to work on and one of the world's best piano technicians to take care of it. A bad instrument confuses and disorients you. A sensitive instrument brings the music out differently—you can do almost anything. What I didn't know was that I would also have at my disposal a two-metre Bösendorfer and a private, locked room to use it in. Nor did I know that the first year there would be only seventy-nine days of work, leaving the rest of the time for practicing. The work varied constantly. One day, it would be with the full orchestra, and the next with a smaller group with French horns, and the next with the orchestra and a choir. The marvellous thing was that you were physically surrounded by all that music—a luxury that overdubbing has just about eliminated. At the end of 1980, they discontinued the orchestra, and I free-lanced around Europe. Then I was asked to teach at the Hochschule, which is a conservatory for the arts. I had forty-two students this year. I gave most of them a private one-hour lesson each week. Then I met with everybody for two two-hour classes, in which the students play for each other and I comment. I was going around the clock. The work almost killed me, but I loved it. I've always tried to work myself to death, just as my mother did before me. I live in the center of town, on the same street as the Hochschule. Berlin is a pleasant place. Everything is new. Everything works. The streets are safe. I was first married in the fifties, and I have remarried. My wife is French and has a Dutch name—Marie-Rose van Deinse–Norris. She's a violinist in the Theater des Westens orchestra. She has two sons, who are both very talented jazz players. It's mostly all work for us, but I play with the two of them when we have time. I used to do my bookings in New York, but it's difficult when you're on the other side of the ocean. A couple of years ago, a man named Bob Schillin called when I was here and asked me if he could be president of the Walter Norris fan club, which he was starting, and I told him he was elected. Eventually, he began to do some booking for me. He lives in New Jersey and doesn't have many contacts with New York clubs, but he perseveres, and things work out."

On this visit, Schillin got Norris into a club on the upper East Side, into a club in Greenwich Village, and into a club in SoHo. The first and last engagements worked out well, but the Greenwich Village job was difficult—although Norris never let on in his playing or his demeanor. The piano was out of tune, particularly in the higher registers, and Norris's bassist had his amplifier turned up. Norris has a delicate, spidery touch, and,

caught between the piano and the bass, he sounded like a remote and almost inaudible radio broadcast. But enough of his
playing came through. He admires Art Tatum and Bud Powell
and Charlie Parker, and he also admires Dinu Lipatti and Vla-
dimir Ashkenazy. His style is light and electric. He likes fast
tempos, Art Tatum runs, and staccato, half-time Billie Holiday
ritards. He likes to take his left hand off the keyboard and play
long, winding, intricate single-note lines with his right hand,
sometimes a cappella and sometimes in counterpoint with the
bassist. Then he'll drop his right hand into his lap and let his
left hand loose. The bassist Red Mitchell, who first heard Norris in California in the mid-fifties, spoke of him the other day.
"He is obsessed by music," Mitchell said, "and playing a good
instrument is part of that. Your instrument is an extension of
your arms and legs. Walter practices with a metronome. He's
after perfection. You have to have flawless time when you play
with him. There aren't many bassists who at some point don't
rush the tempo or slow it down. But if you meet Walter on his
level it can be great fun. You don't have to think about one,
two, three, four. The time just sits there and never changes. But
Walter is not a machine. He is a super, gentle person, a lifetime friend. I was taken with his soulful touch when I first
heard him."

Norris talked about himself before his first set at the Greenwich Village club. He is an imposing figure. Thin and slightly
over six feet, he has a large, professorial head. His hair is grayish and receding, and his face is composed of square, flat sur-
faces, like a late Cézanne landscape. He keeps his eyes narrowed,
and he speaks quickly, leaving nice pauses. His voice is high
and slatey, and still has its Arkansas edge. "I teach my students
the musical rules," he said, "but I do it as we go along, almost
indirectly. For assignments, I might ask them to work on a harmonic sequence—say, a ii-V-I progression—and be able to sing
all its parts. Or do a Bach two-part invention by playing the
right hand and singing the left, then reversing the procedure.
Or I might give them rhythmic exercises to be played against a

metronome. Or I might ask them to learn a pieces in all the keys. I want them to be able to play any interval in a chord and be secure, and I want them to be able to play in any rhythm or at any speed and be secure. Finally, I want them to develop a sense of coloring and dynamics—important refinements that many jazz pianists ignore. Then, after all this, I tell them *not* to think. I ask them when they are improvising to concentrate on their breathing—in-out, in-out—and not on what they are play-ing. So much improvisation is intuitive. I learned that by listen-ing to street-corner singers in Little Rock when I was a kid. They would scat-sing or cup their hands in front of their mouths and pretend they were trumpets or trombones. They were very good, and they didn't know an A from a C. Maybe they only used three or four notes, but they realized that when they hit a wrong note all they had to do was move up or down a half tone to be in the right place. I tell my students to compare the cave paintings with modern art. The cave painter had the same tal-ent as the modern painter. That talent has always been in us. It simply hadn't been documented much until the last three thou-sand years. There is every chance that there were musicians and singers in the cave painters' tribe who were just as good as the painters.

"Of course, jazz improvisation is not unique. Improvisation of some sort keeps resurfacing. We know that Bach improvised, and apparently Beethoven was a way-out improviser, a kind of charter Parker-Coltrane. Mendelssohn improvised, and so did Czerny and Chopin. And Rachmaninoff and Prokofiev. And Art Tatum worked things the other way around. The drummer Billy Exiner told me that he heard Tatum get a Chopin étude down letter-perfect in one hour. When I improvise, I let the harmonic vibrations pull me into the harmonic center of each number. I do not think ahead. It's an unnecessary distraction. I have to use my thinking energy for each instant, for what is coming out. It's my belief that every note we have ever played is pro-grammed in our subconscious, and that when we play the sub-conscious clicks on and notes come out in combinations that we

may have used before or that may be close to those combinations. Our task is to alter those patterns and make something
new in the instant they hit the ear—or even before. We must
play the way Picasso painted—in one continuous improvisatory
motion. But eventually improvising has to be regarded as spiritual, as beyond ordinary secular knowledge. I am skeptical about
any musician over forty who is not spiritual."

Norris settled into his first set with two rich ballads, "The
Best Thing for You" and "Never Let Me Go." Both began a
cappella and ad lib, then went into tempo. Norris's a-cappella
chords were loose and spacious; they seemed to rain on the melody. He did a fast "I Get a Kick Out of You," a digging, sombre
"Lover Man," and a fast number of his own, "Spacemaker." He
hums a rough melodic counterpoint to what he is playing, and
he moves constantly. Sometimes his hand shoots into the air at
the end of an arpeggio, and when he goes into a fast tempo he
jiggles and shakes and looks as if he might fly apart. He wears
heavy aviator glasses, but midway in the set he took them off.
He also removed his jacket and loosened his tie, folding the
jacket and putting it on the piano next to the music rack—an
echo of the way the old stride pianists used to fold their coats
inside out, so that their sensational custom-made linings would
knock their listeners' eyes out. When the set was over, he put
his jacket on and straightened his tie. He cleaned his glasses,
and ordered a cup of coffee. "Once, in Los Angeles, I went to
hear Art Tatum at a club not far from where I was working,"
he said. "The piano he was playing sounded wonderful. The
day after, at a jam session at the same club, I played that piano, and it was horrible. It was out of tune, and the action was
unbelievable. I went back that night to hear Tatum, and the piano sounded perfect again. He transcended any piano. His mind
went into it and made it sound wonderful. Playing this piano
reminds me of what a perfectionist my mother was. She'd stand
behind me, and when I made a mistake—*whack!* across my
shoulders with a switch. I did progress rapidly, but I already

had music in me, and I think I would have progressed anyway.

"I was born in Little Rock on December 27, 1931. On a Sunday. I was an only child who always wished he had brothers and sisters to make up a rhythm section or horn section to play with. My father came from a village in northeast Arkansas called Poughkeepsie. He worked for the Federal Reserve System. He was mild-mannered, and he had a natural understanding of other people's situations. He could always see clearly both sides of a problem. He was not an intellectual, but I think he would have liked to be one. When I was five years old, he began to teach me not to be prejudiced. Little Rock was integrated in the sense that there were white sections and black sections side by side. My father told me that the black people wanted to eat and have a place to live in and raise their children in, just as we did. He said that if black people got hurt the pain was the same as the pain we felt. He said that if something bad happened to a black child the parents felt the same sadness that he and my mother would feel if something bad happened to me. This made great sense to me, and I accepted it. He was always stretching my horizons. When I was older, he'd take me out to lunch at a Greek restaurant or an Italian restaurant or a German restaurant. It gave me a very open feeling about people from other countries. My mother's name was Mary Metcalf. She came from Evening Shade, Arkansas. She was highly energetic: Do more, push, push, push. She was like a racehorse. She played the piano, and started me in at four and a half. I was bad in school. I thought only of music. When I was eight, I heard a boogie-woogie piano player on the radio. I couldn't believe it. I sat down and taught myself boogie-woogie that day. I had thirteen years of classical training. My teacher, John Summers, was a church organist and choirmaster in Little Rock who improvised in the manner of church music. When I was ten, I was asked to join a band. It eventually grew to nineteen pieces. We'd rent an auditorium and give a dance after a football game, and have a packed hall. We even rented the municipal auditorium in Little Rock, and sometimes we traveled two hundred miles to play after a game. The money we made went into subscriptions to *down beat* and *Metronome* and to the purchase of the newest 78s. We had Charlie Parkers and Dizzy Gillespies two or three months after they were released. The band was integrated, and we never had any problem.

"Three months after I graduated from high school, in 1950, I was drafted for the police action in Korea. I ended up in the Air Force sixteen miles behind the lines, where suicide planes sometime exploded. I tried for two years to get into the service band, but, because of red tape, I never made it. When I got out, I worked in Houston for a great tenor player named Jimmy Ford. In 1953, I went to Los Angeles. It was a golden age in L.A. Before I settled in, though, I heard about a job in Las Vegas. It didn't sound like much, but I went, and it was nine months of paradise. It was in a black club called the El Morocco, which was on an unpaved street on the wrong side of the tracks. I worked in a trio, first as a sideman, then as the leader. The owner of the club was a black man named Oscar Crozier, and he was a marvel. He told us not to honor requests—he'd say to the audience, 'Man, don't bother my musicians.' And when I had to discuss business with him the give-and-take was first-class. The black entertainers on the Strip would come in after work, and so would visiting musicians, and we would play into the next morning. When I got back to Los Angeles, I couldn't believe the amount of music there was—the number of jam sessions. We'd play all Friday night and all Saturday and Saturday night and sometimes through Sunday. We'd go from club to club to club. I'd fall asleep at the keyboard and wake up and wonder what I was playing. This happened every weekend. I was never without work in Los Angeles—the Tiffany, the Haig, the Lighthouse, Zardi's. Two-week engagements in each. And the musicians who were around! Teddy Edwards, Sonny Criss, Lawrence Marable, Leroy Vinnegar, Joe Gordon, Zoot Sims, Herb Geller, Joe Maini, Frank Butler, Jimmy Rowles, Art Tatum, Frank Morgan, Ornette Coleman. I was on Ornette's first recording, 'Something Else!' It was done for Contemporary Records early

in 1958. We rehearsed five months, and every time we played
Ornette changed his music. When we got to the studio—Don
Cherry was on trumpet, Don Payne on bass, and Billy Higgins
on drums—Ornette changed everything again, but by this time
we were used to it. The session had that good pressure where the
music was pulled out of your bones. I'm still happy with that
date. The sad side of those years was that so few musicians
stayed straight. I had a junkie trio once, and the trouble just to
get them started every night! Anyway, I got married in Los
Angeles, and we had two children. Then we moved to New
York. It was 1960. Very few musicians who come to New York
from out of town stay. It's too difficult. They'll stay awhile and
go home, come back and go home again, and maybe, if they're
good enough and tough enough, come back for good. But I was
lucky. I found work right away, and I gigged around until
1963, when I went into the Playboy Club. Kai Winding was
the musical director, then Sam Donahue, then me. I worked
there eight years, in every sort of musical situation, and I also
went to the Manhattan School of Music, where I studied with
the great Heida Hermanns. I played so much I developed a
muscle spasm in my right forearm. The forearm became as
hard as a tabletop, and I couldn't play. I treated it in a whirl-
pool, and it finally eased. I learned about muscles and playing.
I can tell now when it's starting up again. I taught privately
after I left the Playboy Club, and in 1974 I joined the Thad
Jones–Mel Lewis band. I would rather have worked in that
band than in any other band in the world. Thad had written
many of the arrangements around his brother Hank, but Hank
was generally too busy to show up on Mondays when the band
played, so I would take all those solo spots. In 1976, I got the
chance to tour Scandinavia as a soloist, but the tour collapsed,
and I was stranded in Stockholm. Red Mitchell was living there,
and he saved me. It took me seven months to get back to New
York. Charlie Mingus hired me. He had Dannie Richmond on
drums and Jack Walrath on trumpet. I knew about Mingus's
reputation for physical violence, but I thought he was an angel.

We had long talks. He was very pleased that I liked the solo pi-ano album he made. He had been stepped on and scarred most of his life. He wanted to be warm, but instead he'd be violent. I think I generally played beautifully with Mingus, because it was so dangerous. I had heard that he had slammed the key-board cover on Jaki Byard's fingers. When it came time for my solo, Mingus would say, in that guttural mutter, 'Blow, Norris!' And I *would*. Then Rolf Ericson told me about the S.F.B. job in Berlin."

It was time for Norris's second set. He pushed his coffee cup aside and rubbed his fingers together. "Jazz improvisation is do-it-yourself music," he said. "You create it with your two hands. It's the free American spirit. In classical music, it's do-as-you're-told. And that's generally the European way. New York, in particular, wakes up the musical vibrations in the jazz animal. New York has more energy than any other city I've ever been in. You feel it in the street. You feel it at night. You'd feel it if half the buildings were torn down. I remember that about New York when I'm not here, and it helps sustain me. I would like to establish the jazz program at the Hochschule firmly, then move on to another city, set up a similar nucleus of playing musicians, and move on again. Maybe every four or five years, like a Johnny Appleseed. Jazz should be far more widely accepted in the world than it is. Do you know how many Europeans learn English just so they can take up jazz?"

[1987]

GOODBYE
OOMPAH

~~

In the early eighteen-forties, Hector Berlioz made an exploratory musical tour of Germany, and in one of the exhaustive letters he sent back to France he said, "The bass tuba . . . has completely dislodged the ophicleide in Prussia. . . . [It] is a large brass instrument . . . fitted with a mechanism of five rotary valves which gives it an enormous range in the lower register. The lowest notes of all are a little blurred, it is true; but when doubled an octave higher by another bass tuba, they take on amazing richness and resonance; and in the middle and upper registers the tone is impressively noble, not at all flat like the ophicleide's but full and vibrant and well matched with the timbre of trombones and trumpets, to which it serves as a true bass, blending perfectly with them." For all of Berlioz's perspicacity, about the only thing that happened to the tuba during the next hundred years was its absorption into the symphony orchestra and the marching band. Then, twenty years ago, Ralph Vaughan Williams wrote his pioneering Concerto for Bass Tuba and Orchestra, which was followed by Paul Hindemith's Sonata for Tuba and Piano. Before that, tubists had eased their urge to solo by playing transcriptions of Bach and Beethoven and by transposing solo pieces that had been written for other instruments. Vaughan Williams and Hindemith broke a vicious circle: no one had written pieces for solo tuba because there were none to point the way, none to suggest the marvellous tonal and lyrical possibilities of the instrument, and there were none to point the way because—and so forth. In the fifties and sixties, post-Vaughan Williams–Hindemith, a further trickle of tuba compositions appeared, many of them written by Alec Wilder, and in the seventies this freshet suddenly became a river. There are now almost four hundred solo compositions for tuba—for tuba and piano, for tuba and string quartet, for tuba and nine French horns, for tuba and horn and piano, for tuba and woodwind quintet, for tuba and four horns and percussion, for tuba and small orchestra—as well as tuba octets, quartets, trios, duos, and solos.

The ongoing elevation of the tuba from the laughingstock of musical instruments to one of its kings is mainly the doing of Harvey Phillips, a tubist and a professor of music at Indiana University, who has spent over half his life in the service of his instrument, which he plays better than anyone else in the world. (Tubists are multiplying in direct ratio to their repertory; there are now nearly a thousand members of TUBA—the Tubists Universal Brotherhood Association, an organization Phillips helped get on its feet.) Many of his colleagues rank him the finest living brass player and, by extension, one of the certified virtuosos of his time. But Phillips is not interested in pecking orders, real or imagined. His passions are the betterment of the tuba, the betterment of those who play it, and the betterment of American music. "It's a time of marvels in wind playing," James T. Maher, the omnifarious writer and a close observer of Phillips, has said. "There have been and are an extraordinary number of good players, like Julius Baker on flute and Reginald Kell on clarinet and Bernard Garfield on bassoon and Leon Goossens on oboe. And horn players like the late Dennis Brain and the late John Barrows. Harvey Phillips certainly belongs in that company. He also belongs to the American school of wind playing. The English school—Brain, Kell, and the like—has its elegance, its sense of *ensemble;* the American school has more sinew, even a little roughness. The players in the American school take incredible chances, despite the terrific problems wind instruments inherently have. Harvey has uncanny phrasing— which is not the right word. It makes him sound too technical. What he does is point up the poetry in what he plays. And he is apt to play anything, since there is really no longer a sharp division between jazz wind players and classical wind players and the like. Wind players now move in a great gray area, in which the best are apt to play a different kind of music every day of the week. It doesn't matter if it's a TV commercial or a recital or a jazz date or movie music, but it does matter how well they execute. Harvey wants to be the best tubist there is, and he wants to shape a new world of sensibility in all music. He's willing to tackle every side of the problem. He keeps a pleasant demeanor, but he's tough and he's obsessive. Along with all the order he professes to exhibit in his comings and goings, he likes a bit of daily chaos. Then he has something on which to demonstrate his ability to impose order."

Phillips is over six feet and of considerable girth. His fingers are sausages and his feet gunboats. He has a long, full face and wavy black hair, and he wears glasses. His cherubic lips bear the pinkish aureole that is the unmistakable badge of the professional brass player. He has an old-fashioned, almost goody-goody look. But his deep-set eyes are savvy and laughing, and his generally placid expression conceals a mischievous intelligence. Phillips is celebrated for his outsize ways, for his studied chaos, but his excesses—harmless except when the exhaustion they lead to topples him and he goes down like a sequoia—are positive and even altruistic. Here are half a dozen instances of his Paul Bunyan ways:

When he was on the road in Kansas, 1960, with the New York Brass Quintet, he suggested that the group spend a night with one of his sisters, who lived on a farm handy to their next concert. He drove the unwitting musicians twenty miles out of the way to an abandoned farm he knew of. There he went through an extended routine of calling his sister through the gaping front door of the farmhouse and then, scratching his head, hallooing into the swaying barn, all the while furtively studying the frozen expressions on his colleagues' city-slicker faces.

In 1962, he carted enough hickory wood from the Midwest to the Aspen Music Festival to smoke twenty-eight sides of pork, twenty hams, and twelve trout. He also transplanted enough mint to furnish several hundred mint juleps. And when the Festival officials refused to specially honor Gunther Schuller, who was coming to the Festival and is one of his heroes, he hired an Aspen restaurant and threw a party himself.

Phillips always needs money for tuba-uplift events. He has recently financed four—the First International Tuba Symposium-Workshop, held in the spring of 1973 at Indiana University and attended by four hundred interested composers, professional tubists, and students, and three Octubafests, the first of which was held at Indiana in the fall of 1973 and was attended by many of his students and former students. Whenever Phillips says "Octubafest," a "good pun!" light goes on in his eyes. And it goes on when he talks of his most recent tuba-uplift idea— a toothpaste called Tuba.

During the past twenty-five years, Phillips has played with or been a member of the New York Philharmonic, the Metropolitan Opera Orchestra, the New York City Ballet Orchestra, the Ringling Brothers and Barnum & Bailey Circus Band, the Sauter-Finegan orchestra, the NBC Opera orchestra, the United States Army Field Band, the "Bell Telephone Hour" orchestra, the New York Brass Quintet, the Symphony of the Air, the Goldman Band, the "Voice of Firestone" orchestra, and Orchestra U.S.A. The result is an inveterate traveler who cannot stand being late or missing engagements. He once started out from New York for a one-night stand in Springfield, Massachusetts, on a train to Scarsdale, where an oboist he had just met was to pick him up and drive him the rest of the way. But he fell asleep on the train and woke up at the end of the run, in White Plains. He couldn't remember the oboist's name or phone number, so he hailed a White Plains cab and took off for Springfield. The tab was seventy-five dollars, but he walked onstage just ahead of the conductor.

While he was assistant to the president of the New England Conservatory of Music, in Boston, he kept his chair in the New York City Ballet Orchestra. During the season, he'd finish a full day's work in Boston and take the six-thirty flight to New York, arriving at eight-fifteen at Lincoln Center; then he'd catch the last flight back. Once in a while, he'd fly to New York in the morning for a recording session, fly back for an afternoon meeting at the Conservatory, take an evening shuttle for his New York Ballet performance, and be home in bed in his Boston suburb by one-thirty. During this period, his practicing often fell into arrears. He recalls getting back to Boston early one morning and finding his wife, Carol, and their three children (Jesse, Harvey, and Thomas) asleep spoon-fashion in bed together. Phillips is as passionate about his family as he is about the tuba. Knowing that he had to practice but wishing to be with them, he turned on a light, sat down with his tuba, and played until dawn. It was a perfect session: nobody woke up, and he proved to himself again that when it is properly played the tuba is the softest instrument in the world.

Phillips refuses to be separated from his family for any length of time. He and Carol went everywhere together during the childless years of their marriage, and after he was injured in an automobile collision in New York she carried his tuba to every gig for six months. Nowadays, when an engagement keeps him away for more than five days Carol and the children join him, no matter the time of year. On the way home, Carol drives and he sits in the back and practices.

In 1974, Phillips decided that New York was ready for the tuba, and he organized two extraordinary events. The first was a concert of Christmas carols in Rockefeller Plaza, in front of the big tree, by 250 tubists who had come, at Phillips's invitation, from all over the country at their own expense. A couple of dozen carols had been freshly scored by Alec Wilder in four- and six-part harmony, and the massed sounds were unique and stirring and noble—so much so that the concert, by 400 tubists, will be repeated this year on December 21st. (The music at the 1974 rehearsal, held in a long, low, steaming corridor on the second floor of the RCA Building, was, by virtue of being compressed and yet augmented by the milieu, even more spectacular. Phillips, in his shirtsleeves, closed the rehearsal by shouting to his tubists, *"Now* let them talk about their oompahs!"*) His second New York event took place early in January of this year. He rented Carnegie Recital Hall for four evenings and an afternoon, and gave five marathon tuba recitals, during which he played thirty-nine pieces. He was abetted by a small jazz group, the New England Conservatory Chamber Orchestra (shipped south at his expense), a string quartet, a woodwind quintet, several pianists, a host of horn players, two percussionists, and three tubists. There were jazz numbers arranged by Dick Cary and Johnny Carisi; lyrical serenades and sonatas by Alec Wilder; the Hindemith and Vaughan Williams pieces; David Baker's jarring, complex exercise for tuba and string quartet; Bernhard Heiden's brand-new piece for tuba and nine horns; a short, pastel composition by Eddie Sauter; Richard Peaslee's spooky, melodramatic "The Devil's Herald," its ink barely dry, for tuba, four horns, and percussion; and Gunther Schuller's Capriccio for Tuba and Small Orchestra. During the eleven days the recitals involved, Phillips rehearsed sixty-six hours, and on two days he did his old New York-Boston-New York shuttle act. Not only did his lip survive seventy-six hours of playing, but immediately after the final concert he went to the Roosevelt Hotel, where he performed the Baker tuba-and-string-quartet piece again for a conference of brass men. The next day, he drove Carol and the children through a blizzard to Boston to record Schuller's Capriccio. And the day after, he recorded the Vaughan Williams Concerto.

Phillips started rehearsing in New York a month or so before
the recitals. The rehearsals were held in half a dozen of the
plethora of studios scattered about the city. He went to two or
three or four a day, and most lasted three hours. To relax, he
talked a good deal during the cab rides between studios. He
keeps his eyes closed when he talks at length, as if he were
watching his words on a screen inside his head, and he speaks
in a deliberate, quietly swinging way.

"The origins of the tuba are not at all clear. But I do know
that it followed the ophicleide, which followed the serpent. I
also know it became possible through the invention of valves.
The serpent was made of wood and leather, and it had finger
holes. It looked like an S with a big curlicue at either end, and
I think it appeared around 1600. The ophicleide was invented
in 1817 by one Jean Hilaire Asté, and it was a tall, thin tuba, a
kind of spinster tuba. Not long after Berlioz made his German
discovery, the ingenious Adolphe Sax was at work in Paris
making tubas. Eventually they came in many shapes: some
bells pointed up, some pointed backward, some were like tear-
drops. One model straddled both shoulders. But eventually Sax
determined pretty much what we now know as their shape—
valves and all. The tuba inherited the ophicleide orchestra parts,
and since the tuba has about five times the resonance of an ophicleide, which had a wispy, anemic sound, you sometimes hear
tubists in an orchestra overblowing. The worst thing a tuba
player can do is dominate an ensemble, and the best thing he
can do is blend and balance and affirm.

"The tuba is at the tonal bottom of the brass ladder. At the
top is the trumpet, then comes the French horn, which is not
French and should simply be called a horn. The trombone is
next, and then the tuba. Each rung has its subdivisions. There
are piccolo trumpets, F trumpets, cornets, B-flat trumpets, C
trumpets, and bass trumpets. There are F tubas, E-flat tubas,
CC tubas, and double-B-flat tubas. The breathing for singing is
parallel to the breathing for brass instruments. One must have
breath support, and breath support is being able to contain a

full volume of air in your lungs without coughing or exhaling. Breath control—what you do with the air when you release it—is the key to artistic execution. But there can be no breath control without breath support. In one way, the tuba is the most comfortable of the brass instruments, because it has the largest mouthpiece. In another way, it is the most difficult, because one has to move so much air. It's extremely hard to play a C above middle C, and it's equally difficult at the low end of the instrument. You have to constantly clarify the tones down there. You can't just hope the right note will come out. A lot of tubists have no sense of control; they let their lips flop around inside the mouthpiece. The tuba has, after all, two main parts—one is flesh and the other metal. All the metal part can do is accommodate the flesh. If you play a beautiful phrase, the tuba will amplify it. If you play a bad one, the tuba will amplify it. One must learn to *practice*. The definition of practicing is when you go into a room by yourself with your instrument and make a lot of terrible sounds, because you're working out things as yet unrefined. You are not performing or even rehearsing. You are practicing."

•

"There are three reasons why the tuba still suffers a ridiculous image. One is the inept playing of many tubists. Another is the dreadful comic—in quotes—sounds tuba players are asked to make in the line of duty, and that includes the classical and jazz worlds. And still another is that the tuba solo repertory is so new. The horn had its own concerto in Mozart's time, but the tuba had to wait until Ralph Vaughan Williams produced his Concerto, in 1954. So when I first came to New York, in 1950, the only tuba solo with orchestra I knew was George Kleinsinger's 'Tubby the Tuba,' which was written in 1941. People have unthinkingly laughed at it, but there are many lovely things in that piece. We also had such treats as 'When Yuba Plays the Rhumba on the Tuba' and 'Asleep in the Deep' and 'Down in the Deep Cellar.' Since the late fifties, the tuba repertory has grown faster than any other instrument's. I want the tuba player to have an in-depth legacy to lean on. I want him to know he has roots. Any time I meet a composer I admire, I don't let up on him about writing a piece for the instrument until I get a positive answer—which may take as long as twelve years. The air that lets performers exist is created by composers, and you have to have plenty to survive. Hell, if Prokofieff and Stravinsky and Ravel and Schoenberg and Webern and Bartók and Berg and Tchaikovsky and Berlioz had each written a concerto for tuba, it would be a recognized solo instrument now and every orchestra would have a tuba section instead of one tuba, and we wouldn't have well over a hundred tubists applying for the tuba chair in the Baltimore Symphony, which happened not long ago."

"I went to Indiana in the fall of 1971. I replaced my friend and teacher William Bell, who had retired. I came over from the New England Conservatory, where I'd been helping Gunther Schuller. When he was made head of the Conservatory, in 1967, he asked me to be his assistant. He had never run a music school, or any school, and he needed some armor. The place was in dreadful shape, spiritually and financially, and I at least had had some administrative experience along the way in bookkeeping, personnel, and managing. I learned something about teaching at the Conservatory, and I'm still learning. I don't just teach the tuba to my students; I teach them life, if you will. I tell each student he only has one musician to compete with the rest of his days—himself. And I try to make him understand the ethical responsibilities of being a professional musician. Musicians have been laughed at and considered loony long enough. If a student of mine plays badly at our weekly meeting, I want to know why. Is he sick? Is one of his family sick? Is it drugs, love—what? I get to the problem while it's festering. So we indulge one another, and eventually we have a feeling of partnership. Which is what made the first Octubafest possible. I wanted my freshmen and my recent graduates to get acquainted musically and socially. And I wanted everyone to perform a solo.

We had five recitals—one each night for five nights. Forty-six major works for the tuba were played. On Sunday, when the Octuba was over, we had the Fest—a party that went on out at my farm, which has eighty acres and a lot of animals, from twelve noon until the next morning. This year, we had fifty-three Octubafests on as many campuses. I want, eventually, to expand and coördinate these so that a composer can have a première in a hundred or more places at once. Why should a première be heard only by the occupants of a single hall?"

"I graduated from high school in Marionville, Missouri, in 1947, and I got a summer job playing tuba with the King Brothers Circus. This came about through Homer Lee, who taught music at my school and had got me started on the sousaphone. He looked like Ichabod Crane and was a retired circus bandleader. When the word reached our Methodist preacher that I was joining a circus, he came out to the house and Mother received him in the parlor. 'That boy will be destroyed if he works in a circus,' he said to my mother. 'Circuses are full of the wicked and degenerate. He will be lost.' Tears came to my mother's eyes, and she said, 'You don't have much faith in Harvey, do you, Reverend? Well, I do,' and she showed him the door. Homer Lee found me a York BB-flat tuba, and Mother made me a modesty cover for it out of a blanket. The taxi man in town was going to visit a relative in Syracuse, and he said he'd drop me off in Binghamton. From there, I got a bus to Waterbury, Connecticut, where the circus was. I was met at the station by a trumpet player with one leg and a drummer who was afflicted in such a way that he couldn't close his mouth. The leader of the band, A. Lee Hinckley, kept a wad of tobacco in each cheek when he played. I'll admit the sight of those three made the Reverend's words pass through my mind. Also, I'd never been farther from home than a Boy Scout camp, so the food, which I couldn't eat, and the three-inch mattresses and no sheets took me by surprise. But eventually I got on top of things and began enjoying myself in all ways. They paid me five dollars extra a week to drive a truck and carry the blues, which is what the planks used for bleacher seats were called. There were no maps to get from location to location; you just followed arrows marked on phone poles and trees. One time, the brakes on my truck failed. I rocketed down a long hill, and what saved me was jamming the gears into compound low when it ran out of steam halfway up the next hill. After nine weeks, I left to go to the University of Missouri, where I had a scholarship.

"I was miserable there. I slept in a rickety bunk in a basement with a local boy, and I carried my room and board by raking leaves and stoking the furnace and cleaning the house. I had eighteen hours of subjects and worked nights at the School of Music. Then a telegram came from Merle Evans, the leader of the band with Ringling Brothers and Barnum & Bailey Circus. He offered me a job on tuba at eighty-seven fifty a week, and I was to go to Sarasota right away if I was interested. Well, I called Homer Lee, and he said immediately, 'Harvey, get down there with Merle.' They knew each other, and, of course, to Homer, Ringling Brothers was it. So I closed up at the university and went.

"It was some different from the King Brothers. Ringling had a thousand or so on the payroll. The band traveled in its own railroad car, with a porter and a kitchen and clean sheets every week. Merle had his own stateroom. Johnny Evans, who was no relation to Merle, was the tuba player, and sitting beside him every day was a free lesson. I think the greatest compliment I ever received was after I'd been with the band six months and one of the trumpet players said, 'Harvey, I couldn't tell whether it was you or Johnny playing tonight.' The drummer was Red Floyd. He had a lined, pruny face, and looked like Old Man Time. I think he had played in New Orleans. He had a crippled left arm, but he was an extraordinary musician. He played all the mallet instruments, and he did a beautiful snare-drum roll with one hand by holding two sticks parallel in that hand like extra fingers and seesawing them so fast they became a blur. When we played New York, Sidney Catlett would spend all afternoon at the Garden watching Red, and then ask him to autograph a pair of his sticks. One of the trumpet players was Al Hiltensmith. He was red-faced and had a waxed mustache, and he'd been with John Philip Sousa. He chewed ginger root all day, and lived for the trip his first glass of beer gave him when it hit his ginger mouth. One of the band's jobs was to give the alarms. We played 'Stars and Stripes Forever' when a disaster impended, like the Midwestern storms that lifted the great center poles in the big top four feet off the ground. And we played the 'Twelfth Street Rag' when a high-wire act fell, which I saw happen one night. The tune was a signal for the clowns to come out and distract the audience. My first year, we hit every state in the Union. I stayed at the old Forrest Hotel, on West Forty-ninth Street, in New York, and between shows I didn't know what else to do, so I'd play duets with the sounds in the pipes in my room. During my second visit to New York, I met Bill Bell, who was the tubist with the Philharmonic. Johnny Evans didn't come on the trip, and Bill Bell replaced him at the Garden. I got to know him, and I fell in love with the man. He was a marvelous human being, who had a grace and distinction I've never run across in anyone else.

"I stayed with Ringling Brothers until 1950, and I'd be there still—I consider it my career—if I hadn't got a wire from Bill Bell when we were playing in Los Angeles. It said I had a full scholarship at Juilliard. This was the second time someone had grabbed my shoulders and turned me around and given me a push in the direction I was supposed to go in. I went to New York, and I was in Juilliard off and on for four years. I lived for a while in Bill Bell's studio, on 121st Street, in a back room with a man named Eric Hauser. He was a fine horn player, or had been. But he'd become alcoholic, and Bill took care of him. He'd sit on his bed and criticize everything I played. I learned that way, and I learned from playing duets with Bill Bell and by going to rehearsals and record dates with him. In 1953, I joined the Sauter-Finegan band for about six months. It knocked me out with its fantastic arrangements and crazy instrumentation. Then I started with the New York City Opera and the New York City Ballet, and, except for a fine two-year stint in the U.S. Army Field Band, I stayed on the New York scene, working twenty-four hours a day, until I joined Gunther Schuller in Boston and had to commute to keep my hand in."

●

"My first method book—and without question the best—was a hymnal. I'd play out of that for hours. Even now, I have my students use a hymnal, so they can learn the effects of lyrics on music."

●

"The tuba is not accepted in jazz the way I'd like it to be, so it will be a great day when the first Clark Terry of the instrument comes along. They used the tuba in the early days before the string bass was adopted, and it reappeared in the Claude Thornhill band in the late forties, when Gil Evans was the arranger. Miles Davis had a tuba in his Nonet recordings in 1949 and 1950. I think he used Bill Barber. The finest jazz tubist is Rich Matteson, who has played with the Dukes of Dixieland and is on the faculty at North Texas State. I wish I had more opportunity to improvise. When I was with the Ballet in New York and doing the Conservatory gig, I'd sit in at Jimmy Ryan's sometimes before I took the plane back to Boston. But there doesn't seem to be time for things like that now, and improvisation comes a lot easier if you do it steadily. Jazz players grow and change like stones in a stream—from rubbing constantly against each other."

●

"I was born the tenth child of ten children on December 2, 1929, in Aurora, Missouri. I had six sisters and three brothers. My oldest brother was born in 1905 and didn't get married until 1949, and he was a second father to me. Another brother, Jesse, which was my father's name, died the year before I was born, and once in a while my parents would call me Jesse by mistake. My father came from a family of farmers. He was born in 1882, in Shelbyville, Tennessee, and his family moved to Missouri in 1887. He had four brothers and two sisters. Like many people during the Depression, my father did anything—plumbing, carpentry, electrical work, farming, barn-dance fiddling. He had a great sense of humor and a terrible temper. A couple of cows that belonged to a neighbor strayed into our yard once, and my father put them in the barn lot for safekeeping. The neighbor came by and saw the cows in the lot and accused my father of stealing them. My father went purple, and the neighbor jumped in his car and bowled out of the yard, but not before my father had thrown a hammer clean through his rear window. He used to tell us stories every night when we went to bed, and sometimes he was so tired he'd fall asleep in mid-sentence. On Saturdays, after we'd been to town, where they'd try to help people out of work by throwing free chickens from the upper windows of the courthouse, which used to bother me, he'd play the fiddle for us and we'd pop corn and eat apples from the cellar.

"My mother was—is—very tiny, very feminine, and very hardy. She was born in Marionville, Missouri, in 1888. Her father was a blacksmith. When she was four or five, he locked up his shop one day and nobody ever saw him again. My mother was married when she was seventeen, on New Year's Day, 1905. She handled the feeding and dressing of ten children without applause. She did her laundry with a scrub board, and she made her own soap. She didn't enjoy the benefits of plumbing and electricity until she was almost sixty. She baked bread every day, and in the spring she'd pick wild greens—lamb's-tongue and dandelion and poke and dock—and cook and can them. We all picked blackberries and hazelnuts and walnuts and gooseberries, which had to be stemmed on both ends. We'd have contests to see who could de-stem the most. I've never seen my mother raise her voice in anger. I've seen her show disappointment in her eyes and face, which is far more devastating than any words of anger. When we were little, she'd sit at table and wait until everyone had finished before she took anything—if, indeed, there was anything. Like many Southern country people, her favorite word is 'well,' but stretched out to several syllables. It's generally said in response to any kind of news. When I called her from New York to tell her that Carol and I were going to get married, she let loose a terrific 'Well,' paused, and said, 'There've been two deaths here.'

"All four of my father's brothers were farmers, and their land, together with my father's, was near their parents.' They had something like twelve hundred acres in all. But when the Depression came, my father had to give up his land. The primary reason was that although the farms were owned by his flesh and blood, each brother bought his own equipment instead of chipping in to buy common tractors and harvesters and the like. That pig-headedness wiped them out. After that, my father harvested wheat in Kansas and worked for the W.P.A., which, God knows, kept our part of the country going by allowing people their pride. From the time I was born until I was ten, we lived in nine different houses, which we called by their owners' names. The first was the Demond place, and the only thing I recall was nearly being flattened by a mad sow when I dropped my straw hat into her pen and went in after it. I started school at the Burney place, and I also plugged every last one of my father's acre of watermelons to see if they were ripe, and killed them all, which got my reputation for two whippings a day going. I was six when we moved to the Bacon place, and in time I had fourteen rabbit traps that I ran every morning, so we could have fried rabbit for breakfast and I could collect my eight cents a skin. I also went to a one-room schoolhouse and won all the ciphering matches, some of them against eighth-graders from other schools. At the Smith place, we raised beef and sheep, and I drove Aunt Sally from down the road to church in her horse and buggy. We finally settled in a three-room house near Marionville. We bought it for $800—a hundred down and five dollars a month. This was the house I finished growing up in, and it was the house my father made something livable out of. He picked it up off the ground four feet and put a foundation under it. He put in a furnace and plumbing. He wired the house. He added a wing with three rooms, and he built a shed and a garage. And he did it all with used wood—which added to the work, because you had to find it first. And he planted a lot of trees, which are huge now.

"I did what I could to help out financially. I picked strawberries and apples and peaches for a penny a box. I took care of a neighbor's mule for fifty cents a month, and I worked in a grocery store on Saturdays. I worked with the movie projectionist Saturday nights, and ran the projector myself when I was eleven. I worked at the funeral home, where I mowed the lawn and unpacked caskets and went with the town ambulance when a deceased had to be picked up. I was given a lot of responsibility early."

Phillips's five recitals at Carnegie Hall could be considered a bust. They were, with the exception of the last one, poorly attended (there was no Phillips money for publicity), and they were given just two short notices in the *Times*, neither of which said anything about Phillips's extraordinary playing. On top of that, *Newsweek* ran a "funny" tuba piece and interview with Phillips in conjunction with the series, and that almost unhinged him. Nonetheless, there was a triumphant air about the concerts. Most tubas engulf their players, but Phillips holds his so that it looks no bigger than a flügelhorn or a French horn. He rests it easily on his right thigh, its bell up, and he secures it with his left hand, which he flops casually over the top tubing. He plays effortlessly, and the only indication that he is maintaining his breath support is the sharp, windy intakes of air at the end of his capacious phrases. He is a magisterial yet invariably accessible player. At slow tempos, his timbre is soft and smoky and somewhat like Tommy Dorsey's trombone, which is held in high esteem by brass men. At greater speeds, his playing hardens in a muscular, singing way, but he is never brittle. His tone is light and direct, whether he is hitting a C above middle C or whether he is rummaging in the huge lower register—an area where the finest tubist can grope, his candle blown out by his own bearish notes. Phillips's sound is unique. His tuba suggests a graceful trombone, or a horn minus its nasal quality, or a baritone saxophone of the most velvet persuasion. His technique is astonishing. His arpeggios are glassy and clean, the alarming intervals he sometimes has to play are deft and exact, and his staccato passages are cream. Most of the composers who write for him purposely include passages of such complexity that it is possible no other tubist could maneuver them.

The final recital was suitably climactic, and it came to its peak in Alec Wilder's 1959 Sonata for Tuba and Piano. The first and third movements are slow and unabashedly lyrical, and Phillips made poems of them. His tone was soft and daringly burred, and his vibrato barely moved. He slid from phrase to phrase with the warmth and spontaneity of improvisation. He made Wilder's melodies—so close to his beautiful popular ones—three-dimensional. Afterward, Wilder expressed his pleasure in Phillips's rendition indirectly by saying that although Phillips had told him the series had been a financial disaster, he felt the tuba had been furthered in New York. "Anyway, I'm not at all worried about him," Wilder went on. "I was in his hotel room before the concert, and I watched him wrap a package of sheet music to mail back to Indiana. You wouldn't believe the things he did with mere paper and twine, the tightness and neatness and finality of his wrapping, the *strongbox* look of the package when he was finished. The only way to open it when it gets there will be to blow it up."

[1975]

FORTIETH

~~

The brilliant explosion known as Benny Goodman went off in 1935, and it hasn't gone out yet. Born to parents of Russian-Jewish extraction in Chicago in 1909, the eighth of eleven children, Goodman became a proficient clarinettist in his early teens. When he was sixteen, he was hired by Ben Pollack, who brought him to New York in 1928. He quit Pollack a year later, and for the next four years he was a busy New York radio, pit-band, and recording musician, who appeared with André Kostelanetz, Bessie Smith, Paul Whiteman, Enric Madriguera, Sam Lanin, Red Nichols, Ruth Etting, Hoagy Carmichael, Ted Lewis, and Bix Beiderbecke. He put together his first band in 1932 (for Russ Columbo, at the Woodmansten Inn, on the Pelham Parkway), and another in 1934, which became a weekly fixture on the three-hour Saturday-night "Let's Dance" radio show. ("If anyone were to ask what was the biggest thing that has ever happened to me," Goodman said recently, "landing a place on that show was it.") In the middle of 1935, Goodman and the band set out on a cross-country tour, and for a long time it was disastrous. The band bombed in Michigan and then in Denver, where it competed with and lost to Kay Kyser (who later traveled as Kay Kyser and His Kollege of Musical Knowledge). Jess Stacy had just joined the band, and he describes Goodman's reaction: "Goodman began saying he was going to quit this nonsense and go back into radio in New York. I said, 'Benny, get over the mountains first and see what happens.' I didn't tell him 'I told you so,' but when we got to Sweet's Ballroom in Oakland they were standing in lines a block long, and when we got down to the Palomar Ballroom in Los Angeles everybody went crazy. And on our way back it was that way in Chicago, at the Congress Hotel, and then in New York, at the Pennsylvania Hotel and the Paramount Theatre." Goodman was on radio almost nightly after his success on the Coast, and the near-riot that attended the band's Paramount Theatre appearance was the first instance in this country of the frightening power of electronics. He kept a band together for ten years, finally disbanding after graduating from his Swing Academy the likes of Bunny Berigan, Bud Freeman, Harry James, Ziggy Elman, Gene Krupa, Jess Stacy, Charlie Christian, Teddy Wilson, Lionel Hampton, Mel Powell, Billy Butterfield, Lou McGarity, Stan Getz, Zoot Sims, and Jimmy Rowles. Since then, a man of means, he has worked as he has seen fit, with jazz and classical groups of all sizes and in every imaginable place. He is not a sentimental man, but on January 17 he will celebrate the fortieth anniversary of his famous 1938 Carnegie Hall concert with another Carnegie Hall concert. There has been no need to advertise, for the old Goodman power prevails. The day tickets went on sale, the concert sold out.

Most eccentrics are private people, and Goodman is no exception. As a result, he has long been surrounded by legends, some true and some not. One is the legend of the Jack Benny skinflint who delights in paying his musicians low wages and then cadges their cigarettes. Zoot Sims, who first played with Goodman in 1943, once brought an apple with him to a recording session and put it on his music stand. When Sims took his first solo, Goodman picked up the apple and started eating it. After Sims's first chorus, Goodman had him take another and then another. Sims was only seventeen and never said a word, but it is the longest solo Goodman has ever given him. Another legendary Goodman is a Simon Legree at rehearsals and on the stand. Goodman is a perfectionist about his own playing, and he expects no less than perfection of his musicians. When he is displeased by a sideman, he fixes him with a stony look that has come to be known as "the ray." Still another legendary Goodman is the befuddled, inarticulate maestro. Instances abound of elaborate anecdotes left hanging, of sentences delivered in low gargles. When he was questioned not long ago about having fired the great drummer Sidney Catlett in 1941, he replied, "It's always been one of my enigmas—drummers." But there has never been any confusion about Goodman the musician. He was one of the first jazz virtuosos, and the first jazz musician to cross the barrier between jazz and classical music and become an adept and respected classical soloist. (It is not a move he is settled about yet; he feels his jazz playing may have suffered because of his adventurousness, and he knows he is not the best of all classical clarinettists.) Though it was once a pervasive jazz instrument, the clarinet has had little influence outside its own intense and difficult discipline. So it is not clear how much effect Goodman's playing has had on jazz improvisers. He helped iron out the rhythmic chunkiness that had afflicted jazz phrasing since the twenties. He made jazz musicians more conscious of tone, which had been wholly intuitive. He was the first serious improviser to champion melodic playing. Entire solos followed the melody closely or were ingenious and subtle paraphrases. And when he broke loose, his improvisations, no matter what their speed, were a flow of new melodies that continually intimated their originals: the flicker's sharp undulations constantly suggesting pure arcs. Goodman was also a *hot* player, of which there have been surprisingly few. He used a "dirty" tone and intense on-the-beat and staccato phrasing, and he frequently sank into the chalumeau register, which endows the clarinet with great intimacy and lyricism. He favored fast tempos—the high winds of jazz playing, which invariably give the effect, even when the musicians are being blown galley-west, that everyone is swinging like crazy. But, above all, there was a rare ease about his playing. Bix Beiderbecke and Frankie Trumbauer had it, and both Goodman and Lester Young learned from them.

By 1938, Goodman was almost as famous as Franklin Roosevelt, and when it was announced that he was going to give the first jazz concert ever held in Carnegie Hall, the tickets went so fast he had difficulty getting his family in. The concert consisted of twelve numbers by the big band (chief soloists: Goodman, Harry James, Jess Stacy, Vernon Brown, Gene Krupa), two numbers by the trio (Goodman, Teddy Wilson, Krupa), five numbers by the quartet (the trio plus Lionel Hampton), re-creations of the Original Dixieland Jazz Band, Ted Lewis, and Louis Armstrong, and three numbers by a group of ringers (Bobby Hackett, Count Basie, Freddie Green, Walter Page, Buck Clayton, Lester Young, Cottie Williams, Johnny Hodges, Harry Carney). Irving Kolodin had suggested that the evening include a brief history of the previous twenty years in jazz, and John Hammond had suggested that some Basie and Ellington sidemen might add texture and color to the proceedings. Hackett played a Beiderbecke solo, and the Ellington musicians did "Blue Reverie." The Ellingtons and Basies, together with Goodman, Krupa, James, and Brown, played a long "Honeysuckle Rose" that was designed as a jam session. The recording of the concert brought out twelve years later by Columbia—it is one of the biggest-selling jazz albums of all time—reveals a curious evening. The band sounds aggressive, and Krupa, who was inadvertently overrecorded on the single microphone, is loud and uneven. The trio and quartet numbers are too long, and three are taken at dismaying killer-diller tempos. The jam session is stiff (Basie, Young, and Clayton were used to Jo Jones's bicycling drumming, not Krupa's piston attack), and so is "Sing, Sing, Sing," the band's pièce de résistance—except, of course, for what has come to be recognized as the single classic stroke of the concert: Jess Stacy's unscheduled two-minute solo, an airy, calm, circular improvisation that rises heedless into the noisy air. Bob Bach, a longtime jazz fan, was there. "I went with a friend and his mother," he said recently. "She was an elegant Park Avenue lady who attended the opera and the Philharmonic. Her presence created a certain amount of tension, because everybody knew how much the older people looked down on the concert. Of course, we had our own nervousness, too. The atmosphere was like having someone in your family bar mitzvahed or doing the valedictory at commencement. We were deeply immersed in the Goodman band. We hung out in the Madhattan Room at the Pennsylvania Hotel, and we knew Gene Krupa and Harry James. We'd been to Central Park to the softball games between the Goodman band and the Basie band. Harry James pitched for the Goodmans, and Gene Krupa and Harry Goodman and Babe Russin and Chris Griffin were the infield. Lester Young pitched for the Basies, and Herschel Evans played first and Earle Warren caught. Basie and Jimmy Rushing would come out in their fedoras, and so would the song pluggers and the flotsam and jetsam of the music business, but you never caught Benny there. We knew what we'd hear at Carnegie—the trumpet riffs in 'Sing, Sing, Sing' and the rideouts in the last chorus of the hot numbers and Gene Krupa wrapping everything up with a solo, but we didn't know what would get the biggest applause, what would blow the roof off. Truthfully, nothing really did. The jam session didn't catch fire, and Martha Tilton's singing was pretty dull. But there was a real jam-session moment—a moment of unexpected greatness—and that was when Jess Stacy suddenly took off near the end of 'Sing, Sing, Sing.' It made all the excitement we'd suffered for weeks worthwhile." Another longtime jazz enthusiast, William Shawn, remembers the concert somewhat differently: "Two things have stayed in my mind about the evening. The first was 'Don't Be That Way,' which the band started off with. The atmosphere was very highly charged in the hall. In fact, I can't remember any other musical event quite like it, unless it was a particular Toscanini concert or Oistrakh's first appearance here. So when 'Don't Be That Way' came rolling out, it was as if a hundred-piece band were blasting at you. It was even brassier and louder and more hard-driving than we had dreamed. The other thing that has stayed with me was Jess Stacy's solo. For some reason, I was standing in the back of the hall when it started, and a magical stillness came down immediately over the audience. I recall thinking, This is certainly the finest thing that has happened tonight. One has to remember that Goodman's band was simply a *dance* band. Wherever it played, people danced to it. Jazz concerts hadn't begun yet—or, rather, they began that night—and the sitting-and-listening places, like the clubs on Fifty-second Street, were just getting started. Hearing the Goodman band in Carnegie Hall wasn't just startling. It somehow gave jazz an aesthetic stature it hadn't had before."

The concert was held on a cold Sunday night. The *Times* sent its first-string music critic, Olin Downes, who wrote at considerable length for the Monday editions. It took him several paragraphs to warm up, after which he announced:

> Jazz has given way to "swing." "Swing" is that subtle creative something, the je ne sais quoi in popular music, which has superseded the older product and gained a greater power of popular appeal . . . than jazz ever exerted.

Having unwittingly put his thumb in jazz's terminological soup, Downes continued:

> It may therefore be imagined with what a thumping of the heart the present scribe got into his seat, in good time before the concert began, to hear the very first notes of Goodman's orchestra. It may be said immediately that he was enormously impressed, though not in the precise way he expected. When Mr. Goodman entered he received a real Toscanini send-off from the excited throng. It took some minutes to establish quiet. There was quivering excitement in the air, an almost electrical effect, and much laughter. The audience broke out before the music stopped, in crashing applause and special salvos as one or another of the

heroes of the orchestra rose in his place to give his special and ornate contribution to the occasion.

He then bore down on the music:

> This form of sound is a curious reduction, almost disintegration of music into its component elements. There is hardly an attempt at beauty of tone, and certainly none at construction of melody. A few fragments of well-known popular tunes suffice for a sort of rough material, subject to variation by the players. They do such feats of rhythm and dexterity as occur to them on the tune's basis. The tone of the brass instruments, almost continually overblown, is hard, shrill and noisy. The other instruments add what they can to swell the racket. . . . The playing last night, if noise, speed and syncopation, all old devices, are heat, was "hot" as it could be, but nothing came of it all, and in the long run it was decidedly monotonous.

Goodman, Wilson, Hampton, and Stacy played up to and over their heads at the concert, and so did the Ellingtons and Basies in their brief stints, but Downes, as Lester Young used to say, had no ears for what he was hearing. He boomed on:

> Nor is Mr. Goodman, when he plays his clarinet, anything like as original as other players of the same instrument and the same sort of thing that we have heard. Nor did we hear a single player, in the course of a solid hour of music, invent one original or interesting musical phrase, over the persistent basic rhythm. Not that they lacked technical accomplishment and amazing mastery of their medium. Musically, they let us down.

Near the close of his review, Downes looked into the future. " 'Swing' of this kind," he predicted, "will quickly be a thing of the past."

The *Herald Tribune* sent its second-string music critic, Francis D. Perkins, and he was a lot lighter on his feet than Downes. He even managed, after vivid pictures of Krupa and Goodman, some pioneering and quite accurate jazz criticism:

> The foremost contributor to [the visual aspect of the concert] was Mr. Gene Krupa, the group's super-expert

percussionist, whose gestures and facial expressions proved unusually engrossing for those near enough to note them in detail, and suggested that he has talents as an actor as well as an instrumentalist. In the usual symphony concert the conductor has the major share of the gesturing, but here Mr. Goodman was the calmest in mien, even when he did incredible work on his clarinet, and he presided over the sessions of the trio and the quartet with an air of paternal benevolence.

To an incompletely initiated listener, last night's swing had not altogether departed from certain fundamental features of the jazz set forth by Mr. Whiteman fourteen years ago [the Aeolian Hall concert at which Whiteman introduced George Gershwin's "Rhapsody in Blue" but played just two jazzlike numbers], except that it suggested a turning away from the trend toward politer music and more sophisticated forms represented in more recent programs of Messrs. Whiteman and Grofé. The fundamental rhythmic one-two beat pervaded the program throughout, as in the jazz of yore, although the variations of rhythm over this basic beat have become freer, more changing and higher-flying before returning home; the individual soli are more elaborate, more venturesome and considerably more brilliant and effective. As before, there is a notable range of instrumental sonorities and colors, from proclamative, ear-filling plangence and rousing brilliance to mellow smoothness, and another prominent feature was the expert dynamic control of the orchestra, especially in long gradual crescendi which aroused the audience to roars of applause.

Goodman himself is of about the same heft he was forty years ago. His face is bigger, and whereas he once had a grocery-clerk look, his expression is now owlish and quizzical. His patent-leather hair has become tousled and somewhat thinner, and his rimless spectacles have given way to horn-rimmed ones. His once tight-lipped mouth bears permanent clarinet scars; that is, it slopes toward his right, forming a kind of sluice, out of which his words come. Goodman talks in clumps, which may last two or three minutes before ending suddenly in reverberat-

ing silences. His speech resembles his playing. He often starts
in a hoarse, dog-eared voice, which suggests his chalumeau
tones. His voice slowly ascends until it reaches the clearer,
lighter middle register, and as he gathers momentum he occasionally lets loose a falsetto phrase before abruptly falling back
to the chalumeau. His words follow each other closely, and
sometimes they pile up; then he clears his throat vigorously,
and the flow resumes. He laughs a lot, but it is not the kind of
laugh you laugh along with, because it demands a great deal of
breath. It goes on and on metronomically on the same note, and
it calls to mind a stone skipping across the water. A few days
ago, Goodman talked about the fortieth-anniversary concert, in
the living room of his East Side apartment, where he carries on
his business (planning some seventy appearances a year, collecting art, jamming with musicians like Jimmy Rowles, listening to records).

"It's remarkable after forty years that I'm still here," he said.
"Particularly when you think of all the musicians at the 1938
concert who are gone—Carney and Hodges and Lester Young
and Hackett and Gene Krupa. But I think we should have this
little celebration. You can't go back forty years musically any
more than you can put together the New York Yankees of Joe
DiMaggio and Lou Gehrig. But we can do a show with a good
air about it. Lionel Hampton and Jess Stacy are set, and I *think*
Teddy Wilson will work out. Vernon Brown called, but I don't
know whether he'll make it. Harry James can't do it, because
he'll be in Hawaii. I suppose the original concert changed the
nature of the business. It wasn't very long afterward that everybody was playing concerts. I wish I could say that the whole
thing was my idea, but it wasn't. In fact, a press agent named
Wynn Nathanson came to me and asked, 'You want to play
Carnegie Hall?' I remember saying, 'Are you out of your mind?
What the hell would we do there?' I acquiesced, but there was a
certain reluctance, an apprehensiveness. I went to see Bea Lillie
after I'd accepted, to talk her into doing a skit. I was a great fan
of hers, and I thought it would relieve the monotony, and any-

way the stage shows we played in theatres always included comics. She was smart enough to say no. Sol Hurok's name was on the evening, but he had nothing to do with it outside of sending me a wire reminding me to tell the musicians they would be playing in Carnegie Hall and to be on their best behavior. That was an interesting band. It didn't get uptight about anything. It had its good and bad nights, but that particular night it was on. The only reason the concert was recorded was because of Albert Marx, a booking agent, who was married to Helen Ward, who'd been my vocalist. In those days, I had air checks of the band made all the time—just to hear how new things sounded—and my hotel room was flooded with them. So I thought I'd skip having the concert recorded. But when Marx told me he was going to record it and would I like a copy, I said sure. I think he sent the acetates in two tin boxes. I had them in my office for a while, and then I took them to my apartment on Park Avenue and put them away and forgot them. When I moved, my sister-in-law Rachel took over the apartment, because it was rent-controlled, and she found the acetates in a closet. She told me I'd better take them before her son did. I had them played at the Reeves sound studios, because I didn't know what shape they were in, and felt a tape should be made. It was quite something hearing the concert again. We'd rehearsed for it a couple of days in Carnegie to get used to the acoustics, which is what you might call bringing the musicians in to hear the hall. We'd been playing in the Madhattan Room, where the sound was stuffy and dense, and to go into a place where it was so lively was very upsetting at first. Big bands were always difficult to handle acoustically anyway, because of their unorthodox instrumentation."

Then Goodman talked about clarinet playing. "Jimmie Noone was one of my favorite players, and Leon Roppolo was another," he said. "Noone had a clarinet clarinet sound, but Buster Bailey had an academic sound. Bailey and I shared the same teacher in Chicago, and we used to do duets together. Frank Teschemacher was talented, and I liked Volley De Faut, whose

name was Voltaire De Faut, and Larry Shields, who was with
the Original Dixieland Jazz Band. I think Pee Wee Russell was
kind of an anachronism. I first heard him in St. Louis. I don't
think he knew much about the clarinet. In fact, I think his
clarinet was leaking air half the time. Artie Shaw was a hell of
a clarinet player. My time was always more legato than his, but
his sound was more open. It carried a lot farther. And, of
course, Bob Wilber is a superb clarinettist.

"Hindemith wrote a clarinet concerto for me in 1947, and I
played it with the Philadelphia. I listened to it recently—the
version by Louis Cahuzac, the great French clarinettist. It takes
some doing, that piece. You always have to have chops if you
play classical music. I studied with Reginald Kell, and he was
the sort of teacher who analyzed every inch of what you were
playing. He was terrific in that sense. He wanted to know what
you were *doing*. The pressures are quite violent in classical
music. You reach your art on the far side of technical matters,
yet every once in a while you have to go back to the basics.
People have often said to me, 'You're so relaxed when you
play.' Relaxed, my elbow. It's practice. You do the same thing
over and over so many times that it comes to sound relaxed and
easy. But, to turn it around, I've never been able to play one of
my own transcribed jazz solos. Louis Armstrong and Lester
Young and Bix Beiderbecke and Earl Hines didn't learn to improvise out of a book. They learned the tradition of it first.
When Mel Powell joined me on piano, Dixieland was about
finished, but he knew all the old pieces, like 'That's a Plenty'
and 'Riverboat Shuffle.' It was the same with Charlie Parker.
His blues were older than time. When you improvise, you're
thinking partly about the chords and partly about the melody.
You think about a scale you might have been working on, or a
motif that's been in your head. Improvisation also depends on
the tune you're playing. Fletcher Henderson tried to arrange
songs that swung to begin with. Good improvising has to be
done with complete authority, and with taste and grace. And I
always have to know the lyrics first. I sing them to myself, and

that helps to get the tempo right. The quality of a lyric—the way the words fit the melody—can affect the way you play. You don't always put the greatest things down. You have moods about music, just the way you have about sunshine or darkness. Jazz is very romantic. I've frequently thought of Brahms as one of the great jazz composers. The last movement of his first clarinet sonata sounds like Bix Beiderbecke." Goodman hummed a melody rapidly, in falsetto. "The *sound* of instruments doesn't seem to matter the way it used to. Bix and Louis and Chu Berry all got big, fat sounds. Sometimes I think about the jam sessions we used to have. The whole damned thing was quite beautiful. You were sent—to use an old expression. I've occasionally thought about my position in music, then discarded the thought. It's terribly hard for one who has made history to talk about it, to be objective. As a musician, I see myself in others' reactions, and that stretches all the way from Glenn Miller to Dennis Brain. I don't think I'll ever stop playing. The clarinet is difficult to play as you get older—just as difficult as a brass instrument. There's a good deal of physical wear, I've noticed, and you have to pace yourself. I'd miss all the problems if I quit. But I'm very lucky. I can pick and choose the problems I want."

[1978]

AESTHETIC
VITAMINS

~~

First-rate jazz trumpeters tend to be diminutive. Consider Louis Armstrong, Bix Beiderbecke, Roy Eldridge, Charlie Shavers, Bobby Hackett, Billy Butterfield, Ray Nance, Ruby Braff, and Miles Davis. The larger the lyrical soul, it would seem, the smaller its house. This is certainly true of Braff, an eloquent five-foot-four-inch featherweight. In addition to being wispy and poetical, Braff is also an anachronism. He came to the fore in the mid-fifties, as part of a tradition (Armstrong, Eldridge, Buck Clayton) that had been declared dead, or at least obsolescent. Young trumpet players were no longer idolizing Armstrong; instead they followed the mercurial, multi-noted ways of Dizzy Gillespie and Fats Navarro. When Braff appeared, the florid, brilliant Clifford Brown, created largely by Navarro and killed at twenty-five in an automobile accident, was the new, young, champion trumpet player. Braff, by contrast, was a throwback, a return to an unfashionable way of playing that was devoted to melody, lyricism, and grace. But none of this matters anymore. Gillespie's academy grew old and gave way to the avant-garde of the sixties, while Braff, perfecting his anachronistic form and battling the whims of fashion and economics, has become a tradition unto himself.

Braff is, in the best way, a rococo performer who uses a lot of notes, sagacious flourishes, and a scarlet tone. He favors the middle and lower registers; daring and frequent intervals; fast, short runs; mix-'em-up rhythmic tricks (legato/on-the-beat/double time/legato); and melody. He achieves an expansive cave of sound in the lower registers. "I love the bass and the cello," he explains. "I love the low register of the clarinet. I love Harry Carney. I have a great need for those sounds. I change my embouchure when I move down there, and I move into another room, another world." Braff is, as well, an extraordinarily precise horn player, whose exactness recently caused Alec Wilder to observe that "every note he plays is the *center* of that note." Braff loves melody, and he plays it in a way that lies between embellishment and full-scale improvisation. He does not, in the manner of many improvisers, impose himself on the tunes he plays; rather he heats them up so that their colors and curves and textures gleam and shine. He points up their treasures, but he leaves them intact. He will start a slow ballad by playing the notes as they are written, but he will celebrate them by moving along just behind the beat. Then he will descend, suddenly and softly, into his lowest register, roam there almost inaudibly, and rise swiftly to the start of the second eight bars of the tune, which he will play on the beat but which he will alter by skipping certain notes and by adding others, in the form of miniature calligraphic flourishes. He will be more adventurous on the bridge, and, raising his volume (as the years have gone by, he has taken to playing softer and softer, without setting aside his mastery of dynamics), bob up and down through several big intervals, duck downstairs again, and then start the final eight bars a beat or two late. He will restate the melody, again gently subtracting and adding notes, and go out with a series of low tones, the last one terminated by a barely wavering vibrato.

The house that shelters these graceful sounds is oddly built.

Braff is cylindrical, and he has substantial feet, small hands, and long arms. His head, with receding brownish hair, is round and affirmative. He has a trumpet player's mouth, wide and rather flat, and he has heavy-lidded hazel eyes. These eyes, continually at half-mast, move like lighthouse beacons, and they dominate his face. His voice, anchoring all, is heavy and sonorous. When he plays, he stands motionless, his legs slightly apart, his horn pointed just above the horizon. The only parts of him which move are his lips and his fingers. He keeps his eyes mostly closed, occasionally opening them halfway and rolling them back when he takes a breath and is ready to start a salutary phrase. He radiates the stone-stillness of absolute concentration.

Braff is obsessed by two things: talking and playing. So he recently spent a perfect day, talking out the afternoon in a midtown luncheonette and playing out the evening in a recording studio, where he rehearsed rigorously with the group he leads with the guitarist George Barnes.

Braff at the coffee shop: "Louis Armstrong's playing was a fat, warm, glowing thing," Braff said. "It gave me butterflies. When I got to know him, I knew I was dealing with a musical genius. He was deadly serious about music, and he had a fantastic degree of concentration and energy. Think of playing improvised music for fifty-five years! But there was no end to the amount of steam that he could turn up, even at the end. He told me once that when you play there are always two bands—the one you hire, and yourself. When the hired one is good, you turn them up mentally and dig them. But when they're not, you turn them off and *you* become the band. "If you spend your life depending on other musicians,' he'd say, 'it's too bad for you.' Louis laughed a lot at life, like when he had that all-star group in the forties, with Sid Catlett and Jack Teagarden and Earl Hines and Barney Bigard, and he told me, 'Man, that band! Pretty soon I'm going to surprise them and let all those leaders go.' He was a very joyous host. He took real pride in making you comfortable, even in his dressing room, with fifty people standing around. He had total recall, and he loved telling stories. He'd act out every part, and I'd always think, What a pity he'll never have the chance to do straight acting roles. There was no phase of the entertainment business he didn't understand, and I *know* he could have been a great hard-core actor. He also remembered every smell and taste and feeling he'd had. He once described how as a kid he'd seen this circus trumpeter with his uniform and shining buttons and shining trumpet, and how good it made him feel, and suddenly *you* felt the way *he* did when he saw that circus cat. He also carried every bit of music he'd ever heard in his head. He was intelligent and he was tough, in that he did what he felt he had to do in this world. Louis was no cream puff. And that sense of time he had! He even laughed in time and told his stories in time. When one of his sidemen was doing his feature onstage at a concert, he'd step into the wings and tell me a story, and the last word always came the split second before he was supposed to be back onstage to play. He could play four quarter notes a certain way, and you could stand beside him and play the same notes in the same way, but your time would not be as good as his.

"Louis knew that emotion without skill is no good, and I think I've finally reached the point where the two are working together. I never used to practice at all, but several years ago I became aware that there was something wrong with my embouchure. It was very rubbery, and I had to fake certain things, like getting quickly from upstairs to downstairs on my horn. I started going to Joe Shepley's house. He's a studio trumpeter, and studio musicians don't fail when they play. I watched him practice for hours, and got inspired and started taking lessons from another trumpeter, Bernie Privin. He got me going enough so that I can practice now from the exercise books. It's hard, heavy labor—those exercises. But I play better now than I ever have. I also studied a couple of years with Sanford Gold, the piano teacher. He showed me how to take chords apart, and he showed me I could write my own things. And Louis taught me another way of practicing. 'Make up a two-bar phrase or a four-bar phrase,' he'd say, 'and keep working at it until that two-bar phrase or four-bar phrase is a complete and perfect thing, a small jewel.' It sounds easy, but it's unbelievably difficult. All this new knowledge gives me the freedom to excel, to use to the fullest what I have.

"A performer is a person who needs immediate communication and an immediate reward. Of course, you're naked when you perform. So you must always know how good or how bad you are. The only way to do that is to carry a yardstick in your head—a yardstick made up of a great Armstrong solo or of a good solo of your own—and measure yourself constantly against it. A jazz musician doesn't have time to wait around for inspiration. You create it yourself, and the way you do it is to recall something that made you happy and inspired before, like Louis's remembering that shining circus trumpeter. That way you summon up feelings of warmth and joy. And you have to keep a backlog of music in your head; you have to constantly replenish your musical supply by listening to records or the radio. This is all part of the flow of excellence, which has to be checked every day. You have to put your aesthetic vitamins in the pot every morning and stir and pour.

"Improvisation is adoration of the melody. It's imagination coupled with a strong sense of composition. The best improvisations I've heard came out of melodic thinking. When I play 'I Got Rhythm,' I play it because I love the melody, and I keep that melody singing along somewhere in my head. Running its chords doesn't interest me. What does is trying to superimpose a new melody on the original, to build in layers, like Louis did. When I play one of his records, I'm mesmerized at first with what he put on top, with the *surface*. When I play it again, I hear the second layer, and then the third. Every time I play it, I hear something I didn't know was there before. But a great solo is also this: it surprises you each time you hear it, even though you know every note by heart.

"I feel very formal about music, and that includes the way you dress onstage and the way you talk into a microphone. I used to be a wise-ass on microphone, cracking bad jokes and such, but I know now I was trying to make it with the musicians because I was insecure. There's a star system, and it shouldn't be destroyed, like the young musicians are doing now. Fred Astaire is a star. But if he'd worked in sleazy places in disreputable clothes, his talent would have suffered, and he wouldn't have star status. Look at Ellington. I get goose bumps every time that man walks out on a stage. And Goodman—the epitome of professionalism and care and tone. It's based on the understanding that you're an entertainer, and you can't be an entertainer until you play well enough to communicate with your audience. And it has to do with the American dream: if you're good enough, you'll make it because *some*body's going to pick up on you. But if you destroy the star system, what is there to shoot for? It was never the artist's job to play ugly, to parade his ugly dreams in public."

When Braff drives downtown in his Toyota sports car from Riverdale, where he lives, he parks in a municipal garage at Eighth Avenue and Fifty-third Street, which he uses as his "midtown office." At eight-thirty in the evening, he left the coffee shop, got his car, and picked up George Barnes, who lives around the corner. They arrived at nine at the loft building where they were to rehearse. Hank O'Neal, who has a desk job with the CIA during the day and makes records for his own label, Chiaroscuro, at night, rents a couple of floors in the building, and they contain an apartment and three huge workrooms, one of them a recording studio. He is a tall, thin, gentle Southerner, and he greeted Braff and Barnes warmly. The guitarist Wayne Wright and the bassist John Giuffrida round out the quintet, and they were already there. The studio had the usual jungle of cables and microphones, but there were also a sofa and comfortable chairs. A couple of thronelike leather chairs were side by side in the center of the room, and Braff and

Barnes headed for them. Braff had a new cornet, and he shook it and fixed its valves. "Every new horn needs a mouthpiece made for it, and not one from another horn," he said. He chuckled and lifted his eyebrows. "And what do you know—I ain't got one. So it's going to be a bitch getting used to this tonight." Wright and Giuffrida, stationed to the rear of Braff and Barnes, were look-alikes in mod spectacles, monkish hairdos, and work clothes. They smiled whenever Braff or Barnes said anything. (Neither Braff nor Barnes is noted for equanimity.) Barnes got up and walked around. He is the same height as Braff, but he is ovoid. He has a round head, a small, crinkly face, and short arms. He wears his pants high, and they carry him like a vessel. He lit a giant cigar and sat down again, picked up his guitar, and rested his right foot on a brick he carries to every job. He and Braff glanced at one another. Braff leaned back in his chair and closed his eyes, and suddenly they were into a fast blues. Braff soloed first, then Barnes. He has spent much of his career in studios, and he has a curious singsong way of playing. His notes vibrate like Django Reinhardt's, and he has an extraordinary sense of dynamics. Some of his notes whisper, and some ring like a clarinet's upper register. The two men exchanged four-bar breaks and winged through the closing ensemble. One second of silence, then Braff cackled and said, "You see what happens when you lay off three whole weeks. Man! Let's try something else." It is Braff's own "With Time to Love." He played softly, the notes squeezing themselves out of the horn, and there were several deep-register phrases. Barnes was even softer, and the room filled with gentle, stirring sounds. The number ended with a sighing Barnes note, and he and Braff looked at each other. "Hey!" Braff said. "That's togetherness!"

Braff took a sip of coffee, and lit a cigarette. It was three-thirty, and the coffee shop was almost empty. "I was born in 1927 in Roxbury, a suburb of Boston. There were four children—an older brother, who was killed in World War Two;

my oldest sister, who died a few years ago; and my next oldest sister, who lives in Randolph, Mass. My parents were both thrown on boats and sent over here from Russia when they were young. It was the time of the pogroms, and Jews were being slaughtered. But imagine the guts of coming to this country and not knowing the language and going to work in a factory! My mother was somewhere in her teens, and she had a sister in Boston, where my parents met. My father was the same age when he came over, I think, but he was already a carpenter and a cabinetmaker. He had a very inventive head. He once made a window where you pressed a button and it opened into the room so that you could wash it without hanging outside and breaking your neck. And when the office-furniture outfit he was working for bought a new truck, before he'd drive it he parked it in an alley and took it entirely apart, and then put it back together so that he'd know exactly how it worked. My parents live in Brighton now, and I jump up to Boston every six months or so to see them. All their records in Russia are gone, but they estimate they're about ninety, or close to it. They still have things amazingly together, far more than most of the musicians I run into at Jim and Andy's bar. About fifteen years ago, my mother decided to learn English, so she could write to me. My father long ago picked up on English because he was out in the world, but my mother has always been at home. So she started studying the newspapers, and now she writes and I can understand her. Words come out funny. She'll say 'Good lucky' at the end of a letter, and when she really gets up against it she clips out the word she wants from the newspaper and pastes it on the page. It's a Yiddish household, and I still speak it fluently.

"I knew from the time I walked I wanted to play music. But there were many, many fights about it at home. My father's father had been a clarinettist, and most musicians, outside of the symphony, were regarded as *klezmer*, a Yiddish word for a sleazy person. I wanted a tenor saxophone, and I screamed at them for years. Saxophones looked comfortable and shiny, and they had these pearly buttons. There was a strap you put on, and there was the business of choosing the right reed and wetting it and putting it into the mouthpiece. It was a sharp ritual. When I was seven, my sisters went to the Conn instrument company and looked at saxophones, but all they probably saw were baritones and such, which would have been ridiculous with my size. So they bought a trumpet. It looked silly, this puny thing with three valves and a little mouthpiece, and I felt terrible about it. But I took lessons from an old man who had been a circus trumpeter, and then he died. So I played with the radio endlessly, and that way I learned all the tunes. I never practiced from the exercise books when my family was around, because it irritated them, particularly my father when he came home from work. To this day, I use a mute in my apartment, and I can't stand anyone hearing me practice. But maybe this secretiveness helped me get so many quiet tones on the instrument—that and the fact I would *still* like to sound like a saxophone. The trumpet probably saved me. I felt literally imprisoned in school. I never listened to the teachers, and anyway three-quarters of them were not crazy about kids at all. So I continually got poor marks, and of course I'm sorry now. I can write music faster than I can read the papers. Recently, I've been picking up on Alec Wilder's book about American songs, but I have to stop every minute or two because of the big words he uses. When I finish a chapter, I make out an alphabetical list of the tough words and look them up and write down their meanings. Then I take the list and go back and read the chapter again.

"I didn't get into listening to jazz until I was fourteen or fifteen. I knew the Dorseys and Artie Shaw and Ziggy Elman and Glenn Miller, but I didn't know Louis Armstrong or Bix Beiderbecke. I started listening to the poolhall hustlers down the street. They'd go to the Ray-Mor Ballroom all the time, and they were far better critics than the real ones. They'd say: 'Oh, man, I went to see Goodman last night, and you know he had Harry James playing lead on "King Porter Stomp," and that's not right. And that tempo he chose for "Stompin' at the Savoy" was way off.' They were participating, they were deep into it, they knew everything. I began going to people's houses who had collections of Basie and Billie Holiday and Ellington and Armstrong. One was Mayo Duca. He was a marvelous trumpet player and a fanatical Armstrong collector. I think he had every record Louis ever made. In fact, Louis would stay with him when he was working in Boston, and sit at a typewriter and write his letters and listen to his records. When you went to Mayo's house, he had a coffeepot in every room, and he'd run from room to room, drinking coffee and explaining every note on every record before he put it on, so it took all night to hear about three records.

"Around this time, I took some more lessons from a cat named Bob Gordon who came to the house every Saturday afternoon. He was a club-date trumpeter. The things he gave me I learned by ear when he thought I was reading them. I also started playing professionally at places like the Silver Dollar Bar—sometimes in the afternoon, sometimes in the evening, when I had the cab fare to get home. My parents weren't too happy about it; in fact, it wasn't until I was twenty-two that they finally gave in on my becoming a musician. In Boston, there were no steady gigs, unless you played badly. So I'd work here and there a couple of weeks at a time, and the first big-time date I had was at the Savoy, with Edmond Hall. Vic Dickenson was in the band, and Ken Kersey and that beautiful, smiling cat Jimmy Crawford. This was the late forties. I'd already been down to New York and back a couple of times, but I wasn't ready yet, and those were lean times. On one New York trip, I stayed at the Saint James Hotel, in midtown, and tried to get a day job, things were so bad. An agency sent me to a place where they made transformers. They put me in an apron, and I was supposed to wind wire around sharp, nickel-plated things, and right away I cut my fingers to ribbons. By ten-twenty, I'd had it. The next day, the agency sent me to a sweatshop where they drilled holes in pieces of wood to put Christmas trees in, and I lasted until ten-twenty-five. 'You just weren't cut out for work,' the agency said. The only gig I had during this time was a one-nighter in Allentown, Pennsylvania, with Somebody and His Smiling Irishmen. We stood all the way on the bus, and when we got there the leader told us, '*Everybody in this orchestra smiles when I smile, and frowns when I frown, and that goes whether you have a horn in your mouth or not.*' Man, I thought, what have you gotten yourself into? The gig was in a ballroom, and during the first intermission I conned my pay of fifteen bucks from the guy on some pretext and ran outside and asked a cabbie what he'd charge to take me to New York. Fifteen dollars. I was back at the Saint James in two hours.

"After the Savoy date in Boston, I worked with Sid Catlett at George Wein's first Storyville there, and it was Sid who brought me to New York for good. He was something—that great big man with those little balls of drums arranged so tightly around him. He'd say, 'I can swing seventeen men with one wire brush and a phone book,' and he was right. He always had a room with a family, and he'd ask me to come to these rent parties where he lived. Two or three bucks and all the whiskey and sandwiches you could handle. I finally found out that the parties were for *him.* He loved to gamble, and he always needed bread. Before we came to New York, he took me by his place one night, and he showed me how to pack. He had two suitcases and all these camel's hair coats and twenty pairs of shoes and all, and he rolled everything into tight, perfect sausages. When we got to New York, he opened the suitcases and took everything out, and not a wrinkle! Fantastic! I've tried many times to pack that way, but my clothes come out like an unmade bed. Sid took me around town, introducing me to people, and when he played down at Bob Malz's Central Plaza, he made Malz hire me. Then, in 1953, I got a break. I was invited to play at an arts festival at Brandeis University, and John Hammond heard me the first time. After I'd played 'Sleepy Time Down South,' he grabbed the mike and said, 'That's *marvellous!*' John and his way of talking all the time with words like 'marvellous' and 'wonderful' and 'great.' I've had telephone conversations with him that go like this:

'Hello, Ruby. This is John. How are you?'

'Well, I'm in bed with pneumonia and I feel awful.'

'Wonderful, Ruby. Now what I called about . . .'

"Just after Brandeis, John started making his Vanguard recordings with Buck Clayton and Edmond Hall and Mel Powell, and he used me. Those records got a lot of notice, and for the first time I was on the map. I also recorded with Ellis Larkins, just the two of us, and John took it to Richard Rodgers, who was putting together *Pipe Dreams* for Broadway, and I was hired. It wasn't a speaking part. I was supposed to be an idiot wetback, but I did play a couple of times during the show. *Pipe Dreams* was based on John Steinbeck's *Sweet Thursday*, and he was at most of the rehearsals. He even got to be my coffee runner. He also told me all these wild stories. Or lies, which I guess is a writer's right. It's hard to believe that I talked with Richard Rodgers every day and watched him work. If they needed sixteen bars, he'd sit at the piano and write out those sixteen bars just like that, note for note. Then Oscar Hammerstein would fit the words to the music right away. How pleasurable it must have been for those two to work together! After *Pipe Dreams*, which lasted seven months, I worked and recorded with Benny Goodman. People say Benny is a strange cat, and I guess he is, but I got along with him. We were rehearsing at Nola Studios, and they had unhinged a big door to move an organ or something, and the door fell over on me and cut my lip so badly the doctor Benny sent me to said I'd never play again. I lost all feeling in my lips for six months, but Benny *made* me play with him every weekend at Basin Street in that little band he had with Urbie Green and Paul Quinichette. It was terrible, but it probably rescued my career."

At the recording studio, the quartet moved into a medium-tempo version of "Looking at You," notable for the four-bar exchanges at the end, in which Barnes mimicked Braff's pas-

sages so well he made Braff laugh. A fast "Liza" followed, and
then a lullaby reading of the Beatles' "Here, There, and Everywhere." "This horn is much lighter than my old one," Braff
said. "But I've got to get used to it. My old one, I might as well
have been playing a baritone, it was so heavy. You have to be
young and stupid to play one like that." The group settled
down and played a yearning version of Louis Armstrong's "No
One Else but You" that recalled an equally eloquent rendition
that Braff and Pee Wee Russell had played one night at the
Newport Jazz Festival. In the next number, there were several
starts and stops. Wright was having trouble with a tricky two-
bar fill phrase. He tried it three times, to no avail, and Braff
chuckled and said, "Don't worry, Wayne. There are at least a
dozen out-of-work guitarists up at Jim and Andy's this very
minute." Wright maneuvered the phrase and they finished the
number. Braff sat down at the piano and played a pretty tune.
"Duke heard me play this once," he said. " 'Hey, Ruby, You're
going to lay that fine little tune on me, aren't you?' Isn't that
something? Duke Ellington wanting a song *I* wrote!"

The coffee shop was filling up with the early-dinner, Salis-
bury-steak crowd. Braff ordered his third cup of coffee. "The
group was one of those great accidents," he said. "A couple of
years back, when Bucky Pizzarrelli and George Barnes had
their duo at the Upstairs at the Downstairs, I sat in with them.
George knocked me out. He had a way of phrasing with me
almost as if we had the same timbre, as if we were the same
instrument. I kept thinking about this phenomenon, and one
morning not long ago I was driving home and I stopped at Jim
and Andy's on the chance George would be there. It was three-
thirty, but I knew he was an insomniac. By God, he was, and
we talked for a while and I said, 'Let's consolidate forces,' and
he said, 'Right!' At eleven the same morning we met at his
house and played for hours and had a ball. We wanted a kind
of Freddie Green–Walter Page guitar and bass combination
behind us, and we got Wayne Wright and John Giuffrida, and

we started rehearsing like crazy. We made our first public appearance at the Newport Festival, and every notice was good. We recorded what we'd played right after, and since then we've made a record with Tony Bennett, and we're also going to do a documentary film with him, and then go into the Rainbow Grill. I've spent all my life knocking on doors, but now they're knocking on ours. So it's the right combination of souls.

"I've lived up in Riverdale for eighteen or nineteen years. I lived in Pee Wee Russell's building down on King Street before. You'd think my joint was an insane asylum to see it. I never thought it would be permanent, so I've never really furnished it. I thought I'd wait until I had an apartment in New York and one in London and one in Paris and maids and chauffeurs and then buy some decent furniture. I cook everything in a frying pan, and I cook and eat and wash up in twenty minutes. I don't think food should be too important. When I was on tour in Europe with George Wein, we'd go to a fancy restaurant in Paris and spend about three hours, and then George would say he knew another place that had fantastic desserts, and we'd go there for another hour, and then somewhere else for coffee. It sent me up the wall. I've come close to getting married a couple of times, but I married music a long time ago, and a wife would have to understand that. Anyway, there's only room for one nut in a household, and I have first claim on that.

"I don't feel right if I'm not playing, but there have been times when I haven't had a gig in six months. What I'd do, if I couldn't call a session, was go through an entire concert in my mind—an invented concert, note for note, right down to the lights and the applause. If it went well, I'd sometimes make actual notes about it: that's something to remember, something to use. But how to keep your spirits up when you're not working is another kind of discipline. One thing, I stay away from the negatives; they can bring you down and tear you apart. Another is a one-night gig. It can wipe out months of difficulty. Otherwise, it's just get through the week and then everything will be cool. But you can't abuse your music at such times by going and making a rock-and-roll record or something. If you do, your music will somewhere along the line up and punch you in the nose. But I'm an optimist. I've always felt that things would be all right, that I'd be rewarded. I know I'm good and I know I'm unique. If I had to go out and hire someone just like me, it would be impossible, because he doesn't exist."

[1974]

BIRD

~~~

Charlie Parker died at the age of thirty-four, in 1955, and he was one of the wonders of twentieth-century music. Like his all but interchangeable spiritual brother, Dylan Thomas, who died a year earlier, Parker was labyrinthine. He was a tragic figure who helplessly consumed himself, and at the same time he was a demon who presided over the wreckage of his life. He was an original and fertile musician who had reached the edge of self-parody. He was an irresistibly attractive man who bit almost every hand that fed him. He lived outside the pale of his own times, yet he indirectly presaged, in his drives and fierce independence, the coming of Malcolm X and Eldridge Cleaver. And he was, albeit succored by a slavish cult, largely unknown during his life.

Parker was born in a Kansas City suburb to a knockabout vaudevillian, Charles Parker, and a local eighteen-year-old, Addie Boyley (or Bayley). When he was eight or nine, his parents moved to Kansas City proper, and when he was eleven his father, who had become a Pullman chef, disappeared almost completely from his life. Grammar school went well, but after he had spent two years in high school as a freshman he dropped out, and by the time he was sixteen his life had already begun to accelerate dangerously. He had got married, he had become a professional, self-taught alto saxophonist, he was a member of the musicians' union, he was a neophyte figure of the teeming Kansas City night world, and he had begun using drugs. When he was eighteen, he went to Chicago and then to New York, where he became a dishwasher in a Harlem restaurant and fell under the sway of its pianist, Art Tatum. He also played in a couple of taxi-dance-hall bands, and jammed tentatively around Harlem. In 1939, he went home, joined Harlan Leonard's band, then Jay McShann's Kansas City band. John Lewis, then a student at the University of New Mexico, has noted the effect that McShann's radio broadcasts had on him: "The alto solos on those broadcasts opened up a whole new world of music for me. I'd known Jay McShann from the time he used to barnstorm in the Southwest . . . but the alto saxophone was new and years ahead of anybody in jazz. He was into a whole new system of sound and time. The emcee didn't announce his name [and] I didn't learn it was Charlie Parker until after the war." The effect of a McShann broadcast on the black members of Charlie Barnet's band was no less electric. Somebody played ten spectacular choruses of "Cherokee" during a McShann broadcast they heard backstage at the Newark theatre where they were working, and when their show was over they rushed to the Savoy, found out who the soloist was by asking McShann to play the tune again, and took Parker out to dinner. Parker quit McShann in 1942, and, after a period of rootlessness and semi-starvation in Harlem, joined Earl Hines's big band, a crazy, warring group made up almost equally of old-line musicians and young beboppers. He then passed briefly through the brilliant, short-lived avant-garde big band led by Billy Eckstine, and by 1945 had settled down with the many small bands he would lead and/or record with until his death.

He had also settled, irreversibly, into the role of Gargantua. He was divorced and remarried when he was twenty-two, and the new marriage was, as far as anyone knows, the last legal liaison of the four he had. He lived in hotels and boarding houses. He had become a baffling and extraordinary drug addict—one who, unlike most addicts, was also a glutton, an alcoholic, and a man of insatiable sexual needs. He would eat twenty hamburgers in a row, drink sixteen double whiskeys in a couple of hours, and go to bed with two women at once. At times he went berserk, and would throw his saxophone out a hotel window or walk into the ocean in a brand-new suit. His sense of humor was equally askew. Early one morning he took a cab to the trumpeter Kenny Dorham's apartment (Parker spent a good part of his life in cabs, using them as his office, as rendevous, as places to sleep, as compact, mobile fortresses), got Dorham out of bed, asked for a light, and went on his way. In 1947, he collapsed, and spent six months in a state mental hospital in California. (He had gone to the coast the year before with the first bebop band to travel west of the Mississippi; it also included Dizzy Gillespie, Al Haig, Milt Jackson, and Ray Brown.) During his stay in the state hospital, where his astonishing recuperative powers soon became evident, Parker was cared for by a doctor who was also a fan. Ross Russell, Parker's first biographer, has set down the doctor's thoughts about him: "A man living from moment to moment. A man living for the pleasure principle, music, food, sex, drugs, kicks, his personality arrested at an infantile level. A man with almost no feeling of guilt and only the smallest, most atrophied nub of conscience. Except for his music, a potential member of the army of psychopaths supplying the populations of prisons and mental institutions. But with Charlie Parker it was the music factor that makes all the difference. That's really the only reason we're interested in him. The reason we're willing to stop our own lives and clean up his messes. People like Charlie require somebody like that."

Parker's wild excesses never seemed—at least until the very end of his life—to interfere with his music. It is now agreed among jazz musicians that drugs dislocate and dilute their improvisations; it was just the other way with Parker. The only time he could not function were when he was strung out and needed a fix. His style had matured completely by the time he made his first small-band records, in 1945. Parker's playing did not, as has often been claimed, spring magically from the virgin soil of the Southwest. Other musicians had a hand in its creation. When he was a teenager, Parker bathed night after night in the unique, rocking music of Kansas City. No matter where he went, he heard the blues—the heavy, sad, windblown blues of Lips Page, Pete Johnson, Joe Turner, Herschel Evans, and Buddy Tate, and the light, rolling, new-coin blues of Count Basie and Lester Young. Young became his idol, and when Parker first went on the road he took along all Young's records and committed his solos to memory. Parker also worked in Kansas City, with Buster Smith, a saxophonist whose style bears a speaking likeness to Parker's early playing. He picked up technical advice from a well-trained local bandleader, Tommy Douglas, and when he got to New York he studied Art Tatum, who unwittingly showed him how to play at lightning speeds, and how to devise wholly new harmonies. Some of these early wingings into the blue were disastrous. When he was fifteen or sixteen, he brazened his way onto the bandstand during one of the tough, endless Kansas City jam sessions, and, trying some fancy stuff in a roaring "I Got Rhythm," lost his way. The drummer, Jo Jones, stopped playing, grabbed a cymbal, and threw it on the floor at Parker's feet: He had been "gonged off" the stand. From such embarrassing acorns Parkers grow.

Parker had a unique tone; no other saxophonist has achieved as *human* a sound. It could be edgy, and even sharp. (He used the hardest and most technically difficult of the reeds.) It could be smooth and big and sombre. It could be soft and buzzing. Unlike most saxophonists of his time, who took their cue from Coleman Hawkins, he used almost no vibrato; when he did, it was only a flutter, a murmur. The blues lived in every room of his style, and he was one of the most striking and affecting blues improvisers we have had. His slow blues had a preaching, admonitory quality. He would begin a solo with a purposely stuttering four-or-five-note announcement, pause for effect, repeat the phrase, bending its last note into silence, and then turn the phrase around backward and abruptly slip sidewise into double time, zigzag up the scale, circle around quickly at the top, and plummet down, the notes falling somewhere between silence and sound. (Parker was a master of dynamics and of the dramatic use of silence.) Another pause, and he would begin his second chorus with a dreaming, three-note figure, each of the notes running into the next but each held in prolonged, hymnlike fashion. Taken from an unexpected part of the chord, they would slip out in slow motion. He would shatter this brief spell by inserting two or three short arpeggios, disconnected and broken off, then he would float into a back-pedaling half-time and shoot into another climbing-and-falling double-time run, in which he would dart in and out of nearby keys. He would pause, then close the chorus with an amen figure resembling his opening announcement.

But there was another, quite different Parker—the Parker who played extraordinary slow ballads, such as "Embraceable You" and "Don't Blame Me" and "White Christmas." Here he went several steps farther than he did with the blues. He literally dismantled a composer's song and put together a structure ten times as complex. New chords and harmonies appeared, along with new melodic lines that moved high above the unsounded original. (He would, though, always inject pieces of the melody as signposts for the listener.) He could do anything he liked with time, and in his ballads he would lag behind the beat, float easily along on it, or leap ahead of it; he would do things with time that no one had yet thought of and that no one has yet surpassed. His ballads were dense visions, glimpses into an unknown musical dimension. Although they were perfectly structured, they seemed to have no beginnings and no endings; each was simply another of the fragmentary visions that stirred and maddened his mind. Thus his 1947 version of "Embraceable You" (first take), which, so intense, so beautiful, remains one of the sensations of music. Parker's fast thirty-two-bar tunes were meteoric. He used multitudes of notes but never a superfluous one. His runs exploded like light spilling out of an opened doorway. His rhythms had a muscled, chattering density. He crackled and roared.

Parker turned the world of jazz around, and the effects are still felt. One hears him in the work of such saxophonists as Charlie McPherson and Phil Woods and Sonny Stitt and Sonny Criss, and less openly in the playing of Sonny Rollins and John Coltrane and Ornette Coleman. One hears him in almost every guitarist, pianist, trumpeter, bassist, drummer, and trombonist over forty, and he is still audible in the instrumentalists of the present generation, although most of them may not know it. But Parker's legion of admirers have, by and large, missed his main point. He widened the improvisational boundaries of time and harmony and melody, but he did not reject what had come before him, for at bottom he was a conservative, who found new ways of expressing the same things that King Oliver and Louis Armstrong and Sidney Bechet had said earlier. His admirers donned his form and ignored his content. Countless players appeared who used a thousand notes in every chorus, who had hard, smart tones, and who indulged in fancy rhythmic patterns. Yet they sidestepped the emotions that governed all that Parker played. The ironic results were the hard-boppers of the late fifties and the cul-de-sac avant-garde of the early sixties. Fortunately, most of this happened after he was dead, and so he did not suffer the horrors that Lester Young endured during the last decade of his life—the musical claustrophobia of hearing yourself reproduced again and again in the work of almost every young saxophonist and of knowing, at the same time, that your own powers have dwindled to the point where the new men are playing better than you are.

For a time after his release from the hospital in California, Parker cooled it. But the pace of his life quickened again, and by the early fifties it had got completely out of control. He collapsed on the street, he got into fights, he tried to commit suicide. He slept, when he slept at all, on floors or in bathtubs or in the beds of friends. He cadged drinks, and he panhandled. His horn was usually in hock, and he missed gigs. And at last his playing faltered; he began to imitate himself. One reason was physical; he no longer had the stamina to sustain his brilliant flights. The other was more subtle. Like Jackson Pollock, he felt that he had reached the end of his explorations. The blues and the thirty-two-bar song no longer were challenges. He had, he thought, discovered every chord change, every rhythmic turn, every adventurous harmony. He talked of big orchestral works, and he considered studying with the composers Stefan Wolpe and Edgard Varese. But there were exceptions, and one of them was the famous concert given in May of 1953 in Massey Music Hall, in Toronto. On hand with Parker, who arrived without a horn and had to borrow one from a music store, were Dizzy Gillespie, Bud Powell, Charles Mingus, and Max Roach. Parker had long had ambivalent feelings about Gillespie. He admired him as a musician, but he resented Gillespie's fame—the story in *Life* about Gillespie and bebop, in which Parker was not even mentioned; the Profile of Gillespie written for *The New Yorker* by Richard O. Boyer. Gillespie, though, has long had life in sharp focus. Parker was the opposite—a closed, secret, stormy, misshapen figure who continually barricaded himself behind the put-on (using his deepest voice, he announced at the concert that Gillespie's "Salt Peanuts" was by "my worthy constituent"). Gillespie was a challenge that night, and so was the rhythm section, which played with ferocity and precision. Parker responded, and in "Wee," "Hot House," and "Night in Tunisia" he soloed with a fire and a brilliance that match anything in his earlier work.

Parker's death was an inevitable mixture of camp, irony, and melodrama. He had been befriended by the Baroness Pannonica Koenigswarter, a wealthy, intelligent eccentric who lived in the Stanhope Hotel and drove herself to jazz clubs in a silver Rolls Royce. Her apartment had become a salon for musicians. In March of 1955, Parker secured a gig at George Wein's Storyville, in Boston, and on his way out of New York he stopped at the Stanhope to say hello. The Baroness offered Parker a drink.

To her astonishment, he refused, and asked for ice water. His ulcer was acting up, and cold water would, he said, quench its fire. Suddenly he started vomiting blood. The Baroness's doctor examined him and said that he would have to go to a hospital at once. He refused, so he was put to bed and given antibiotics. Several days passed, and he seemed to improve. On a Saturday night, he was allowed to sit in the living room and watch Tommy Dorsey's television show. He was in good spirits. During a juggling act involving bricks, which he remembered having seen in Kansas City as a child, he started laughing, choked, and slumped in his chair. He died a minute or two later. At that instant, according to the Baroness, she heard a single huge clap of thunder. The official cause of death was lobar pneumonia, but Parker had simply worn out.

The tenor-saxophonist Buddy Tate had run into Parker not long before. "I first knew him in Kansas City in the thirties, when I was with Andy Kirk," he has said. "He hadn't gotten himself together yet, but he was admiring Buster Smith, who always played Kansas City style. When he first came to New York, we'd hang out together some. He didn't have any work, and nobody knew who he was yet, but he'd be up at Monroe Clark's Uptown House every night. I'd have him over to the house, and my wife would put on a pot, but he would never eat. I tried at the time to get him into Basie's band, but Basie wouldn't have him, and he never forgot that. But he was always nice and kind and soft around me. I never saw him mad at anybody.

"One morning a week before he died, I was walking down Forty-second Street toward Grand Central. It was about ten o'clock, and I'd been on some sort of big-band record date, just playing clarinet. I saw this man way down the sidewalk, and it was Bird. He was hard to miss, with those out-of-style suits that didn't fit, and those big, old, wide granddaddy suspenders he always wore. When I got close, I saw he was all swollen up. I knew he'd been very sick and in the psychiatric part of Bellevue. He said, 'I'm so glad to see you. How you been?'

"I told him fine, and he said, 'Take me for a taste.'

"We went into a bar, and I thought he'd settle down for a few, but he only had two shots. I'd heard he was so strung out he was sleeping on the stand at Birdland and that they'd had to fire him and that he owed the string section that had been backing him up $2500, which he didn't have. We talked about an hour. He said he wished people would call him for record dates like the one I'd just been on, and I told him they probably didn't because they'd think he'd want a thousand for a little old forty-two-dollar date, and he said no, he'd do it for free, just to sit in a section again and play with the other guys. Of course, he rarely had his own horn. He'd play anybody's, any old Sears, Roebuck job, so long as it had a mouthpiece and a reed. I told him I was working up at the Savoy, and he said, 'Oh, I been hearing about you, and I'm going up there to listen.' Bird had played with Jay McShann at the Savoy one of the first times he came to New York. But he never did come uptown, and I never saw him again."

[1974]

A DIFFICULT
INSTRUMENT

~~

For a long time, jazz was dominated by clarinettists. The earliest members of this ruling class were from New Orleans, where they flourished between 1890 and the First World War. They included the Lorenzo Tios, father and son, Alphonse Picou, George Baquet, and Big Eye Louis Nelson Delisle. The next generation of clarinettists, also from New Orleans, is more familiar: Johnny Dodds, Yellow Nunez, Larry Shields, Jimmy Noone, Sidney Bechet, George Lewis, Albert Nicholas, Edmond Hall, Omer Simeon, Leon Roppolo, Raymond Burke, Barney Bigard, Louis Cottrell, Jr., Irving Fazola. The New Orleans clarinettists used the Albert-system clarinet, which had exceedingly difficult fingering and a woody, generous, pleased Edwardian sound. They were, by and large, legato, baroque players, who swooped and soared, who bent notes and loved glissandos. They translated the fretwork around them into sound, and they made the New Orleans ensemble work. They lighted the dark, rough sounds of the trumpet and trombone, and they made the ensembles melodically and harmonically tight. The third generation of clarinettists, often influenced by the New Orleans clarinettists who had gone north after the First World War, were a more disparate group, and they came from everywhere. The New Orleans players Edmond Hall, Barney Bigard, and Irving Fazok moved among them easily, and they were, for lack of a better term, swing clarinettists. Some worked in small bands, but most ended up in or at the head of big bands. Their ensemble function reduced to occasionally floating angelically over the band in the closing chorus, the swing clarinettists became primarily soloists, and few bands in the thirties and early forties lacked their star clarinettist. These included Benny Goodman, Artie Shaw, Jimmy Dorsey, Woody Herman, Joe Marsala, Ernie Caceres, Danny Polo, Jimmy Hamilton, Frank Teschemacher, Pee Wee Russell, Buster Bailey, Johnny Mince, Lester Young, Benny Carter, Prince Robinson, Jerry Blake, Clarence Hutchenrider. Goodman and Shaw governed from opposite poles. Goodman, an arpeggio player, had great facility and passion. He had a fine tone and was a first-class melodist. In the late thirties and early forties, he seemed one of the finest of all jazz players. Artie Shaw was cooler, narrower, and deeper. He was an even better melodist, and though his tone was smaller than Goodman's, he was more interesting harmonically. Musicians tended to relish Shaw. Some of the clarinettists between Goodman and Shaw, though less skilled, were stunningly original. Lester Young summoned up lemons and small rooms. Irving Fazola, using an Albert-system clarinet, had a portly, brocaded tone, while Edmond Hall, also using the Albert system, had a harsh, reedy, jumpy attack. Pee Wee Russell was staccato, exhilarating, absurd, and beautiful. Benny Carter was oil and ease and elegance. But the big bands, with their four- and five-man reed sections, caused saxophonists to proliferate, and by 1945 they had just about replaced clarinettists as the principal reed soloists. At the same time, bebop, which was simply too difficult rhythmically and harmonically for most clarinettists, arrived, and the clarinet, king for almost fifty years, fell out of jazz. Nonetheless, a fourth and final class of jazz clarinettists appeared, and it contained just two members—Tony Scott and

Buddy De Franco. Scott, a restless, volatile, gifted man, moved on the edges of bebop for a time, then went abroad and into avant-garde jazz. De Franco, unbearably challenged by Charlie Parker, attacked bebop head-on and mastered it. He developed such fluency and invention and speed that he was considered the supreme jazz clarinettist. His work has never faltered, and he has kept the instrument alive in jazz simply by playing it so well. In the late sixties and early seventies, he put his clarinet aside in order to lead the perennial Glenn Miller band. The rest seems to have refreshed him. The coolness and near arrogance of his earlier playing has given away to thought, and warmth, and even passion.

De Franco appears in New York occasionally, and he talked about his life during a visit. He is a tall, handsome, kingly man. He has brown hair, a high dome, a long delicate Roman nose, a serious chin, and blunt clarinettist's fingers. His eyes are large and clear, and he talks quickly and with great assurance. His smile eases his imposing face. He is a constant student of his instrument: "There are several reasons that the clarinet is such a difficult instrument. The oboe, the flute, the saxophone are all octave instruments, but the clarinet's three registers—chalumeau, middle, and altissimo—are built in twelfths. If you press the octave key on a saxophone, you go up or down an octave, but on a clarinet you go twelve tones, from, say, low F to middle C. Saxophones have pads over the air holes. When you press a key, the pad closes the hole and you get a note. Clarinets have seven tone holes and no pads, and you have to close them with the ends of your fingers. So you have to have absolute finger control. If any air escapes, you get a terrible squeak or no note at all. Going from the middle register of the clarinet to the altissimo is very awkward because the fingering changes completely. That's the reason so many clarinettists seem to lose control when they go into the top register, why they tend to shriek. Clarinets are made of granadilla wood, which comes from the south of France and North Africa. It is one of the hardest of woods, almost like a metal, and it has to be seasoned several years after it is cut. Even so, heat and cold affect the wood to an astonishing degree. A night club's heating up during a set will make your instrument sharp, and air-conditioning will do the reverse. Too much expansion and contraction of the wood can ruin the bore. You have to develop an embouchure that is good enough to compensate for this constant fluctuation. If I were a symphony clarinettist, I'd use a closed mouthpiece and a soft reed. But to play jazz, I use a stiff reed and an open mouthpiece. That way, I can get percussive effects and be heard over a loud rhythm section, and even over a big band. Most bassists and some drummers are electrified now, and I have to use a very stiff reed and twice the lung power. It is quite exhausting. What is also exhausting is the amount of time you play on the average night in a club. If you play three one-hour sets, you may play a third of that time, which means one solid hour of clarinet playing. Perhaps that is why there have been so few good clarinettists.

"I was with Tommy Dorsey off and on between 1944 and 1949, and that toughened and strengthened me as a player. Dorsey wrote the book on show-biz types. He was all the good and bad characters in one. He was voluble, generous, prejudiced, dirty-mouthed, impatient, a terrific musician. He'd call in a specialist if you were sick. He'd help you out if you were having financial troubles. He had the highest-paid band in the business, and after he'd bought a yacht from Walter Chrysler he took us all on a cruise through the Florida Keys. For a time, we had our own railroad car. But he could be very rough. He loved the shock. Two old ladies came up to him once during an intermission and one of them said, 'I know your mom's sister,' or some such, and Dorsey said, 'Why don't you talk to her and not bug me?' A kid who had just joined the band told Tommy a bad dirty joke, and Tommy laughed, 'Ha, ha, ha,' and said, 'You're fired.' We had our first falling out over my solo on 'Opus 1,' which was a big hit record in 1945. Wherever we went, he wanted me to play the solo that was on the recording because he said that was what people expected—what they came to hear. I was an itchy kid, so I kept changing the solo, and he got more and more unhappy. Finally, he told me he wasn't interested in my creativity, and he fired me. I settled in New York, and things didn't go so well. A few months later he called: 'You little shit. You got enough wrinkles in your belly yet?' I told him I was doing great when the fact was I had checked into the Piccadilly Hotel and got the first week's tab— three hundred dollars, which would be like fifteen hundred now. I told him I'd want three hundred a week if I rejoined and five hundred right away. He turned away from the phone and said, 'I knew it. The son of a bitch is broke!' He said yes, and I went back. The next uproar, I quit and settled in California, and the strangest thing happened. For six months, I couldn't get work, and I couldn't understand it. Well, I found out later that Tommy, who had a lot of influence and sway, had black-balled me, and to please him nobody would hire me. But I rejoined him again, and we became quite friendly and were close until he died. There was no nonsense on the bandstand. There was a ten-dollar fine if you weren't present a half hour before the show, a twenty-five-dollar fine if you missed the show, and a ten-dollar fine if you smiled on the stand. When you soloed, he'd never take his eyes off you, and if he felt a little malicious, he'd make you go on and on until you were ready to drop." De Franco told the British jazz critic Steve Voce this Dorsey story in *Jazz Journal:* He and the pianist Dodo Marmarosa missed the band train from Louisville to St. Louis and caught up with it by hiring a private plane for three hundred and fifty dollars. Dorsey was in the diner. "He got up from his seat and suddenly he saw us," De Franco told Voce. "It seemed like a full two minutes we watched him, and he went through all the phases of emotion in that time. I grabbed a ketchup bottle, because 'Step outside' was one of his frequent ideas. The veins stood out on his forehead, his face got red, he was flexing his muscles, grunting and groaning, and he came over and glared at us for a long while. Then he suddenly started to laugh. 'You guys are ridiculous,' he said. 'You remind me of when I was a kid. I can't get mad at you. You tried to get there, you hired a plane. Stick around, I'll give you both a raise.' "

De Franco is all business when he plays. He stands straight and motionless, and points his clarinet at the floor—unlike Benny Goodman and Artie Shaw, who in exultant moments would rear back and point their instruments directly at God. De Franco's playing is constant motion. The clarinettists who preceded him seemed to hang their melodic lines between their notes. De Franco doesn't appear to use notes. His solos are pliable, glistening tubes of sound that move steadily up and down the instrument's three registers. His solos are always disappearing over the next ridge, and it is not easy to keep up with them, no matter what the tempo. He has a sunny, aluminum sound, a Bauhaus clarity and smoothness. His tone, even in the chalumeau register, has none of the plumminess of Irving Fazola or the low-register Pee Wee Russell. He uses almost no vibrato, and he likes avalanches of eighth notes, often repeated two or three times. He uses double-time passages that blur in the ear. He likes little out-of-breath pauses, placed oddly, and he likes to skid from an arpeggio into a glissando, as if he were sliding into base. One of the finest recordings he ever made was with Art Tatum in the mid-fifties, not long before Tatum's death. Both men, masters of the rococo, have jokey tendencies. Tatum mimics De Franco, De Franco races Tatum, Tatum surges up and around De Franco, De Franco floats away, just out of reach, Tatum encircles De Franco with an enormous arpeggio, De Franco ducks away with an equally enormous counter-arpeggio. De Franco recalled the session: "I was sick that day, but it wasn't an occasion I would have missed. It was a game between us of can you top this? He'd play some astonishing figure and laugh, or turn and make a face at me over one shoulder. Or he'd rest his right hand on his knee and play with just his left hand, making it sound like both hands. I think he could have outwitted Charlie Parker.

"I first heard Parker in the mid-forties. It was uptown at

some club. He had just come in from upstate—skinny, with a mop of hair. He borrowed a horn and sat in. I was completely turned around. I couldn't sleep for two days. I decided immediately that that was it: I was determined to articulate like that on the clarinet. I changed my reed and opened up my mouthpiece. I've worked toward that articulation ever since. I've also learned a great deal more about the essence of jazz over the years. I think it began in the mid-forties when I was between bands and sat in with Stuff Smith, the violinist, in Chicago. He had Jimmy Jones on piano and Sid Catlett on drums. My God, the intensity of Catlett's drumming—I got a message, a light went on, I knew what *swinging* was. I feel more, physically and emotionally, than I once did. I used to suffer from stage fright, and that made my playing cautious and mechanical-sounding. You have to show off what you have but control that showing off. Your brain is always miles ahead of your technical facility, and you have to realize that. I see nothing in my head when I improvise, and I'd just as soon forget the chords once I've learned them. But you can sort of see where your solo is going in your mind's eye. You can see your melodic line ahead. When I have a strong piano player, I try and float over his harmonic structure, over the blanket of his sound. We all have our little improvisational patterns, but I try and not put these patterns in at the same time or in the same mix. And you have to keep the melody at hand. It's arrogant to destroy a melody. Listen to Artie Shaw's solo on his recording of 'Star Dust.' It's the greatest clarinet solo of all time.

"My early training was more along the classical than the jazz line. I was born in Camden, New Jersey, on February 17, 1923. My parents moved to Philadelphia when I was three, and I was raised there. My full name is Bonifacio Ferdinando Leonardo De Franco. Bonafacio, which means 'good face,' was my grandfather's name. Leonardo was my father's name and Ferdinando came from an uncle. We were five children. The youngest died at a year. My older brother, Leonard, plays bass and is still active in Philadelphia. I have a married sister in Cherry Hill, New Jersey, and my younger brother, Anthony, who started out as a bassoonist, lives with my Aunt Grace, who has never married. My father's parents and grandparents came from central Italy, where the people have blue eyes and light hair, sometimes blond. My father was tall and heavy—an impressive-looking man and a remarkable man. Most of his life was a thread of tragedy. He lost his sight before I was born—an infection that had been given the wrong treatment. He said that he didn't do a thing for a year after he went blind, except feel sorry for himself. Then he enrolled in the Overbrook School for the blind, and learned how to tune pianos and to cook and type. He didn't catch on right away as a piano tuner, so he tried the candy-vending-machine business, but that didn't work either. Leonard and I would take turns making his route with him, and if we were late, he'd grab his cane and be off by himself. Sometimes we had no money, and had to eat candy bars for dinner. My father was an amateur guitarist, and he joined a band of blind people called the Jovial Night Owls. It was primarily a string band, and they played tunes like 'Sweet Sue.' The thing about my Dad, he always found time to play for us, or to tell us a story. He was born in Philadelphia, like my mother. Her name was Louise Giordano. She was dark and had brown eyes and was frail. She was a high-strung, bright, sensitive woman, who was always correcting our English. She worked as a secretary and in cigar factories to help out, but she finally gave up. There were too many children and not enough money. She attempted suicide, and in the end asked to be put away. Aunt Grace took us in, one by one, after my mother left. She lived in a row house with my grandfather and grandmother Domenica, and with Uncle Anthony and Aunt Lucy. She fed us and clothed us and got us through school. My mother spent the rest of her life in a state institution. Sometimes she knew us when we visited, and sometimes she sat there for hours and didn't say a word. She died in the mid-sixties. My father remarried twice, but only one marriage worked out to any degree of happiness. He died not long after my mother.

"I went to Mastbaum Technical High School, which was almost like a music school. The trumpet players Red Rodney and Joe Wilder were in my class. I started in on mandolin when I was five and switched to clarinet when I was eight or nine. Chap Cottrell was my first teacher, and he also taught me alto saxophone. My next teacher was Wally De Simone. He was in the pit band at the Earl Theatre, and he taught me every Sunday for nothing. He lived nearby, and he'd walk by our house to see if I was practicing. I hate to practice now, but it was fascinating to me then. It was a grand feeling every time you mastered another aspect of the instrument. The first jazz clarinet player who had any effect on me was Johnny Mince, a very underrated player with Tommy Dorsey. Then I heard Benny Goodman, and was enthralled. He had fire *and* facility. I later became an Artie Shaw fan. He was more linear in his musical thinking than the arpeggiated Chicago players like Goodman. And he was more modern harmonically. Those three clarinettists have always been top for me.

"When I was fourteen, I entered a nationwide contest run by Tommy Dorsey to find the best young jazz player. Willy De Simone told me, 'You're going to win, and this is how you're going to do it. You are going to wear shorts, and you're going to play 'Honeysuckle Rose,' and during the last eight bars you're going to hit a high A. While you're punching out that high A, you're going to hold out your left arm to show you are playing the clarinet and holding this fantastic A with just one hand.' I won, and when I met Tommy Dorsey afterward, he said, 'Stick to it, kid, and you'll be in my band.' I sailed through Mastbaum in three years instead of four, and it was the first time I enjoyed school. I had been sluggish before. Around this time, my brother Leonard and I started going to Billy Krechmer's jam sessions in the Downbeat Room. Whoever was in town—Teddy Wilson or Georgie Auld or Charlie Christian—would drop by and play, and we were allowed to sit in with these big-timers. Johnny Scat Davis, a trumpet player and bandleader who had been with Fred Waring, heard me at one of the sessions and offered me a job. I was fifteen. He had to sign special papers so I could travel with him. He paid me sixty dollars a week, and I sent half of it home and lived on the rest. I joined Gene Krupa's band in 1941. He had Charlie Ventura and Roy Eldridge and Anita O'Day. Dodo Marmarosa was on piano. He had been with Scat Davis. I learned then that I could never be a doper—that I could not alter my consciousness and still play well. I had heard an acetate I'd made when I'd had a few drinks, and it was embarrassing. I was with Gene at the Golden Gate Theatre in San Francisco when he was busted for possession of marijuana, and it was a sad business. Krupa was one of the best people in the business. We had got word backstage that agents were searching our hotel rooms, so Krupa sent his valet back to the hotel to get an envelope that was in a jacket pocket. The valet walked through the hotel lobby with the envelope in his hand and was stopped and that was it. Gene went to jail for three months, and it was headlines all over the country. I went from Krupa to Charlie Barnet. He had Pete Candoli and Neal Hefti and Oscar Pettiford, and Gil Evans was writing arrangements. Barnet was a delightful person. His mother had given him the money to get having a big band out of his system, which of course he never did. Everything was a kind of party. Dodo Marmarosa had joined with me, and he featured us both. I went with Ted Fio Rito for a short time, and on to Tommy Dorsey.

"In 1950, after I had left Tommy Dorsey for good, I joined Count Basie's small band. He had Clark Terry and Wardell Grey and Gus Johnson. He made any group sound like him, and he did it all from the piano. I never heard anyone play so much by doing so little. His philosophy was: Settle down, we'll get there. And: Don't smother people with notes. Every once in a while, he'd take the tempo up. All right, he'd say. Now you can smoke, and we would. Boyd Raeburn had a good band, an experimental band, and I went with him. George Handy and

Johnny Richards were doing the arrangements. Then, in 1952, I put together my own big band. I had to be Benny Goodman and Artie Shaw. Willard Alexander, the booker, advised me not to do it, but who do you listen to at that age? Your ego outdistances your brain. I had good people—Jimmy Lyon, Bernie Glow, Lee Konitz, Earl Swope, Gene Quill—but I didn't know anything about leading a big band. The band had no identity, and it was the wrong time—big bands were over. It lasted less than a year, and I lost a lot of money.

"The rest of the fifties, I had a good group for two years with Art Blakey and Kenny Drew. I was hot, and we did good business. I joined Norman Granz's Jazz at the Phil., and made a lot of records for Norman. I had a marvellous but totally unsalable group with Tommy Gumina on accordion, Carl Perkins on piano, Scott La Faro on bass, Pete Jolly on piano, Howard Roberts on guitar, and Billy Higgins on drums. Then 1960 rolled around, and the night clubs went topless or to rock. Concerts dropped off, and nobody would put out a record for you. It was understandable. Kids like to participate when they listen to music—vicariously or as dancers. They couldn't do either with bebop. The music was too complicated to partake in, and you couldn't dance to it. Rock answered their prayers. I did West Coast studio work and school clinics. It was an abyss, and I barely survived. In one year, my income went from six figures to six thousand dollars. Then I ran into Willard Alexander. He said, 'What are you doing?' I said, 'Starving.' He looked at me and said, 'You're going to be the next leader of the Glenn Miller band. I'll get back to you in forty-eight hours.' Willard always said he'd get back to you in forty-eight hours, and mostly that would be the last you heard. But he called the next day and hired me, and I ran the Glenn Miller band for eight years. That band is like a religion. It's booked years in advance all over the world. Our theme song, 'Moonlight Serenade,' made grown men and women cry. We could *hear* the love for Miller's music wherever we went. But I had so much to do running the band that I had to stop playing, and for several years I didn't touch my clarinet.

"In 1975, I decided to start a jazz career again. I also got married. It's taken me three times to find the right wife. Her name is Joyce, and we have a little boy, Chad. I bought some property in Panama City in northwestern Florida, and built a house a hundred yards from the beach. It has the best beaches in the country. I only work about thirty weeks a year. When I go abroad, I take Joyce and Chad. She's in real estate at home. She buys little houses and fixes them up and rents them. When I'm there, I help out. I'll hang a door, fix a lock. Then I'll set up a crab trap off the beach and do a little fishing. It's all the life I need."

[1982]

FIRST AND
LAST

~~

Child prodigies do not grow up easily. Sometimes, burdened by
their gifts, they become quirky and eccentric, and retire from
the world. Sometimes a mysterious stasis sets in, and they sink
into melancholy. Sometimes they suffer temporary reversals,
usually in midlife, then revive and carry on brilliantly. That
is what happened to the virtuoso drummer Louis Bellson. He
began playing at three, owned a set of drums at nine, taught
percussion at thirteen, joined the musicians' union at fourteen,
and, at seventeen, won a nationwide drum contest sponsored by
Gene Krupa. During the next dozen years or so, he went on to
work with the big bands of Benny Goodman, Tommy Dorsey,
Harry James, and Duke Ellington. Then two things happened:
he married the singer Pearl Bailey and became the drummer in
her accompanying big band; and he slipped into the ever-
expanding shadow cast by Buddy Rich, a virtuoso drummer
seven years his senior. Bailey and Rich continued to thrive, while
Bellson, a gentle, self-effacing man, remained more or less in
the wings, despite excellent recordings made in his own name
and occasional, widely praised solo appearances (his stint as the

drummer in Duke Ellington's first Sacred Concert, given twice in 1965). In the seventies, Pearl Bailey's career began to slow (she went to college and was invited to join the United States Mission to the United Nations), and Bellson came out more frequently as the leader of big and small bands of his own, and as a sideman with all-star groups (the two Swing Reunion concerts, given in 1985 on successive nights at Town Hall, with Benny Carter, Red Norvo, Teddy Wilson, and George Duvivier). In 1987, Buddy Rich died suddenly, and Bellson became not only the last of the great swing drummers but the most commanding of all living drummers.

The first—and some think still the greatest—swing drummer was Chick Webb. A hunchback, under five feet in height, Webb died in 1939, at the age of thirty. He was an exhilarating, almost overweening performer, who played with a power and precision and depth of timbre that completely belied his handicap. Buddy Rich learned from him (Webb patterns could be heard in Rich's last recorded solos), and remembered seeing him at the Savoy Ballroom in Harlem, where Webb was in residence with his marvellously ungainly big band during most of the thirties. "Webb was startling," Rich once said. "He was a tiny man with a hunchback and this big face and big, stiff shoulders. He sat way up on a kind of throne and used a twenty-eight-inch bass drum which had special pedals for his feet, and he had those old gooseneck cymbal holders. Every beat was like a bell." Webb took the ricky-tick quality out of jazz drumming, and he was the first to tune his drums in such a way that each had a rich sound. He was the first expert cymbal player, pitching his cymbals to match the general tenor of his various band sections, and using them to wash and thicken his soloists. His own solos, rarely longer than twelve bars, were highly concentrated. He kept to his snare drum, issuing numbing staccato and double-time figures and filling the air with explosive rimshots. The jazz chronicler Helen Oakley Dance knew Webb well, and she has said of him, "Chick couldn't read music, but after the band had run down a new arrangement he would sing every part. If someone hit a wrong note on the stand, he'd know who it was, and he'd call him on it. If he wasn't getting what he wanted from the band, he'd get angry, and they'd whisper, 'Look out, that hump is breathing!' He had tuberculosis of the spine. Like most black people at the time, he wouldn't go to a hospital because he was convinced they'd let him die there. Sometimes he'd come off the stand and faint, he was in such pain. Or he'd send in a sub like Kaiser Marshall. But he was a fighter. There was such fire in his playing. There was such fire in his drums. Before he started a set, he'd hit his big bass drum twice: Boom! Boom! And everybody in the audience would cheer." Every drummer studied Webb, but none achieved the lift and momentum he gave a big band, with the exception of Sidney Catlett, who carried Webb's flag forward after Webb's death. You can still hear Webb today, in the work of the drummers Panama Francis and Gus Johnson—and, in a subtle, oblique fashion, in Louis Bellson.

Bellson is medium-sized and has the cheerful, even-featured handsomeness that mothers and aunts relish and pretty women are at ease with. His feet are small and his hands are like steel. When he picks up a pair of wire brushes and plays, the effect is of great strength effortlessly used. He smiles a lot, and he talks rapidly, with little hitches that are like snare-drum offbeats. He is an emotional man, in a laughing, guarded way. Here is what he recently wrote about two of his idols, Sid Catlett and Jo Jones (the mixed metaphors compound the emotion in his words): "Big Sid and Papa Jo were the Leonardo and Michelangelo of this century. Their drum sets were perfect canvases and their strokes equalled the flight of huge birds in the sky. They left us beautiful paintings and a rich heritage, *never to be forgotten.*"

Bellson is generally in New York when Pearl Bailey is at the U.N., and not long ago he spoke about his life and his career: "I was born July 6, 1924, in Rock Falls, Illinois, but my family moved to Moline when I was eleven or twelve. Moline is about 160 miles west of Chicago, over near the Iowa line. I was christened Luigi Paulino Alfredo Francesco Antonio Balassone. The middle names were for uncles and godfathers. My father, who was in the music business, changed the name to Bellson because it was easier to write and pronounce. There were four girls and four boys, all of them still living. The girls came first—Edie, Dee Dee, Josephine, and Mary. Two live in Las Vegas and one in Moline and one in Kewanee, Illinois. I'm the second of the boys, so it was Frank, me, Anthony, and Henry. Tony and Hank are drummers. Tony lives in Chandler, Arizona, and Hank tests drumheads for the Remo drum factory in Los Angeles. My father was born Luigi Balassone, in Naples. He'd been married to my mother's sister. When she died, he married my mother. She was born Carmen Bartelucci, in Rome. She died at the age of ninety-two, a year ago. She was about five feet tall, and, unlike a lot of short Italian women, she kept her weight down. She did all the cleaning and cooking, and she made everything we ate. She was a firebrand. She loved music and dancing. My father died in 1960, at the age of sixty-eight. He was huge—six feet two and two hundred and fifty pounds. He was quiet and peaceful and had great patience. He read the papers, he was up on politics. He made his own wine. We always had wine at meals, and I used to take some to school in a Coke bottle. The teachers never found out. My dad had a store, the Bellson Music Company. He built the showcases and painted the signs—things he had learned in Italy. He told me that he had an Italian professor who said he had to learn everything there was about music. And he did. He played every instrument except the accordion—his fingers were too big. He taught us the brass instruments and the saxophones and the strings. He taught us the great arias, and he made us aware of everyone from Bach to Ravel. He loved jazz, too. He let us in on everything, and I thank him for that. We lived in an apartment in Rock Falls and a house in Moline with two stories and a basement. After school, we went right to the store. We'd clean windows and put up Christmas decorations and sell records and sheet music. When we were around thirteen, we'd help with the music lessons. I became the percussion instructor.

"There was music every night in the store. Monday, there was a fifteen-piece accordion band. Tuesday, a woodwind ensemble with flutes, clarinets, oboes, and all the saxophones. There was a brass ensemble on Wednesday, and a concert band on Thursday. Friday, a string orchestra. We practiced in the store on weekends, when we had access to the studios. I started playing when I was three. I had a parade drum with gut snares. I studied with Roy Knapp for two years, starting at fifteen. I played at a local tavern called the Rendezvous. It had a piano player named Speck Red and a drummer named Percy Walker. They let me sit in on Tuesday nights. That was where I learned some of the basics of jazz drumming.

"I also sat in with bands that were passing through. One was Ted Fio Rito, the Fio Rito who wrote 'When Lights Are Low' and 'I Never Knew.' He wanted to hire me, but I had three months of high school left. So he said if I was interested to join him at the Florentine Gardens in Hollywood after I graduated, and I did. The Mills Brothers were the main attraction there, and I stayed three months. One night, Freddy Goodman, Benny's brother, told me Benny was looking for a drummer, and would I like to audition? I went to the Paramount Studio, where Benny was making a movie, and the costume people put me in a tuxedo, and I played a quartet number with Benny in the movie. All he said after was that the band was leaving for New York that Thursday and to be at the station. Of course, it helped that before I joined Fio Rito I had won a Gene Krupa drum contest. It was nationwide, and it got a lot of publicity. I worked with Benny at the New Yorker Hotel. In New York, I got to hear and know drummers like Big Sid Catlett and Davy Tough and Jo Jones, people I'd only heard on records. How great it would have been if every aspiring drummer could have listened to Sid play and talk. I played loud then—bang! crash! real gung ho—and he told me never to hit my cymbals too hard. 'Let them breathe,' he said. He also said, 'Your drums are

your own orchestra. Your snare is the soprano, the small tomtom is the alto, the big tomtom is the tenor, and the bass drum is
the bass.' When Sid took a solo, it was as if he was weaving, and
when he finished, there it was, with its colors and flowers and
patterns—a beautiful carpet. Sid and Jo Jones could do time
steps and the shim-sham-shimmy. I took some tap dancing. You
had to do these things. That kind of dancing worked right into
your drumming. I still think like a tap dancer when I play.

"Uncle Sam got me in 1942. I was stationed in Washington,
D.C., at the Walter Reed Annex, in Silver Spring, Maryland. I
was part of a full orchestra, and out of it came a dance band
and chamber groups. A lot of the musicians had been at the
Eastman School of Music. We played for dances at night, we
played concerts almost every day, we played in the hospitals.
When I got out, in 1945, I went back with Ted Fio Rito for
several months, then rejoined Benny Goodman for a year. I
started using two bass drums instead of one when I was with
Fio Rito the second time. I'd had the idea in high school. I drew
a picture of the set I had in mind—two bass drums, measuring
twenty by twenty inches, five small tomtoms stretched across
them, and two floor toms on the side. I took the drawing to
the Slingerland drum people in 1940, but they weren't interested, and it wasn't until 1946 that the first set was built—by
Gretsch. I joined Tommy Dorsey in 1947 at the Casino Garden
ballroom in Santa Monica, and when Tommy saw the two bass
drums the wheels started going. He had a great show sense. He
could look out at an audience and know immediately what to
play for it—tempo, material, mood. He told me, 'I want the people out front to realize you're using two bass drums.' I suggested
we put the drums on a revolving platform. We had a motor
built, and when we opened at the Strand Theatre in New York
there I was on this platform in front of the band. Tommy con-
trolled it. When I soloed, he'd stop me when my back was to
the audience, and the lights would go out. I had a phosphorescent patch on each drumstick and a phosphorescent headband.
All the audience saw was these lights leaping around. It was a

great theatrical gimmick. You *worked* with Tommy. Once, we did six straight months of one-nighters, without a single night off. Some days, we'd be on the bus for five hundred miles.

"I was with Dorsey three years, and then I went with Harry James. Juan Tizol, the trombonist who had been with Duke Ellington, was in the band, and so was Willie Smith, the Lunceford alto saxophonist. I was staying in Tizol's house in Los Angeles, and one day he said, 'Would you like to join Duke Ellington?' Well. We approached Harry, and he said, 'Go,' and we joined Duke. It was 1951. I came to think of Duke as my second father. He paid the same attention to everyone, whether he was a newspaper boy or Toscanini. He was no disciplinarian. Sometimes Paul Gonsalves and Ray Nance would go on a binge for four or five days. He never said a word when they showed up. He'd get back at them that night by making them stand out there—and they probably not feeling too good—and take chorus after chorus, telling the audience how much they loved to play for them. He told me, 'If I had to deal with temperaments, I'd be under the ground.' I was interested in arranging. I had studied it as a kid, and I had written arrangements for Harry James and Tommy Dorsey. Tizol persuaded me to bring them in—'Skin Deep' and 'The Hawk Talks'—and Duke recorded them. Anyway, I asked Billy Strayhorn how he had voiced a certain piece of his, and he hemmed and hawed and changed the subject. I was embarrassed at bothering him, and I apologized. But later Duke sat me down beside him at the piano and showed me how he would give this note to Johnny Hodges and this one to Gonsalves, how he'd put Jimmy Hamilton's clarinet on top and Harry Carney's baritone in the middle and Gonsalves' tenor on the bottom. It was that kind of voicing that made his saxophone section sound like it had ten men in it. Duke wrote all the time. Once, on a plane trip, he turned around and asked me if I had any manuscript paper, and I said, 'Sorry, it's packed.' He took off his coat and drew five lines on one sleeve and wrote out the notes he had in his head. Tizol scored the melody when we got to the gig, and we played it that night. Duke and Strayhorn were full of superstitions. Nobody was supposed to wear anything with yellow in it. Nobody was supposed to button a shirt all the way down the front. Nobody was supposed to whistle in the dressing room.

"Ellington's arrangements never had drum parts. But not once did he say, 'This is how Sonny Greer did it.' He said, 'Do it your own way.' He made you create. He used to call me in for special events in later years. In 1965, I played his 'Golden Broom and the Green Apple' with the New York Philharmonic. There I was with twenty minutes of music to play and a hundred musicians sitting behind me, and all he had told me was that the first part was in waltz time. The same year, he asked me to sit in at the Grace Cathedral in San Francisco for his first Sacred Concert. He said, 'I want you to play a drum solo in church. You are the thunder and lightning.' That's what I thought about when I soloed at the end of 'David Danced Before the Lord,' while the band played and a choir chanted and all hell broke loose. Some nights, the band swung so hard I couldn't believe it. Some nights, it was on fire. Duke introduced me to everything I hadn't known before about music—and life."

Bellson uses a huge set of drums. It includes two twenty-four-inch bass drums and five tomtoms, ranging from a six-inch concert tomtom to two sixteen-by-sixteen-inch floor tomtoms. He also uses two roto-toms (shallow, dishlike drums with just one skin) and a five-and-a-half-inch snare drum. His drums are made by Remo. He generally has five Zildjian cymbals. There are two large ride cymbals, two slightly smaller crash cymbals, and a twenty-two-inch Chinese cymbal. His high hat has fourteen-inch cymbals, with an extra-heavy cymbal on the bottom. When his whole set is assembled, its gold and silver colors gleam and wink and shimmer, and it looks, before he sits down and anchors it, as if it might slowly and soundlessly ascend.

Bellson's accompanying is casual and annealing. It forms a light, steady flow of sounds, made up of suggestive but unobtrusive cymbal strokes and endless accents, carried out on his snare, his tomtoms, and his bass drums. He seems to hear every

note that is played around him and to have the proper comple-
ment for it. He never overpowers, he never underplays. His
solos are logical extensions of his accompanying. They are
louder, they can be melodramatic, but they have the same grace
and motion. He moves constantly from one part of his set to
another, not in the speed-of-light way of Buddy Rich, but in
the legato, melodic manner of Jo Jones and Sid Catlett. The
snare drum is the center of his solos, and he will use staccato strokes, double-time strokes, and quick rolls, all varied by
side strokes to his tomtoms and his cymbals. Fast tempos bring
out the Lear in him. He goes along for a while, doing his roun-
delays, spilling hundreds of rimshots, and gradually preparing
his listeners for the storm to come. This arrives when he begins
what amounts to a single-stroke roll with his feet on his two
bass drums. Soon it is a solid, thunderous wall of sound, decorated by snare and tomtom explosions and occasional cymbal
crashes. A vein stands out on his forehead, his face reddens, and
his feet move faster than feet were ever supposed to move.
When the wall of sound becomes unbearable, he abruptly stops,
flickers around his set in a Catlett, winding-down manner, and
it is over. These theatrics jelly the audience and probably make
Bellson's ankles tremble, but the next number begins, and he
leads the way lightly, a smile on his face, his Atlas strength intact.

When Pearl Bailey is in New York, she is completely absorbed by her work at the United Nations. But this is what she
said one evening about her husband: "We've been married
thirty-seven years. We live together and we work together, but
we haven't hit each other yet. We are very different. I can stay
indoors six weeks and never go out. I have my needlepoint, my
books, my cooking. Louis has to move. He loves that telephone:
'Listen, man. I'll take the gig.' 'Listen, man. I'll call you back.'
He's an introvert and I'm an extrovert. I do the cooking, he
does the dishes. He's neat as a pin. We cross a busy street and
he sees a cigarette butt, he picks it up. If one of my pots gets a
little dark on the bottom, he goes out and buys a new one. Many
people beat a drum; Louis plays it. I see Louis as an awesome

artist. If that man looked at me the way he looks at his drums, I'd be delighted. I love my husband. I don't tell him every day. The deed of love is stronger than words. He is loyal. He's family to the hilt. I believe there's nothing he wouldn't do for me. There is a lot of loving among musicians, too. They have a one-ness. They hug when they meet, and they hug when they part. If music is their God, they are the holiest of men. He sings in his sleep—out of tune. He doesn't read much, so I'll lay a book I think he'll like by his side of the bed. It may take a while, but he gets into it and he'll read it. I first met Louis outside the Howard Theatre in Washington, D.C. Juan Tizol had told me about him: 'You should meet this wonderful young man. He doesn't go out. He has no girlfriend.' Tizol came out of the thea-tre with a young man. 'Hi. I'm Louis.' 'Hi. I'm Pearl.' Two weeks later, we were married in London. We have two adopted children. Deedee is twenty-nine, and Tony is thirty-five. I lay the parables on them, Louis soothes them."

Louis on Pearl: "She's the most honest person I've ever met. She's got tremendous ESP. She scares me the way she psyches people out, the way that she can tell you that this person she's just met will be a friend and that this one is disturbed—the way she gets to the crux of a person. Her natural ability overwhelms me. She has perfect pitch. She can start a song cold without a note. She's a great ad-libber. She has a wonderful theatre sense. She's the same onstage as she is offstage. When our kids were growing up, she was the disciplinarian and I was the softie. She took them to the circus and let them know about museums. She has given them whatever values they have. She's a joy to be with. I haven't figured her out, and I never intend to. Some-times it's tough to go out shopping or to a restaurant. People won't give her any peace. But she doesn't sign autographs. She just says, 'Give me your name and address, and I'll send you a picture.' I come home with my pockets full of names."

Bellson resumed talking about his career: "Pearl and I started going on the road after I left the Duke, in 1953. She had a band with people like George Duvivier on bass, Taft Jordan, Joe Wilder, and Dick Vance on trumpets, Butter Jackson and Jimmy Cleveland on trombones, and Hilton Jefferson and Selden Powell on reeds. We had tap dancers, including Honi Coles and Cholly Atkins and her brother Bill Bailey. We had a choir of twelve or fifteen voices. Don Redman was her arranger and conductor. I think there were sixty people in the package. We played the Apollo Theatre in Harlem, the Howard in Washington, the Earl in Philadelphia. We did Vegas and the Coconut Grove in Los Angeles. It was costly, but it didn't sink. We toured for a long time. Then she gave it up and took the lead in an all-black *Hello Dolly* on Broadway. Walter Winchell counted seven standing ovations one night. She did the show two years, and we went back on the road. When we were home, we lived in Northridge, California, and before that we had a place in Apple Valley, in the desert, a hundred miles from L.A. Seven years ago, we left Northridge and moved to Lake Havasu City, in Arizona. It has nineteen thousand people and London Bridge. We have a little house on the third tee of a golf course. We were on the road constantly until the late seventies. Now Pearl likes to do only theatres and concerts. She's not happy about hotels anymore. Of course, she's still part of the U.S. Mission to the U.N., and that takes several months of the year. When I'm not working with Pearl, I take my big band or a small group out for short gigs. There don't seem to be any more of the two-, three-, or four-week gigs we used to have. It's just a weekend or five days in and out. I have a pool of musicians on the East Coast I call on and a pool on the West Coast. And I still do drum clinics in schools and colleges. I like the kids to know what came before them, who the great masters were, and what they sounded like.

"Pearl and I got racist letters when we were first married, some of them real raunchy. We had trouble in restaurants and hotels, and the like. But we didn't wait around with chips on our shoulders. We figured we were two human beings in the enter-

tainment field. The N.A.A.C.P. asked us to join in the fifties—
for five hundred dollars. Pearl isn't a joiner. Her reply was
'Why should I pay all that money to be part of the world that
God has already put me in?' "